The Great Silence

Also by Juliet Nicolson

The Perfect Summer

The Great Silence

1918–1920
Living in the Shadow of the Great War

JULIET NICOLSON

JOHN MURRAY

First published in Great Britain in 2009 by John Murray (Publishers)
An Hachette UK Company

I

© Juliet Nicolson 2009

Extracts from 'The Waste Land' and 'Morning at the Window' by T. S. Eliot
reproduced by permission of Faber and Faber Ltd.
'Suicide in the Trenches' and 'Blighters'
reproduced from copyright Siegfried Sassoon
by kind permission of the Estate of George Sassoon.
Quotations from Royal Archives material:
p.90 RA/GV/QMD 1919 21 January 'Awfully sad and touching';
p.90 RA/GV/QMD 1919 22 January 'Missed the dear child very much indeed . . .';
p.163 RA/GV/QMD 1919 1 December 'very cheery';
p.163 RA/GV/QMD 1919 1 December 'George made a charming speech
and David made a charming reply'.

A CIP catalogue record for this title is available from the British Library

ISBN 978-0-7195-6256-3

Typeset in Bembo by Ellipsis Books Limited, Glasgow

Printed and bound by Clays Ltd, St Ives plc

J[ohn Murray] policy is to use papers that are natural reable
and rele forests.
The rm to

For my brother Adam
il miglior fabbro

and for my daughters Clemmie and Flora
luces meae vitae

and for my husband Charlie
sine qua non

The lingering emotional effects of the war illustrated by a portrait entitled
'Grief' by Hugh Cecil, *Tatler*, November 1919, a full year after
the Armistice had been signed

Contents

Illustrations

Acknowledgements

During the writing of this book I have had the privilege of talking to several people who remember life in Britain at first hand ninety years ago. Mrs Doris Titley was an effervescent 105 when she described her life below stairs both during and after the First World War. My aunt (by marriage) Pam Leigh, now 93, has spent many precious hours making me laugh and cry at her childhood memories. Miss Elaine Rafter's stories of work in a department store just after the Great War remained undimmed when she spoke of them, at the age of 101, with infectious humour. Mary Stearns' memories of her parents and her Kentish childhood were gold dust. Jeremy Hutchinson and Geoffrey Woolley, both now aged 94, provided the smallest and therefore most absorbing details of two specific days, 11 November 1918 and 1919.

There is one other person who cannot quite remember those events, as she was born in the spring of 1920. However I am indebted to the Dowager Duchess of Devonshire for her acute sensibility of the period and for allowing me to read the wonderful letters of her then schoolboy brother Tom Mitford who was killed in the Second World War.

I am indebted to Her Majesty Queen Elizabeth II for allowing me access to the Royal Archive at Windsor and for permission to quote from Queen Mary's Diaries. I am also grateful to Miss Pamela Clarke and her staff at the archive.

The generation born to those who lived through the events I describe have been most generous with their time and their private family archives. I would like to thank Ronald Atkins for the background material on Tommy Atkins, and Dame Eileen Atkins for giving me such a vivid portrait of her father. I am grateful to Fiona

Clarke Hall for talking to me about her mother-in-law Edna and her husband Denis. Ginny Coombes took infinite trouble in trusting me with the papers and the story of her great-uncle Edward Tester. I am grateful to Michael Ann for the valuable memories of his father, the entrepreneurial owner of Drusilla's Zoo in Sussex, and to John Leigh Pemberton for early memories of conversations with his mother. Adrian Goodman, grandson of Ottoline Morrell, was illuminating about his grandmother and I am grateful to Rosalind Ingrams for showing Garsington to me. Conversations with the Marquess of Lansdowne and Hugh Myddleton brought their 'Granny Vi' Astor to life and Philip Astor kindly lent me many moving letters written to her during the war. I was delighted to speak to Peter Jones, the nephew of the splendid but hitherto elusive butler Eric Horne. Mrs Titley's daughter Dorothy Ellis has been most generous with her time since the death of her mother in 2008.

There are others without whose professional understanding I would not have been able to tackle this period of history. I have been given unparalleled insights into the nature of grief by Patricia Anker and Julia Samuel. The wisdom that shines from them both is shot through this book. Kevin Brownlow's knowledge of the early movie industry is unparalleled. Andrew Bamji has answered innumerable queries about the history and technique of plastic surgery and about Harold Gillies's life. Roger Neil knows everything about Nellie Melba and practically everything else that happened in this period. Alison Thomas has been more than generous with the private papers as well as her knowledge of Edna Clarke Hall. Richard Shone has told me a great deal about art, artists, ballet and ballet dancers in England in the years immediately following the First World War.

Both Andrew Peppitt and Helen Marchant have been their wonderfully helpful selves and thanks also to Hannah Obee and Diane Naylor at the Chatsworth Archive.

I would also like to thank individuals at public and private libraries and archives, among them: Anthony Richards and Richard Slocombe at the Imperial War Museum; Rachel Freeman and Jamie Andrews at the British Library; Bret Croft and Harriet Wilson at Condé Nast library; Sophie Basilevitch at Mary Evans, Oriole Cullen at the V&A,

Susan Scott at the Savoy Archive, Steve Jebson at the Meteorological Weather Records Office, the staff at the London Library and the Fulham and Hammersmith Library.

The lonely business of researching and writing has been greatly cheered by the information and the suggestions, insights and encouragement of so many individuals and friends, among them Nigel à Brassard, Kitty Ann, Philip Athill, Peter Bidmead, Georgie Boothby, Sarah and Kildare Bourke-Borrowes, Charlie and Arabella Bridge, Simon Brocklebank Fowler, Paul Calkin, Linda and Brian Clifford, Artemis Cooper, Richard Crook, Dee Daly, Andrew and Ellie Davidson, Atul Doshi, Sophie Dundas, Max Egremont, Jean Claude Eude, Sabina ffrench Blake, Lady Antonia Fraser (always the best of enthusiasts), Lady Annabel Goldsmith, Kevin Gordon, Ian and Victoria Hislop, Philip Hook, Glenn Horowitz and Tracey Jackson, Dr Jonathan Hunt, Brian Huntley Builders, Kathryn Irwin, Diana Kelly, the Hon. Mrs Charles Kitchener, Fiona Lansdowne, Katie Law (aka Marie Rose), Caroline Levison, Brian Masters, Charles Moore, Charlotte Moore, my lovely nieces Molly and Rosie Nicolson, my sister Rebecca Nicolson and my cousin Vanessa Nicolson (both such loyalists), Mark Norman and his staff, Cate Olsen and Nash Robbins (indefatigable champions of the written word), Mary Pearson, the late Harold Pinter, Shirley Punnett, Faith Raven, David Robinson, Stephen Robinson, Marilyn Stanley, Suzanne Sullivan, Kathleen Tessaro, Joanna Trollope, Aly Van Den Berg, Louisa Vertova, Claire Watson, Claire Whalley, Maggie White, Fred Windsor Clive, Gordon Wise, Wendy Wolfe, Joanna and Richard Woods, Henry Wyndham and the unmatchable duo Hugh Harris and David O'Rorke.

I would like to thank Linda Van for her unfailing helpfulness as well as all the other staff at Ed Victor Ltd, especially Charlie Campbell, Sophie Hicks, Maggie Phillips and Hitesh Shah. As an agent Ed himself devotes more time and encouragement to me than I could possibly deserve. He is the best.

Once again I have been more than lucky with my publishers at John Murray to whom I am immensely grateful, especially to my editor Roland Philipps, and to the indefatigable Nikki Barrow, Caro Westmore, James Spackman, Shona Abhyankar, Helen Hawksfield,

Amanda Jones and Sara Marafini. And I am grateful to Douglas Matthews for his masterly work with the index.

The enthusiasm and initiative of my researcher, Clementine Macmillan Scott has been exemplary. And I cannot imagine where I would be without the invaluable encouragement and friendship of Sarah Raven and Rachel Wyndham.

It is a rare thing for a writer to be lucky enough to have a brother who bestows the level of practical and emotional guidance that I have been blessed with in Adam. And when my preoccupation with the written word threatened to become overwhelming, the loving support of my daughters Clemmie and Flora did not waver once. I am indebted to my husband Charlie who has cherished this author unconditionally throughout the writing of the book. The book is for Adam, Clemmie, Flora and Charlie with my profound love.

Slowly, slowly, the wound to the soul begins to make itself felt, like a bruise which only slowly deepens its terrible ache, till it fills all the psyche. And when we think we have recovered and forgotten, it is then that the terrible after-effects have to be encountered at their worst.

D. H. Lawrence, Lady Chatterley's Lover

Introduction

This is a book about silence, the silence that followed the 'incessant thunder' of the four years and four months of the First World War. At the heart of the book are three specific November days in which silence predominated: the day the guns fell silent in 1918; the day the two-minute silence, then known as the Great Silence, was first observed in 1919; and, a year later, the day when in 1920 the Unknown Soldier was lowered into silence beneath the floor of Westminster Abbey. But this book is also about a more general silence – the silence of grief – that crept into every corner of life during the two years that followed the Armistice of 1918, a time when vitality and youth had been swept aside by a massive, unanticipated mortality.

In one way this is a book about the relief that is brought about by the absence of noise: silence as balm, as a time for reflection and contemplation. But it is also about another kind of silence, the silence of isolation and fear, of the failure and the terror of attempting to articulate misery. It is a book about the silence of denial and of emptiness, of endings and of death. Silence can bring with it a vacancy that in its turn craves the distraction of the human voice or the obscuring impact created for example by music. These distractions can help to stifle the terror of being abandoned to the silence of the noisy mind. Even the silence of sleep can carry with it an added dread, for sleep ends in wakefulness. And as Siegfried Sassoon said, 'to wake was to remember'.

During the summer of 1911, a record-breaking hot season three years before the outbreak of war, the strength of the sun had been sufficient to bleach out the pattern of purple pansies on newly married

Ethel Harrison's dress. Already social fragmentation had started to make itself felt in a peacetime society that on the surface seemed ordered and secure. Women, trade unionists, both Houses of Parliament, the servant class, the poor and the rich were all either seeking or resisting change. Some said that the twentieth century did not begin until 1914, that the extended Edwardian idyll had lulled the English into a sense that not only was everything all right with the world, but that it always would be.

In fact the structure of society had been shifting, sometimes imperceptibly and sometimes, as the reign of George V got under way in 1910, with some drama. The suffragette movement had become increasingly volatile and disturbing. The force-feeding of imprisoned women, whose crime had been to fight for votes for the unrepresented half of society, had become more prevalent. Stones were thrown through windows of municipal buildings across the land; one suffragette tried to push the Home Secretary, Winston Churchill, beneath a moving train, and in June 1913 the campaign for the voice of women to be heard in the democratic process resulted in tragedy. During the Epsom Derby Emily Davidson, at the age of 39, had thrown herself beneath the hammering hooves of Anmer, the King's horse, her skull smashed, her brains – so it was reported – spilling out on to the grassy track, as Anmer did a complete somersault in full view of his owner. Just over six years later women would be voting and one of them, an American divorcee, would be representing a constituency in Parliament.

The outbreak of war had brought with it a healing unity; domestic problems were suppressed, while the country joined together to fight side by side against a common enemy, experiencing a new sense of community across the classes with so many suffering the loss of someone they loved. But with the end of the war, after the immediate relief experienced when the fighting stopped, divisions returned with renewed intensity. In moments of honesty many questioned whether the golden summers of the pre-war world had been as golden as memory willed them to be, or whether instead they had been the mere product of hindsight.

Social discontent returned, and in louder voice. Now, too, a series of new divides had developed: between the men who had gone to fight and the women who had been left behind to manage family life; between those too young to have absorbed the real lasting impact of what had happened, and those who would never get over it. The gulf between those who had experienced the closest thing to hell on earth and those who had only glimpsed it was to prove almost impossible to close.

There were of course those for whom the war changed things for the better – in particular women, who won the right to vote immediately the war ended, though the right was still restricted to those over the age of 30 and conditional on owning a house or being married to someone who owned a house. But women's expectations had changed. Seventy years before the Armistice a columnist in the *London Journal* had written that 'a delicate reserve, a rosy diffidence and a sweetly chastened deportment are precisely the qualities in a woman that mostly win upon the affections of men'. It had taken war and the death of millions to bring about change, although some women, mostly of the older generation, hoped that the natural order of things would be restored. Exhausted by the effort of running the whole family show at home, they longed for the men to return and take charge.

Servants like Arthur Atkins, an under-chauffeur with no prospects, returned from the war determined not to resume his servile duties. Unemployment ran through society with a devastation similar to the 1918 flu epidemic, destroying lives as it spread. Not only had four million men returned from the army and navy looking for work, but a further three million munition workers were now without jobs. Means Test committees presided over by fat women cuddling even fatter pekinese talked about the national necessity for tightening belts. Unemployment meant poverty and an estimated 11 per cent of the population was considered to be living under such circumstances. Poverty meant misery. Nor were other sections of society immune to the taxes and the economic consequences of the conflict. Financial ruin had affected the fortunes of many of the richest members of the aristocracy.

But the class system survived the war in large part intact. Although some *men* retained a sense of equality because of shared experiences between servant and master, aristocrat and postman, women had no such exposure to 'the breakdown of tradition'. As the writer Barbara Cartland, then a young woman from the 'gentry' and on the brink of 'coming out', explained: 'We lived in manless homes. We were brought up by women, and Edwardian women at that. We were fenced round with narrow restrictive social customs, nurtured on snobbery and isolated from any contact with, or knowledge of, people outside our own accepted class.'

This book aims to discover what happened to that peaceful pre-war society after the intervening gash of the war years and the death or injury of more than two and a half million men. How had society changed and how were people adapting or failing to adapt to that change? In 1920 the journalist Philip Gibbs wrote of 'fits of profound depression alternating with a restless desire for pleasure'. I want to know what kind of sound was made by the hinge that linked those two sensibilities.

The bereaved of 1918 were facing what the writer Joan Didion has since called 'the unending absence'. The post-war world was in large part a world paralysed by grief. Such a small tidy word is incongruous for something so messy. Grief is an iceberg of a word concealing beneath its innocent simplicity a dangerous mass of confusion and rage. Bereavement follows stages, and if a cycle can be identified within these stages, then the comfort found in reaching the final stage is often dashed with the realisation that circles have no endings. The cyclical sequence of emotions said to be followed by a person in mourning can in practice be inconsistent and irregular, each part failing to fall into its proper place. Emotional effects can include at first shock, disbelief and denial, followed by guilt, self-reproach (Rudyard Kipling never forgave himself for the encouragement he gave and the strings he pulled to get his short-sighted son John sent to the battle that would kill him), loneliness, hopelessness, relief (and the guilt involved in *that* process), numbness and yearning. Disbelief, hope and denial sometimes jostle one another for pre-eminent position.

After the Great War, in Barbara Cartland's words, 'an atmosphere of gloom, misery and deep unrelenting mourning settled on practically

every house in the British Isles'. Formal occasions of remembr\
designed to comfort often produced the reverse effect. Private anniv\
saries of the day someone was reported missing, the day a final telegr\
was delivered, wedding days and the day you last saw them all prompted
memories so similar to the moment of actual loss that the healing
cycle was derailed. In 1917 in *Mourning and Melancholia* Freud was
emphatic about the flaw in the assumption that grief 'would be overcome after a certain lapse of time'. After the shock of the impact of
the news has softened, grief can be like standing with your back to
the sea. Sometimes a warning rumble gathers momentum in the form
of an approaching birthday or Christmas, bringing with it the fear of
remembered happiness. On other days the approaching wall of water
can appear without any warning at all. On the calmest, most settled
sort of day, there is no predicting when a rogue wave in the shape of
a snatch of music, a familiar phrase, even a shared joke, might suddenly roll in and threaten to topple you.

Bereavement can have profound effects on the body including
exhaustion, uncontrollable crying, troubled sleep, palpitations, short-
ness of breath, headaches, recurrent infections, high blood pressure,
loss of appetite, stomach upsets, hair loss, disruption of the menstrual
cycle, irritability and visual and auditory hallucinations. The bereaved
may turn to alcohol or drugs for the relief and numbing of suffering. All of these symptoms can occur even with the often-cathartic
experience of a funeral. But there were no bodies to bury during
the Great War. A decision had been taken in 1915 that no corpses
of either officers or soldiers would be brought back from the front.
There were simply too many for the authorities to be able to manage
such a task. There was another reason too. Many of the bodies were
unidentifiable, being so badly mutilated, although this detail was not
often made explicit. The dead remained abandoned, drowned in the
liquid mud into which they had slipped or been trampled, and were
buried abroad either in the very place where they had lost their lives
or in vast cemeteries – what Rudyard Kipling called a 'Dead Sea of
arrested lives' – set up by the Imperial War Graves Commission.

Lack of evidence gave rise to an inability to believe in death. Ettie
Desborough lost two sons in the war. The first, Julian, had been
wounded and took two weeks to die, his mother at his hospital

bedside throughout. The younger son, Billy, was killed among hundreds of others in a military charge, his body never identified, buried among his fellow men and never again seen by his mother. She confided to her friend Cynthia Asquith that she had found the complete, sudden disappearance of Billy harder to bear than 'the long loving farewell to Julian'.

Before the war people had tended to die in the place where they had spent their lives, surrounded by the people they had loved and the things they had known. A shopkeeper would live out his last days in the back of his shop, customers coming in to pay their respects but also to buy the things they needed for their tea. Life went on. There was something valuable in this way of dying at home, a comfort not only for the dying themselves but also for those who loved them. Death as with birth formed an integral part of living. And burial, and the ceremonial that went with it, was a fundamental part of that process.

A promotional film made by the Cremation Society called *The Great Purifier*, advocating a cleaner, ecologically sound alternative to burial, had failed to attract many supporters to the cause. After news had got out in 1879 about the experimental cremation of a horse in the country's first cremation oven in Woking, the procedure had seemed doomed never to become established. The public distress caused by the disposal of the horse in such a manner resulted in the Home Secretary's threat to prosecute Sir Henry Thompson, surgeon and President of the Cremation Society of England. The burning of a body, human or animal, was widely perceived by Christians to interfere with or even destroy all hope of resurrection, and although cremation was made legal in 1902, by 1918 only 0.3 per cent of the population chose to take up that option.

By the end of the war the absence of funerals and the strain of maintaining hope had exhausted the nation. The English habit of managing difficult feelings was to suppress rather than discuss them, as if by remaining silent the feelings would disappear. The bereaved feared to pass on their grief to those already burdened by grief themselves and friendship and intimacy suffered as a result.

Before the war, a young designer, Cecil Beaton, had noticed that 'women were more hysterical'. The sight of a fire engine charging down a London street, the white horses 'trained to rush out at the sound of a big brass bell rearing and flaring their nostrils' like stallions, was enough to make nursemaids scream and faint at the thought of impending tragedy. The restraint imposed by the rigours of war had banished all such public display of emotion. Now the phrase 'before the war' came to represent all that was untarnished: a benchmark by which to measure all subsequent standards and aspirations. Compassion became a rationed emotion reserved for only the most intimate of relationships as the individuality of death was submerged in the vast numbers of dead. This collective suppression of feeling often produced a deep underlying fury and in many cases prevented the full expression of mourning, resulting in the pain-filled and often angry silence of unspoken grief.

During the war a curious but widespread assumption had grown up that at the end of the war things would return to normal. Leading society figures, among them the Duchess of Devonshire and the Marchioness of Lansdowne, had founded the Officers' Family Fund, a public morale-boosting exercise, designed to emphasise both the glory of sacrifice and the fact that death could on occasion be an opportunity to rejoice. Both had suffered in the death of Charles Fitzmaurice, brother to the Duchess and husband of the Marchioness. The two women had successfully campaigned for the abolition of wearing of black armbands in public; they favoured white to symbolise pride rather than grief in death.

But a little over a month before 11 November 1918 Cynthia Asquith had written about 'the prospect of peace'. Her brother had been killed along with most of her male friends, and she anticipated the end of the war with a shudder of fear. 'I think it will require more courage than anything that has gone before,' she wrote on 28 September. 'It isn't before one leaves off spinning round that one realises how giddy one is. One will have to look at long vistas again, instead of short ones, and one will at last fully recognise that the dead are not only dead for the duration of the war.'

With the war over, a fragment of a famous sermon, taken out of context, was seized on by many who wanted to believe that this unbelievable thing had not happened. As Edward VII lay in state in his coffin in Westminster in the spring of 1910, Canon Henry Scott Holland had given a sermon in St Paul's on the finality of death. During his long meditation he commented on the curious phenomenon of the vivid physical memory of a recently dead person and the strength of the illusion that they have not really gone for ever.

> Death is nothing at all. It does not count. I have only slipped away into the next room. Nothing has happened. Everything remains exactly as it was. I am I, and you are you, and the old life that we lived so fondly together is untouched, unchanged.

But he had continued by reminding his congregation that 'the long horrible silence that follows . . . will cut its way into our souls'. Conveniently *these* words were rarely quoted.

Ignoring the emotional fall-out from the absence of men, an advertisement in *The Times* on 18 December 1918 now outlined a service for the 'Training of War Wives'. The advertisement was addressed to recently demobilised women, or fiancées or wives of soldiers, and offered 'an opportunity to perfect themselves in household accomplishments which will make the homes of the future ideal for family life'. But with the annihilation of a 'golden generation' a deficit arose of suitable healthy men to love and marry the surviving women. Men with shattered faces hidden beneath tin masks walked the streets, terrifying in their inability to make the mask laugh or cry.

When the emotion of shock began to lessen, people began to look for any possible means of escape from the 'gloom, misery and deep unrelenting mourning'. The passion for movies, mostly of the thrilling and adventurous kind, filled an insatiable appetite for entertainment. Charlie Chaplin had become the most famous man on earth and movie stars, male and female, with all their attendant glamour, attracted and illuminated imaginations dulled by the relentless greyness of war.

But it was music and above all the exhilarating injection of jazz into tired souls that ignited the faltering heartbeat of the nation. Jazzing and its players arrived in England from America's Deep South and transcended all class barriers. Saturday nights at huge and exuberant dance halls became a weekly obsession for all the country's youth.

For some the search for spiritual and emotional well-being or simply for understanding was channelled into the creative paths of writing and painting. For others, love developed in unexpected places, in relationships they might not have considered in the straiter-laced confines of the Edwardian age. The sun-carressed skin and muscular arms of the gardener and the delicate complexion of his lady employer suddenly presented both parties with an attraction no longer worth denying.

Technological progress, particularly in aeroplane and motor-car design, as well as the increasingly pervasive use of the wireless, arrived along with other trends in fashion and the arts from across the Atlantic. The post-war world was rapidly becoming unrecognisable in many ways to those who had lived and died before the war.

In this book I have chosen to look at the lives of several individuals for whom the years preceding and following the Great Silence were especially significant, among them a soldier, an undergraduate, a bohemian, a newly married socialite, a duke, a cook, an artist, a surgeon, a war hero, a ten-year-old boy, a four-year-old girl, a butler, a dress designer and the Queen. Wherever possible I have spoken to the individuals themselves, or to their immediate descendants, as well as consulting private diaries and letters, and other sources published and unpublished.

It was a time when trust had vanished. In a just world the good were rewarded and the bad punished, yet the experience of the war had shown this belief to be faulty. Marriage and parenthood were no longer certain bets. The country that people had fought for was no longer the self-assured place they had assumed it to be. Lloyd George, the Prime Minister, had promised that this would be the war to end all wars. Could he be right?

Fighting and death had only been part of it. The delayed response to sights and sounds, the mutilation, the hammering of the guns, experienced by those returning was just beginning. Would any of them recover? Would any of them find lasting peace? Would a healing silence ever come to them, as they lay awake at night, trying to forget? This is a book about the pause that followed the cataclysm: the interval between the falling silent of the guns and the roaring of the 1920s.

I

Wound

August 1914–November 1918

Arthur Tommy Atkins had been the under-chauffeur for the Marquis de Soveral, the rather rakish but hugely popular Portuguese Ambassador to the Court of St James. The Marquis, nicknamed 'The Blue Monkey' for the six o'clock shadow permanently visible on his swarthy chin and also for his naughty though delightful way with the ladies, had been a close friend of Edward VII and had maintained this intimacy with Edward's successor, George V. The embassy Rolls-Royce was often to be seen waiting for its official occupant in the forecourt at Sandringham, and the driver and his deputy felt themselves to be hovering on the brink of a comfortable lifetime serving the great and good of the land.

Then war was declared. Tommy had since his schooldays fancied himself as something of a linguist and signed up with the London Irish Rifles to see a bit of the world. At the age of 22, he had hoped perhaps to visit Paree ('Well, that's what they call it over there,' he would explain) and to find a bit of 'Ooh la la'. He had longed for adventure, his chauffeuring duties confined to keeping the Marquis's Rolls-Royce in shining order and to prodding his boss, the elderly chauffeur, into staying awake at the wheel. Tommy's dream was to learn to drive, but he had never dared ask for a lesson, after once getting caught taking the gleaming machine out for a sneaky illicit run.

Everyone called Tommy by his middle name because the combination of the two, Tommy and Atkins, had been the army nickname for British soldiers for over 150 years. There was even a Victorian music hall song, with a chorus that went

Tommy Tommy Atkins,
You're a 'good un' heart and hand:
You're a credit to your calling
And to all your native land;
May your luck be never failing,
May your love be ever true!
God Bless you, Tommy Atkins,
Here's your Country's love to you!

The real Tommy Atkins knew all the Edwardian music hall songs and being a natural showman would belt out 'Up a Little Gravel Path' and the old East End favourite 'Have You Paid Your Rent?' Tommy hoped that his feet would stand the trials of war. They were rather flat and to his secret shame he had developed a large bunion on each big toe. He thought the bony swellings might be heredi- tary and hoped that if he was lucky enough to have children one day he would not pass on the lumpy tendency. But he had not let on about the bunion problem to the other lads and had joined in lustily as they sang together 'What a Great Holiday' on the march towards the coast-bound trains.

A sudden overwhelming love for England and an accompanying duty to defend it propelled these young men into France and beyond. Maude Onions, a female signaller with the British Expeditionary Force in northern France, had befriended a young soldier who had been reluctant to join up. 'I'm willing to lend a hand in this war business,' he confided to Maude, 'but when it comes to a change of career, it's off. They want me to sign on for three years – and after that?' he had wondered aloud to her. 'Hawk penny articles, I suppose.'

Another army recruit, a gunner, explained to Maude the process involved in cleaning guns. Showing her the soft white lamb's wool that he used to clean and polish the muzzles of the machine until they were spotless, he seemed to travel in his mind to 'somewhere in England . . . among the green fields' and for a moment Maude glimpsed the real hardship of being away from home for so long. She heard his 'mirthless laugh' as he blurted out, 'It's hard to connect, isn't it? My home is among the green fields in England . . . rearing the sheep and lambs is part of my life's work . . . it's hard to connect.'

In the countryside there was an old rural belief that a white feather in a bird's tail indicated a bird of inferior quality, and in the autumn of 1914 a custom had sprung up for angry women to thrust a white feather into the lapel of any young man of fighting age who was seen in the streets out of uniform. Despite the fairly rare unwillingness to fight, based on conscience, religious grounds or simple sheer terror, the humiliation associated with failing to join up was often overwhelming and young men, even those officially unqualified to fight for medical reasons, felt compelled to sign on. And there was disappointment in rejection. Mr Bickham, a veteran of the Boer War, was turned down on account of his poor teeth. 'They must want blokes to bite the damned Germans,' he spluttered in disgust.

For those left behind, the older men, women and children, the prospect of war was bearable only because the 'official' word promised that the conflict would be over by Christmas. In the town of Salford large queues formed outside Lipton's the grocers and the Maypole Dairy. The quick-thinking poor bought up huge quantities of sugar, which they sold off in small measures to those lacking the entrepreneurial spirit. Two thirds of Britain's sugar was imported and people feared the imposition of rationing. Panic and greed set in.

Parents tried to disguise their fear when saying goodbye to the young sons who had been accepted into the army. In 1916, the 18-year-old John Bullock kissed his mother and, after a moment's hesitation, shook his father's hand. He remembered his mother's last words, full of anxious advice 'to keep your feet dry', but in his excitement to be off, was unaware that her outward look of pride masked her apprehension: she recognised that 'a void had come into her breast that would remain until her son came home again'.

At first there had been no conscription. Kitchener's persuasive finger-pointing poster designed by Alfred Leete, marking out each individual as special, as chosen, had been enough to convince the youth of the country of their duty. They felt proud to be needed. But after the huge losses on the Western Front compulsory soldiering had been introduced in January 1916. The upper age limit for eligible men rose to 50 and was expanded to include married men, while the lower limit stayed fixed at 18, although many younger men lied in order to receive the King's Shilling. And as more individuals were needed to replace the dead, the physical standards imposed by the National Service medical boards were subtly relaxed. Photographic guidelines of newly approved body shapes were issued showing youths with emaciated bodies, alarmingly prominent shoulder bones, knock knees and an appearance of general ill health. Mr Bickham's teeth suddenly became no impediment to serving.

For a young man bored with the peacetime routine of life and the dreary prospect of following a trade that his father and grandfather had followed before him, the chance to escape was exhilarating. Many thousands of apprehensive young men who had originally been hesitant to leave the familiarity of home for the first time were lured to the front by General Sir Henry Rawlinson's imaginative concept of the Pals Battalions, and joined up with the inducement of finding comfort in comradeship. Homesickness vanished at the prospect of being surrounded by familiar faces from a school, village or workplace. The scheme, introduced in late August 1914, appealed to a sense of belonging, as well as to a local sense of pride. And there was another motive for signing up. A third of the British population, particularly those in the North and in the mining districts of Wales and Scotland, were living close to the poverty line. The enticement of the King's Shilling, substantial quantities of good cooked food, and a regular pay packet from the army were enough to outweigh the prospect of losing one's life.

And the reality of death in conflict was hazy. Death was reserved for the old. No member of that pre-war generation had known at first hand what war was like. According to the historian A. J. P. Taylor, young men imagined 'it would be an affair of great marches and great battles, quickly decided'. Public schoolboys yearning for a validation of their pampered way of life took up their officer duties with self-confessed relief at finding a new and exhilarating sense of purpose. At the beginning of the war, many like Julian Grenfell, son of leading society hostess Lady Desborough, were caught up in the novelty and excitement. An ebullient and popular young man, he wrote to his mother: 'It's all the best fun one ever dreamed of . . . the uncertainty of it is so good, like a picnic when you don't know where you're going to.' The society magazine, the *Tatler*, referred to the war specifically as 'The Great Adventure'. But seven months after Grenfell's cheery optimism, the picnic was over. Eton College sent 5,687 pupils into battle: of these 1,160 failed to return, including Grenfell; 1,467 were wounded.

Tommy Atkins had never been abroad before and his fiancée Kitty was looking forward to having him home well before Christmas so he could tell her about the goings-on over the Channel and the different habits of the French and the Germans whom he longed to meet. But the hopes of the Marquis de Soveral's under-chauffeur, like those of John Bullock, for a razzle-dazzle of an adventure, filled with exchanges with exciting foreign voices, were soon shot away. The imagined contact with foreigners was smothered at a few paces by the relentless noise of shellfire. The first few days of the five-month-long battle of the Somme sounded to the untrained ear like 'a colossal roar'. Guns woke you, guns prevented sleep. Christmas had come, and three more Christmases followed before Tommy returned home for good. He had found himself in a war that seemed at times as if it might continue indefinitely: there was no 'ooh la la' to report back to Kitty.

Sergeant Alfred Anderson of the 5th Battalion of the Black Watch did not enjoy his first Christmas in the trenches. For several months he had heard the sound of bullets and machine guns, and in rare moments German voices had drifted across from the other side. The reminder of the flesh-and-blood humanity of the enemy served to endorse a common agreement among British troops that they would try and shoot the enemy in the legs 'and no higher'. Even in hell, a class-rooted sense of common decency somehow struggled to the surface. The *Daily Mail* had sent Christmas puddings which, in a festive reversal of roles, were served to the soldiers by the officers. But Sergeant Anderson desperately wanted to be at home with his family on this most un-Christmas-like of days. 'It was quiet all around. In the dead silence we shouted out "Merry Christmas" – although none of us felt merry. We were so tired.'

Sergeant Anderson had received a Christmas box filled with cigarettes, sent by the King and Queen's daughter Princess Mary, but as he didn't smoke he handed the cigarettes to his friends and found to his pleasure that the Bible given to him by his mother fitted inside the box perfectly. That box containing his mother's Bible was the only thing he brought back with him from the war.

Night-time darkness on the battlefield was sometimes pushed aside by searchlights. A sudden, surprising snapshot of illumination would reveal what D. H. Lawrence, in a journey following the Bavarian army at the foot of the Alps in 1913, described as 'a greenish jewel of landscape, splendid bulk of trees, a green meadow, vivid'. Something 'beautiful beyond belief' would be lit up, only for it to be eclipsed by the return of darkness. War became a series of acts of waiting: waiting for light, waiting for sound, waiting for the next command, waiting for the next piece of news from home, waiting for a few days' leave, waiting for the next death to be witnessed or whispered, waiting for the next bullet to smash a hole in a face or a body, waiting for it to be over, waiting to die, waiting for silence.

As the war continued the *Daily Telegraph* war correspondent Philip Gibbs noted a growing realisation that the situation was 'more complex than the old simplicity, a sense of revolt against sacrifice unequally shed and devoted to a purpose which was not that for which they had been called to fight'. There were 57,470 British casualties on 1 July 1916, the first day of the battle of the Somme, a third of whom died of their wounds.

Officers would delve surreptitiously into leather travelling cases, to find the small pot of rouge with which to brighten their cheeks and disguise from young men who looked to them for confident leadership the paleness of fear that washed across their own faces. The young soldiers had lumbered towards the front line, carrying what was known as 'The Soldier's Christmas Tree'. Bent double under the weight of cartridge pouches, water bottle, gas helmet, entrenching tool, bayonet, groundsheet, overcoat, underclothes, socks, precious letters and cherished photographs, each man tried to make headway through the incessant rain and deep, inhibiting mud. Boots slipped off in the sludge, leaving their bare feet, in the poet Wilfred Owen's phrase, 'blood-shod'.

Over the course of those twenty weeks 125,000 British soldiers were killed, most of them so young that in the words of 22-year-old Violet Keppel, who herself had lost so many friends, they had only led 'half-smoked lives'. A junior officer on the front line was unlikely to survive longer than six weeks. Friends picked up parts of bodies that were no larger than a Sunday roast, gathered them together and buried them as best they could beneath the chaotic surface of the muddy fields, before returning to the slaughter. Confidence in political and military leadership dwindled. In a 1917 London pantomime two farmers sitting under a chestnut tree were hit by a falling chestnut each time they told a lie. When one remarked that Lloyd George was predicting an imminent end to the war, the audience smiled wearily as the entire contents of the tree erupted, bombarding the stage with nuts.

Faith in the classically noble utterances of the classically beautiful Rupert Brooke was shattered. Patriotism had become smudged. Sentiments that expressed the belief that this war was essential if you loved England were shown to be lies. Disillusionment was commonplace in conversation among fighting men, and poets at the front began to reflect the shift in feeling as the war showed no sign of ending.

Fifteen years before Brooke had written of a far away but always patriotic meadow, Thomas Hardy had described in more realistic terms the loneliness of a young soldier, Drummer Hodge. 'Fresh from his Wessex home', Hodge had been killed in the Boer War, his body lying 'uncoffined' for ever under 'strange-eyed constellations'. Here was an unromantic battlefield, one that was no outpost of indestructible Englishness, but one that was instead a lonely, alien and abandoned place. The patriotic sentiments of Rupert Brooke's verses now seemed poignantly misplaced. In poems such as Siegfried Sassoon's 'Suicide in the Trenches' the truth came directly from the voices and experiences of the soldiers themselves.

> I knew a simple soldier boy
> Who grinned at life in empty joy,
> Slept soundly through the lonesome dark,
> And whistled early with the lark.
>
> In winter trenches, cowed and glum,
> With crumps and lice and lack of rum,
> He put a bullet through his brain.
> No one spoke of him again.

You smug-faced crowds with kindling eye
Who cheer when soldier lads march by,
Sneak home and pray you'll never know
The hell where youth and laughter go.

Danger was everywhere, as the noise of the guns gave way to the silent and suffocating arrival of gas. Early German experiments with chemical warfare in the form of poison gas had become refined. The first, thick pus-green cloud of chlorine gas had drifted towards the front line at Ypres in 1915 and by the end of the war the even deadlier mustard gas was in common use, blistering both the body and the lungs that inhaled it, leaving just under 200,000 men guttering, choking, drowning, and prompting the poet Wilfred Owen in 'Dulce et Decorum Est' to write his most devastating lines.

The American portraitist John Singer Sargent had been out to the front line with the former Slade Professor Henry Tonks in order to research a commission from the British Government's Ministry of Information for a planned Hall of Remembrance art scheme. Sargent came across a line of men who had just suffered a gas attack and began work immediately afterwards on a huge painting. A nurse explained what the effect of the gas might be on the men. 'With mustard gas the effects did not become apparent for up to twelve hours. But then it began to rot the body, within and without. The skin blistered, the eyes became extremely painful, and nausea and vomiting began. Worse, the gas attacked the bronchial tubes, stripping off the mucous membrane. The pain was almost beyond endurance.' Mr J. L. Bragg, a baker, ran an advertisement in the personal column of *The Times*, quoting a letter of endorsement:

> Will you kindly send me by post some charcoal biscuits? I find these biscuits have been the greatest benefit to me, and have enabled me to eat more or less normally, which I have not been able to do since I left France in April this year with Gas poisoning.

Mr Bragg promised the readers that on receipt of threepence he would provide sufferers with a sample of his magic biscuits.

A suspicion lurked among soldiers of all ranks who returned home on a few days' leave that those left behind at home had been living in ignorance, whether voluntary or unconscious. There was some truth in this. The happily married Mrs Farr from Somerset had been surviving the war years in the simple unflinching conviction that at the end of it she would be reunited with her husband. One day the telegram boy arrived on his bicycle, painted blood-red for urgency, and handed her a brown envelope that Mrs Farr jammed down the front of her dress. She did not tell anyone of its arrival. The news contained inside the envelope, whether it was the speculative 'missing in action' or the definitive 'killed in action', was she knew instinctively, going to be too dreadful to see written down. Mantelpieces up and down the country contained photographs turned to the walls, often in frames surrounded by small blue-painted flowers spelling out beneath the picture the words 'Forget me not'. Sometimes the edge of an unopened telegram peeped out from behind the frame. For as long as the envelope remained sealed, a flicker of hope edged out the truth.

But as the war progressed hope was clung to with increasing desperation. Ever an evanescent commodity, it slipped through the fingers with an inevitability that grew daily. 'You hope for the best, exhausting though that effort is, until the time comes when hope evades you and all the evidence is conspiring to tell you to behave differently and reality insists you stop hoping. For what is the point?' asked the daughter of a soldier who had been reported missing in action, but whose death remained unconfirmed. Denial acted as the shock-absorber of grief, although sometimes a letter posted to the front arrived too late and was returned to the sender with the single brutal word 'Killed' stamped on the outside.

Meanwhile the Government's morale-boosting propaganda had contributed in large part to the ignorance at home of the true state of affairs abroad. Positive stories written by journalists who feared prosecution if they told the truth, including Philip Gibbs of the *Daily Telegraph*, were designed to put the best possible slant on the news. Soldiers who longed to describe the dreadful reality of warfare had their letters censored. Rumours were rife. The 18-year-old Barbara Cartland believed the stories that 'Germans were extracting fat from human corpses which were tied together and sent from France in cattle-trucks'.

An impression of amateurishness, even larkiness at home disturbed the sceptical soldier. Girls from munitions factories spent their wages on gramophones and tickets to dance halls and cinemas, while smug young women from the aristocracy considered themselves heroic in adopting flattering nurse's uniform though wholly unqualified for the task. Country girls working on the land paraded around in 'some kind of fancy dress with buttons and shoulder straps, breeches and puttees' as Philip Gibbs scathingly described the land army outfits, while at the same time there were men working the land who were morally opposed to killing, and had remained in England, struggling with their consciences, often restless and troubled by the decision they had made.

Censorship operated on newspapers, especially on Lord North-cliffe's *Daily Mail*, while sections of the Home Front tried to continue with their lives in much same way they always had, the upper classes in particular clinging to the old existence. Octogenarian Lord Fitzhardinge remained at his twelfth-century, 'pink mammoth' tur-reted, silver-roofed Berkeley Castle in Gloucestershire, continuing to hunt four days a week across the water meadows that led to the Severn. To the delight of Violet Keppel his young house guest, daughter of Edward VII's long-standing mistress Alice Keppel, his huntsmen dressed 'in saffron yellow', while his Lordship wore a Persian cat called Omar wrapped around his neck like some exotic serpent.

Lady Diana Manners, daughter of the Duke of Rutland and a leading society beauty, felt that many of those left at home were 'fren-ziedly dancing a tarantella' in order to prevent the increasingly fatal news damaging an increasingly fragile national morale. Footmen still served at the grand tables and were still, Diana Manners noticed, 'blinded by powder' used for whitening the hair: the excess floated towards the soup bowl as the servant bent forward to ladle out the vichyssoise. In 1916 a sexy, teasing song and dance routine called 'Tanko', designed to poke fun at the new armadillo-like war machine, the tank, was causing hilarity at the Palace Theatre in London. Siegfried Sassoon was enraged by the irresponsible descriptions in the press of these 'waddling toads' and by the amused public response. Watching a London theatre audience laughing while men were dying inspired his poem 'Blighters' in response to the inappropriate mockery.

I'd like to see a Tank come down the stalls,
Lurching to rag-time tunes, or 'Home, Sweet Home'
And there'd be no more jokes in music-halls
To mock the riddled corpses round Bapaume.

How were soldiers to find a way to describe to their isolated, sometimes disbelieving families what happened out there? Although the sound of gunfire was occasionally audible on this side of the Channel, there was an inevitable remoteness about the battlefield. Comfort for those in love but separated might be found in pulling a ragged silk stocking belonging to a sweetheart over the head before hoping for sleep. The soldier's way of life in war remained unrecognisable to anyone who had not experienced it. One soldier, Alfred Finnigan, called it 'hell with the lid off'. How were these men to convincingly describe the rats as large as otters who gorged themselves on the human flesh that lay rotting all around them, or the stomach-churning death-reek whose smell could not be shifted even by the scent of the strongest Turkish cigarette? The rats had developed a reaction to the meat of dead men. Eating it would make their faces swell and whiten visibly at the top of their greasy, grey bodies. Luminous in the darkness of the bottom of a muddy trench, these ghostly creatures would move swiftly towards sleeping men, waking them with a start as they dragged their tails across the men's faces in the constant search for another meal. Lice were transparent when hungry, but turned black after sucking on blood. The poet Robert Graves met a group of men trying to remove the lice from one another. They were discussing whether to kill the young or the old insects. 'Morgan here says that if you kill the old ones, the young ones will die of grief,' Graves was told as the men continued their debate. 'But Parry here says that the young ones are easier to kill and you can catch the old ones when they come to the funeral.'

Crawling lice crept in a steady file over the soldiers' filthy clothing. They could be temporarily halted by turning a vest inside out or by lighting a match along the seams of trousers, only for the insects to re-emerge moments later. Body heat itself encouraged the hatching of the eggs. Bluebottles and cockroaches fed off the live bodies.

The mud, the rats, the wet, the dirt and the lack of medicine meant that almost every soldier in the trenches was affected at times by trench foot. The infection, an extreme form of athlete's foot, produced a swelling the pain of which was so acute that men dreaded the slightest physical proximity, lest the foot be casually brushed against, causing them to scream out in agony.

The daily food rations included twenty ounces of bread, three ounces of cheese, eight ounces of vegetables, four ounces of jam, four ounces of butter – flavoured by half an ounce of salt, one thirty-sixth of an ounce of pepper and one twentieth of mustard. But the irregular supply made meals achingly inadequate. The quality was disgusting, the quantity pathetic. The bully beef and bullet-hard dog biscuits provided little comfort or nourishment. Twenty ounces of tobacco a day was allocated per man and the rare treat of a bar of chocolate, to be shared between three. Half a gill of rum, amounting to one double measure, or when supplies were exhausted, a pint of porter (the soldier's version of lager) had promised a tantalising moment of numbness before the recipient was expected to go and fight for his life. One soldier, Albert 'Smiler' Marshall, who did not like the taste, saved his ration, finding that the alcohol helped as a sort of anaesthetic for the pain he suffered from trench foot.

In between the conflict, boredom was intense. Albert remembered from his childhood the 'glamour of the redcoats' as he watched them in admiration returning to his village after the Boer War. There was little glamour surrounding him in his trench. He missed four village Boxing Day celebrations, a day when the villagers would tie a lead and collar on all the pets, making a fine procession of pigs, goats, ferrets, cats, dogs, tame mice, and the splendid cockerel. The menagerie would race towards a greased pole in the middle of the green. The first to reach the dead duck attached to the top was the winner. Sergeant Jack Dinham found himself thinking of Otford, his village in Kent where at the Boxing Day meet the hounds would be treated to porridge bubbling in huge steaming metal pans, while in summer the Vicar, the Reverend William Lutyens, cricket-mad brother of the famous architect, would be seen in church, his white cricket flannels just visible beneath his cassock. Jack had wondered if his job at Knole, the big house nearby where he worked as Lord Sackville's coachman, would still be open to him after the war.

While away at war, Siegfried Sassoon missed any sense of intellectual stimulus, or even the reassurance of clarity of thought. 'Mental
activity was clogged and hindered by gross physical actualities.' Loneliness was constant. Men missed women. Most of all they missed
their mothers and called aloud for them with increasing frequency.
They sang a song together:

H stands for happiness that you should find there
O stands for old folks in the old armchair
M stands for mother; you'll never find another, no matter where you
    roam
E stands for everyone as everyone knows
H.O.M.E. spells home.

The men missed their wives and their fiancées, too. The Government and the army chiefs were well aware of the physical longings
and the dangers of frustrated abstinence in an army made up largely
of thousands of lusty young men, confused and ashamed of their feelings. Thousands of young British men had grown up in families where
bodily functions and the natural instincts and affections of marriage
went largely unmentioned. Even the coy enquiry concerning the
proper functioning of the digestive system, 'Are you consti?', from a
mother to her child was too intimate to express in full.

Not many men however remained ignorant of the ever-widening
spread of venereal disease. Just behind the battle lines only a mile
or two from the front, girls waited to 'comfort' men, irrespective of
whether they were German, British or French, waiting for them in
abandoned chateaux, village houses, hay barns, caravans, farm buildings and the upper floors of inns. Different coloured lanterns
indicated the rank of clientele allowed entry. Blue denoted a place
reserved for officers, the light sometimes swinging from a pole that
stood next to a sign declaring 'No Admittance for Dogs and
Soldiers'. Common soldiers were directed towards the red light
establishments. Sometimes the queues outside these places could
number a hundred men or more, with three worn-out French
women waiting inside.

The price per slot varied from two and a half to ten francs or
two to eight shillings, although a bartering system involving bread

and sausages was also prevalent. One innocent young officer, hearing his turn called, made his way to room number six where in the bitter-sweet, dirt-smelling near darkness he could see the outline of a female figure who, turning towards him, hiked up her black night-dress to her waist and fell backwards on the edge of the bed. He realised that the highly anticipated delights of seduction were already over. She was ready.

These women estimated that operating a strict schedule of ten minutes per man, they could service an entire battalion every seven days, a production rate that most were usually able to sustain for only three weeks before retiring exhausted, and invariably unwell, but proud of their staying power. This experience had been, for many of the prospectively syphilitic young men, their introduction to the 'joy' of physical love. Even the virginal Prince of Wales went in 1916 with some fellow officers to watch naked girls performing erotic poses in a brothel in Calais, concluding from his own 'first insight into such things' that it was a 'perfectly filthy and revolting sight'.

Only the Austrian army paid much attention to either contraception or hygiene, the prostitute requiring her 'guest' to use a 'preventative instrument'; if he refused, the girl was to 'lubricate his organ with borated Vaseline', a paste made of boric acid, and after the experience was concluded, he was required to visit the 'disinfectant room'. No such rules had applied to British troops and the threat of venereal disease sometimes led soldiers to seek sexual relief with each other. *The Field Almanac* issued to Lieutenant Skelton cautioned men not to 'ease themselves promiscuously', although the detailed instructions on the necessity for cleanliness of the body at all times were impossible to implement in the filthy conditions of the camps. George V, hearing of the extent of homosexual activity in the army some two decades after the imprisonment of Oscar Wilde, had been heard to mutter: 'I thought men like that shot themselves.' There was also a belief that homosexuality might be infectious and Scotland Yard kept a register of known homosexuals. Recovery from prosecution was at best rare and in reality unknown. Two hundred and seventy soldiers and twenty officers were court-martialled for 'acts of gross indecency with another male person according to the Guidance notes in the Manual of Military Law'.

At home morale was shored up by the belief in the value of sacrifice and the reflected pride it bestowed on those who survived. Edward Grey, the former Foreign Secretary, had said, 'None of us who give our sons in this war are so much to be pitied as those who have no sons to give.' For those who had died young, the lines of Laurence Binyon's 1914 poem with its Shakespearian echoes continued to reverberate as the idealisation and myth-making of sacrifice was encouraged.

> They shall grow not old, as we that are left grow old:
> Age shall not weary them, nor the years condemn.

Nearly ten million dead soldiers and sailors and airmen had died in the conflict, three quarters of a million from Britain. A further twelve and a half million had been wounded; nearly one and three quarter million of these were British. An estimated 160,000 women lost husbands and double that number of children emerged fatherless at the end of the war. An estimated 30 per cent of all men aged between 20 and 24 in 1911 were now dead. There were no figures for the fiancées, girlfriends, mothers, children, grandmothers, grandfathers, aunts, uncles, cousins and friends for whom life had changed for ever. On 11 November 1918 the colossal roar finally stopped. Those who had survived hoped the wound would begin to heal in silence. After the catastrophic death of Victorian certainties, silence was beginning to seem like the only possible articulation of the truth.

2

Shock

Armistice Day, 11 November 1918

Just after breakfast on a Monday morning in the middle of November, Maude Onions, the young woman from Liverpool who had become a signaller with the Women's Auxiliary Army Corps, sat down at her stenograph, the shorthand machine she used in the little signal office at Boulogne. Her job was to relay messages to the front. That morning she tapped out the following words:

> Hostilities will cease at 11.00 a.m. November 11th. Troops will stand fast at the line reached at that hour which will be reported to army headquarters. Defensive precautions will be maintained. There will be no intercourse of any description with the enemy. Further instructions follow.

Three hours after she had sent the communication, Maude took 'an involuntary glance' at the clock in her office and saw that the moment the world had been waiting for had arrived. But nothing happened. There was silence. It was, observed Maude, 'as though France had just heaved a vast sigh of relief'.

Maude had arrived in Boulogne eighteen months earlier on a lovely June day in 1917. She was excited at the prospect of joining her country's young men in teaching 'the Hun a lesson'. Soon after her arrival, she had made friends with some of the men. Her skill at the piano was warmly welcomed as she tried to please them with song after song, the requests coming with 'merciless rapidity'. She had asked a Scottish private in the packed canteen how long he thought the war would last and was surprised by his disillusioned response. 'I don't care,' he had replied, 'all I want is home and wife and kiddies and I don't care who England belongs to.'

Maude's earlier mood of eager anticipation gave way to a sense of unease as she worried that 'the seeming futility and endlessness

26

of the war was eating into the souls of men'. One of them, 'a look of inexpressible weariness' on his face, described to her a job worse than that of fighting: 'I've been digging up dead bodies – digging them up for their identification discs so that we can send word home . . . the fellow I was working with dug up his own brother and cried like a child.' Maude found it impossible to look the man in the eyes as he spoke.

Later that day, as Maude walked down towards the port the eerie atmosphere persisted. Then as the church clock struck three, 'Every siren and hooter was let loose, every church bell clanged out – a deafening roar.' But things were still not right. Even though the streets were packed with people, 'not a word was spoken, not a single cry of celebration was made'. To Maude it seemed as if 'the stricken soul of France had not been able to find within itself the desire to rejoice'.

Suddenly her attention was caught by a sound, 'the noise and din, the sobbing of a woman, a few yards away, finis – finis – incroyable'. Later on she remembered that almost unconsciously she had found herself 'in the little military cemetery behind the congested street of the town where our men were buried three deep, for land was dear in France, and where the graves had been so beautifully kept by the loving hands of a khaki girl. I could not distinguish the names for the mist of tears.' Barely able to drag herself away, Maude stumbled and then almost fell over something in the ground; a broken piece of wood that had sunk so deep that it was scarcely visible. She had come across the grave of a German soldier and, anxious not be spotted, she hurriedly laid a few flowers at the foot of the broken cross. She knew that 'somewhere a woman was sorrowing'.

As soon as Maude's signal reached the field units, messengers on foot, bicycle and horseback spread out in all directions, carrying up to the troops at the front line pink slips of paper torn from signal pads on which news of the ceasefire was written.

But the announcement that the war was over did not deter all those still caught up in the process of slaughter. Three hundred and twenty American soldiers lost their lives at Meuse on the morning of the 11th with a further three thousand wounded. General Pershing, Commanding General of the American Expeditionary

Forces, remained stubbornly reluctant to observe the ceasefire before teaching the Germans one final lesson.

Many British soldiers on the front line were too exhausted to celebrate. A muted cheer and a half-hearted attempt to send a hat spinning in the air was the most that some could manage. There was no crossing over into the enemy lines for the gentlemanly shaking of hands. The comradeship felt for fellow human beings during the Christmas truce four years earlier had evaporated.

In the northern French village of Malpaquet on the Belgian border, Brigade Major Wilfred House of the 57th Brigade wanted to demonstrate his gratitude for having survived the last four years. 'We hurriedly organised a tea with rationed food for all the children in the village school', and in their turn the villagers arrived with flowers and wine and pâté, and some rationed eggs and butter. Major House found the party to be 'very moving and very simple'.

In Paris as the bells of Notre-Dame began to ring, flags sold out in every shop; so the scientist Marie Curie, with the help of the daily lady from the Radium Institute, stitched together some blue, red and white material and hung the home-made flag from the Institute's window.

In Germany a young corporal of the 16th Bavarian Reserve Infantry lay on his hospital bed wondering if he would ever fully regain his sight. A few weeks earlier he had been blinded in a gas attack after four years of fighting at the Western Front. The gas had begun to gnaw at his eyes and although the cloudiness was beginning to clear, his vision was still hazy. The news of the Armistice, given to him in the convalescent hospital by the local padre, reduced him to a state of despair as he thought of 'so many a dear friend and comrade' who had died in the fighting. On hearing the news the young soldier had 'tottered and groped' his way back to the ward and at the thought of defeat 'threw myself on my bunk and dug my burning head into my blanket and pillow'. The medical staff were worried. They wondered if Corporal Adolf Hitler was going out of his mind.

In Holland a train was on its way to Arnhem. Inside a curtain-shuttered carriage sat the white-faced Kaiser Wilhelm. A chink in the curtains made it impossible for him to ignore the thousands of people who stood on the banks shouting abuse as the train passed by, indicating with a swipe of the hand how they would like to cut the former leader's throat.

In the English Channel the crew of HMS *Amazon*, which was patrolling the stretch of sea at Beachy Head, were amazed to see a French fishing boat covered in flags. As fishermen shouted out that the war was over, the incredulous captain of the *Amazon* retorted that the boat should return to harbour at once and stop giving false hope to other passing ships.

In London, a young diplomat Harold Nicolson was working in the basement of his office in Whitehall, sufficiently confident in the imminent announcement of an armistice that he was already drawing up plans for the proposed peace conference. In fact he knew the ceasefire agreement had been signed in a railway carriage nearly six hours earlier in Compiègne. Leaving his desk for a moment in search of another map, Nicolson passed a window that overlooked the Prime Minister's official residence. The time was five minutes to eleven on 11 November.

At that moment the door of number 10 was flung open and a hatless Lloyd George emerged. His thick white hair, barely restrained behind his ears, reflected the eagerness of his mood. 'At eleven o'clock this morning the war will be over,' Nicolson heard Lloyd George cry out as if he was a street newspaper seller hoping to attract the attention of anyone who might be listening. He repeated the words several times. As Nicolson watched, the street began to fill up and within a few minutes there was no room to move. There was silence in the crowd, an interruption for cheering and then silence again. But by this time Lloyd George appeared flustered, his flushed face in contrast to the bright white of his hair which, owing to the absence of his customary homburg, was now flying all over the place in the wind. After a burst from the crowd of 'God Save the King', Lloyd George pushed his way back again through the mass of people towards the sanctuary of his famous front door.

That afternoon, on the first day the guns fell silent, the announcement of the Kaiser's abdication and his flight to Holland was posted outside *The Times*' office in Printing House Square. A group of passers-by gathered around the billboard and began to cheer. But the newspaper staff noted that the tone of the cheers was not 'hilarious'. 'The shadows of the last few years remained,' the reporter noted, even though 'the silver lining of passing clouds' seemed to be reflected in the eyes of the passers-by.

A week earlier, although there had been no official word that the Germans were planning a surrender, hundreds of German guns without public explanation or fanfare were placed along the length of the Mall from Buckingham Palace. Brought directly from the French battlefields, they resembled the wounded enemy soldiers themselves, pockmarked and stained. Final, brutal evidence of the war had arrived in the heart of the capital.

In New York there had been a muddle. On Thursday 6 November rumours that the end of the war was imminent had become so pronounced that they were taken for fact. Glancing out of the window of her couture cutting room on to the pavement below, Lucy Duff Gordon, the famous British dress designer, New York resident and survivor of the *Titanic* disaster six years earlier, was amazed to see old men letting off fireworks and staid-looking fathers kissing lovely young women who were quite clearly perfect strangers. At 2.30 p.m. the Stock Exchange closed and one hundred and fifty-five tons of ticker tape fluttered down into the street. Lucy found herself swept up in the excitement and, although her couture business had not been thriving in the manner she would have liked, she impulsively offered all her dress-cutters time off and unlimited champagne for the rest of the day. The day passed, Lucy noted, 'in an orgy of celebration'. As dusk was falling another official announcement was made. It had been a false alarm. There was no armistice as yet. America who had joined the war nineteen months earlier remained at war.

Five days later, on 11 November New York felt both sheepish and exhausted and Lucy noticed that the champagne they still felt compelled to drink had lost its fizz.

In London, the newspaper compositors had been given six hours' notice for assembling the size of type suitable for announcing the news that people had been longing for. The Armistice headlines were an inch high and small boys on bicycles careered through the rain-drenched streets carrying bundles of damp newspapers yelling the single word 'Victory'.

In front of Buckingham Palace the white marble statue of Queen Victoria turned black with the number of people who had climbed into the old sovereign's lap and clung to the winged statues that surrounded her seated figure. The royal family appeared briefly on the balcony acknowledging the cheering crowds, a reassuring symbol for some that Britain was returning to normal.

In London's East End, the eleven o'clock sirens were at first confused for those that announced an air raid. The death of several children in Poplar two years before, when a Zeppelin had exploded in the grounds of a school, had not been forgotten. Children in Canning Town were terrified when a shop handed out armfuls of free fireworks. The noise made by the rockets and Catherine wheels were frighteningly reminiscent of the deadly German bombs.

Duff Cooper, glamorous diplomat and Grenadier, had returned from the battle lines a few days earlier. Back in London he felt overcome with despondency and unable to go down into the streets and join the Armistice Day party. As he watched the scene below him, with the coloured fairy lights threaded through the tricolour draperies, the cheering and the waving of flags, he was 'overcome with melancholy'. He shuddered at the dancing and the noise of celebration and could think only of his friends 'who were dead'. After dining at the Ritz on food that was 'cold and nasty' he slipped away as soon as possible, feeling the infinite sadness of loss wash over his girlfriend, Diana Manners, reducing her to tears. There was another reason, however, for Duff's low spirits. He had a temperature of 102 and he suspected that he might be suffering from 'a sharp attack' of influenza.

Florence Younghusband, wife of General George Younghusband who had commanded British and Indian troops during the Turkish invasion of Egypt, was travelling on the top of a London bus at the moment of the ceasefire. In front of her was a soldier, his face shattered by a shell. As Florence watched, the soldier 'looked straight ahead and remained stonily silent'. Suddenly the lady bus conductor collapsed into the seat beside her and, leaning her head on Florence's shoulder, she wept. Her husband, she confided to Florence, had died two months before and she felt incapable of celebrating. Florence, whose husband had been invalided home in 1916, felt herself to be a lucky one.

Susan and Tom Owen listened as the church bells of Shrewsbury began ringing, and said a prayer of thanks that their three sons had been spared, before going to answer the knock on the front door. A young man stood outside patiently, a telegram in his hand. The news concerning Wilfred, their eldest boy, could not have been more terrible.

Vera Brittain heard the sounds that signalled of the end of the war through the window of the London hospital annexe where her hands were buried deep in a basin of pinkish water. Standing in her nurse's uniform she continued to wash out and disinfect the bloody dressing bowls. Her pointed chin was set firm in concentration at her task. She did not interrupt her work, because 'like a sleeper who is determined to go on dreaming after being told to wake up' she had no interest in the jubilation going on outside the window. Only three years earlier she had written to her fiancé contemplating this exact moment. 'Would she be one of those who take a happy part in the triumph?' she had wondered, or instead would she 'listen to the merriment with a heart that breaks and ears that try to keep out the mirthful sounds?'

A few weeks after receiving the news in December 1915 that her 20-year-old fiancé Roland Leighton had been killed, Vera Brittain had gone to the house of Roland's parents. That morning the postman had delivered a large brown paper packet. When Vera walked into their sitting room she had seen Roland's clothes laid out all over the floor encrusted with mud. Here were clothes that showed what even a bluntly worded telegram could not show. The mud on this bedraggled set of garments 'had not the usual clean smell of earth but it was as though it were saturated with dead bodies'. Here was mud of a different kind to ordinary English mud or even ordinary French mud. This was mud that clung, tenacious even when the struggle was over. This was death mud. In that moment, breathing in the dreadful smell of the jacket, the waistcoat, the breeches soaked in the dying blood of the man she had loved, Vera understood the reality of war, of decay, of mortality. Buried deep in an inner pocket she had found the only possession of Roland's to escape the stench of death: a photograph of Vera herself. The warmth of his body had never lost the power to repel the damp and decay.

Walking through the rain on 11 November 1918, with some fellow Voluntary Aid Detachment nurses, Vera slowly registered that the streets were brightly lit for the first time in four years. Her joylessness grew with the same speed as the elation that surrounded her. No adored brother and no longed for fiancé were here to celebrate with her; there was therefore nothing to celebrate. That evening, finding it impossible to recapture 'the lost youth that the war had stolen', she too realised for the first time 'with all that full realisation meant' that the world had altered irrevocably and that 'the dead were dead and would never return'.

The novelist and spiritualist Sir Arthur Conan Doyle was sitting in the lobby of the Grosvenor Hotel in Park Lane. Exactly two weeks before Maude Onions' signal had gone out along the wires, Conan Doyle's son, weakened by a wound he had suffered in the war, had caught influenza and died. As Sir Arthur sat in the lobby, still barely able to register the catastrophic news, he saw a well-dressed woman push her way through the revolving doors of the hotel. Carrying a Union flag in each of her hands, she slid into a solitary waltz, slowly, elegantly and silently making her way around the large lobby before spinning her way back through the circling door, then out again into the street.

The novelist Arnold Bennett welcomed the damp foggy day because at least it was 'an excellent thing to dampen hysteria and bolshevism'. He had noticed that in places there was a sort of madness in the air. Siegfried Sassoon was disgusted by what he saw. The poet was on sick-leave in Oxford where in the Cornmarket he saw that a woman had tucked her skirts right up to her naked waist and was playing to the cheering crowd, waving a Union flag at the army and navy cadets with unashamed abandon. Taking the train up to London, Sassoon found 'an outburst of mob patriotism . . . a loathsome ending to the loathsome tragedy of the last four years'.

The morning's peace announcement had come as something of a surprise and so it was not until later that many of the celebrants found their stride. But for some the effort was beyond them.

Ottoline Morrell, hostess, socialite, bohemian, friend of Virginia Woolf, felt 'too numb to respond' to the news, her thoughts turning to the distress of the young children of German prisoners of war as she wondered how she could contribute to their new life in England. Perhaps she could arrange Morris dancing or carpentry lessons in the village hall where she lived at Garsington in Oxfordshire? That evening she emerged with the painter Mark Gertler into Charing Cross Road from a performance of the ballet at the Coliseum and was confronted by a disturbing scene in the street. The lifeless arms of a very drunk young boy with one leg were being hauled over his crutches by two 'rough, thick set' men but the arms would not stay in place. As the limp youth collapsed, his companions tried to drag him along the ground. Ottoline and Gertler crossed the road towards them but the men spoke angrily, snapping at them to go away and leave them alone. War's contribution to this young man's life, Ottoline wrote later in her diary, had been to 'maim him in body and ruin him in soul'.

The Russian impresario Serge Diaghilev was back in London on Armistice night and had dined with the writer Osbert Sitwell in Swan Walk in Chelsea. After dinner the party went up to Trafalgar Square where they found a packed crowd 'sometimes joining up, linking hands, dashed like the waves of the sea against the sides of the Square, against the railings of the National Gallery, sweeping up so far even as beyond the shallow stone steps of St Martin's in the Fields'. Packed between the flag-waving, hat-brandishing revellers, cigarettes stuck to their lower lips, mouths opened wide to yell out the cheers, Sitwell examined Diaghilev's reaction to the scene. 'With something of the importance of a public monument attaching to his scale and build, bear-like in his fur coat, [he] gazed with an air of melancholy exhaustion at the crowds'.

Diaghilev often appeared exhausted. Excessive consumption of food seemed in particular to sap his energy. The French couturier Coco Chanel had noticed how, forehead already perspiring, the impresario would not even bother to remove his white gloves before helping himself to a proffered box of chocolates, continuing to 'finish the box, his fat cheeks and his heavy chin wobbling as he munched . . . his trousers held up by a couple of safety pins'.

Cynthia Curzon (known as Cimmie to her friends), younger daughter of the former Viceroy of India, was also in Trafalgar Square, straddling a stone lion, a Union flag wrapped around her shoulders, watching the German guns (that had been brought into the square from the Mall) being set alight. While Cimmie joined in with all those around her belting out the rousing words of 'Land of Hope and Glory' into the night air, a dark-haired officer of athletic appearance stood watching her, a look of despair on his face. On her descent to the pavement he challenged her elation.

'Do any of you think for one moment of the loss of life, the devastation and misery?' he asked a somewhat abashed Cimmie. The officer introduced himself. He was Oswald Mosley, and at the age of 21 was standing as Coalition candidate for the Harrow seat at the following month's general election.

Doris Scovell, assistant cook, was out on the town that night, her hand tucked into the crook of the arm of her sweetheart, the footman Will Titley. They had both been given the evening off from their domestic duties below stairs at the grand house at 142 Piccadilly. The night of 11 November 1918 was an occasion for courting couples to go out and celebrate.

Not far from number 142, a celebratory evening at the Savoy was threatening to get out of hand as delirious members of the RAF swung from the chandeliers. The following morning the dustbins of the hotel contained 2,700 smashed glasses. Nearby in Regent Street an exuberant young woman was sitting on the roof of a taxi waving flags that she had snaffled from the shelves of Selfridges department store. Restaurants and cafés that had been closed after three hours each evening for the last four years remained open to revellers until 11.00 p.m. by special order of the Prefect of Police.

At the Apollo Theatre the production of *Arlette* starring Miss Winifred Barnes was interrupted as Herbert Buckmaster, husband of the actress Gladys Cooper, watched a young man leap from a box on to the dress circle tier. Landing neatly on the stage, he threw himself into the leading lady's arms and gave her a resounding kiss. The audience 'howled with delight'.

Violet Keppel was in a mood to feel 'a reckless sense of combined release and anti-climax'. Despite the death of so many of

Violet's friends, making her accustomed to requiring 'superhuman courage to open a newspaper', the end of the war coincided with the intense flowering of a great love affair. Although the object of her passion was in bed alone being monitored with some concern by her husband after an outbreak of flu, nothing could diminish Violet's personal happiness that day, not even the absence through illness of her lover Vita Sackville-West.

On the evening of the ceasefire David Garnett, a pacifist who had been working as a farm labourer at Charleston, the East Sussex farm of the painter Vanessa Bell, found the London streets milling with lorryloads of ecstatic factory girls, bearing the yellow stains of acid that had leaked over their hands and faces as they made up the munitions. Exhilarated by the sight, Garnett met up with the artist Duncan Grant and together they went to a flat in the Adelphi to join the critic Clive Bell, the painters Roger Fry and Dora Carrington, the economist Maynard Keynes, the Russian ballerina Lydia Lopokova (who had come straight from her performance in *Schéhérazade* at the Coliseum) and Lytton Strachey, the fêted author of the recently published biographical sketches *Eminent Victorians*. Osbert Sitwell and Diaghilev arrived at the party directly from Trafalgar Square and Sitwell watched in surprise as 'the tall flagging figure' of Strachey 'with his rather narrow angular beard, long inquisitive nose . . . jigg[ed] about with an amiable debility'. Strachey, Sitwell concluded, was 'unused to dancing'. Sitwell's brother Sacheverell was there too, confusing the uncomprehending Diaghilev, whose most fluent expression in English was 'more chocolate pudding', and who could not understand why Sacheverell insisted on catching the last train to Aldershot. 'Who was this Aldershot? She must be very beautiful.'

Soon D. H. Lawrence arrived with his wife Frieda but Garnett was shocked by his friend's appearance. The light had left the famous novelist's eyes and Garnett's loving greeting was received with a flatness bordering on indifference. Another friend, Cynthia Asquith, had noticed that the war had given Lawrence the appearance of someone in 'acute physical pain'. Grief and anger combined to prompt him to confess to her that his soul had been 'fizzling savagely', and despite 'radiant lucid intervals' Cynthia Asquith thought him to be in a state of 'delirium'. Garnett, hurt by the rebuff and incapable of an articulate response, gathered Carrington into his arms and whirled her into the centre of the room as someone began to play on the piano.

But Lawrence's presence was impossible to ignore and Garnett returned to hear him speak. 'I suppose you think the war is over and that we shall go back to the kind of world you lived in before,' Lawrence snapped, in a tone of deep scorn. 'But the war isn't over,' he continued, answering his own question. 'The hate and evil is greater now than ever . . . It makes me sick to see you rejoicing like a butterfly in the last rays of the sun before the winter . . . hate will be dammed up in men's hearts and will show itself in all sorts of ways which will be worse than war. Whatever happens there can be no peace on earth.' And with his words joy and merriment left the room.

Later, at Waterloo Station Sacheverel Sitwell, who was trying to catch the last train to Aldershot, saw groups of women staggering along the platform, so drunk that they had to be rolled along 'like milk cans and piled into the guard's van'.

The Countess of Fingall, the half English, half Irish society hostess, was also unable to see the promised benefits that a British victory would bring. 'I used to think and say during the war that if ever that list of Dead and Wounded could cease, I would never mind anything or grumble at anything again,' she recalled. 'But when the Armistice came at last, we seemed drained of all feeling. One felt nothing. We took up our lives again or tried to take them up. The world we had known was vanished. We hunted again but ghosts rode with us. We sat at table and there were absent faces.'

Monica Grenfell, the sister of Julian and Billy who had both lost their lives to the war, wrote to her mother Lady Desborough that day of how she felt there to be 'agonising sadness in this calm after strife'.

There had been no armistice celebration in East Peckham in Kent where kindly Elizabeth Tester managed the village laundry. Despite her son Edward's efforts to be brave, his letters from the trenches had been profoundly upsetting. Mrs Tester sensed the loneliness barely concealed between the jokey but highly accomplished line draw-ings. Ted, as he was known by all those who loved him, always had a talent, she told her friends, but the drawings and the cheery requests for a pot of his mother's home-made jam, the thought of which 'makes my mouth water', did not deceive his mother. Occasionally his homesickness slipped right through the bravado. 'I don't think I shall grumble much about anything when I get back again,' he had written to his mother. 'I shall know how to appreciate a good home.'

And then, after 2 October 1916 Edward had fallen silent. At the urging of her husband Robert, on 15 November that year Elizabeth Tester had sent a letter to the Chaplain of the 11th Battalion of the Queen's Regiment to ask if they knew where Ted could be contacted. The final letter from France arrived just before Christmas, but it was not from Ted. Instead the Commanding Officer wrote to tell Mrs Tester that her 'much liked' son Edward had been killed by a shell on 21 October. Two years later his father Robert, who had suffered for many years from a weakness of the lungs, confided to his remaining daughter that with the death of Ted he had 'lost the will to live'.

A broken-hearted man, Robert had succumbed to the vicious influenza that had started to appear in communities up and down the country. Two of the Testers' other children, Arthur and Daisy, had never known about the war, as both were too fragile to live beyond their second birthdays. Bobby, the youngest boy, was suffering from a condition that severely restricted the maturing of his mind. But Norah, the eldest child, despite the loss of her brother and her fiancé in the trenches, was eager to help her mother. They both loved children. And Elizabeth had a canny business sense that helped to ensure her decimated family would remain clothed and fed. They would continue their pre-war practice of taking foundling children into the laundry. The small sum paid to them by shame-faced relations for looking after children conceived but unwanted would be a help. And if Elizabeth was to face life without her husband, or Ted, Daisy or Arthur, at least she could show her love to those children denied a loving home.

Ten-year-old Tom Mitford, lover of food, books and football in that order, was halfway through the autumn term at his boarding school in the country when the ceasefire came. For three days the pupils of Lockers Park in Hemel Hempstead had been practising singing 'O God Our Help in Ages Past' in preparation for a service to be held just after the announcement. A collection would be taken for the school Memorial Fund, and plans for a memorial window dedicated to the pupils who had died in the war were already under discussion. But in his weekly letter to his mother, Tom was more preoccupied with the cigarette cards that he collected than in the declaration of peace, begging her to send the cards as soon as possible so he could show his friends a complete set of fifty 'gems of Belgian architecture' and the matching collection of 'military motors'.

His mother was not resistant to his request, and it made a change from the usual weekly plea for cake. No one was capable of refusing Tom anything, even if he coveted something that already belonged to someone else. His sisters knew of the trick that he had been perfecting since the age of seven and which between them was referred to as 'The Artful Scheme of Happiness'. Tom was so practised at getting his own way that he could make his voice 'positively sag with desire'. But annoying as he could be, the five daughters adored their only brother and always showed that they, in his eldest sister Nancy's words, had missed him 'dreadfully' when he returned for the holidays. His mother secretly hoped that she might one day have another child and that it would be a brother for Tom.

Three-year-old Jeremy Nicolas Hutchinson was caught up in the excitement of the day. Standing with his parents in the garden of their rented house at Robertsbridge in Sussex he suddenly heard a whoop and a cheer. Galloping towards them bare-backed on the farm pony and at an unnerving pace was the figure of the farm boy from next door. In his urgency to deliver the most dramatic piece of news of his life, he had completely forgotten to saddle up. Unable to control the speed of the animal, he attempted to come to an elegant standstill in front of his small astonished audience but instead was catapulted into the November mud, landing face down in the country muck. The spread-eagled imprint that remained in the mud after the boy had stood up and breathlessly announced the end of the war was pronounced by the amused adults to be the boy's 'trademark'. This was the first long word that young Jeremy had heard and he knew that he would never forget either the word or the circumstances in which he had first heard it.

For ten-year-old Daisy Brooker, the day was one of the rare occasions when her parents and all her nine brothers and sisters were together in one place. Now that she knew the war was over, she was looking forward to getting rid of the hated oblong ration books, 'with a sort of faint paisley pattern on the pages', that entitled the huge family to one tiny allocation each of margarine and plum jam. 'The faggots were so full of pepper and the peas pudding so dry it was agony to get it down my throat,' Daisy grumbled. 'I vowed I'd never buy it when I had a choice.'

To celebrate the Armistice the whole family, including baby George, went on an outing to the sea front at Brighton and along to the West Pier. 'Everyone seemed to be singing and dancing, soldiers and sailors in uniform the worse for drink, staggering around. We then walked back through the town and we all went in a café where Dad bought a large jug of tea and one cup which we took turns in drinking out of. My legs ached with walking and I longed to have a ride in the pram, if only someone would carry George, but no, it did not happen.' But being with her family, knowing the war was over, made 11 November 1918 a day she would never forget.

That evening Lloyd George made a speech at the Guildhall. Those who heard it and those who read the reports the following day should have been in no doubt. Despite the millions of deaths that had occurred in the name of love of country, patriotism remained undiluted. The Prime Minister was cheered at almost every phrase. He spoke of 'the unity of effort, sorrow and sacrifice'. 'Now', he declared, 'we have our brotherhood of joy.' And to enthusiastic cheers he cried: 'Let it not end here. Let us resolve that we shall place loyalty to the land we love first and last, the land whose efforts on sea, in the air, and on the earth have done so much to redeem the world from a scourge that was menacing its liberties.' And rising to his emotional theme he concluded: 'We sank all our sectional interests, all partisan claims, all class and creed differences, in the pursuit of one common purpose.' Such patriotism, he hoped, would continue to unify the British throughout the challenges of the coming years.

On the same evening, a young mother was spending a few days

at her family cottage in Cornwall. She was alone there with Denis, her eight-year-old son, who thought of his mother as a magical figure. Edna Clarke Hall had been a student at the Slade but her unhappy marriage as well as her grief at the death eighteen months earlier of a beloved friend, the writer Edward Thomas, had propelled her into a state of emotional paralysis. Painting had become impossible for her. Instead she had become accustomed to writing poems, sometimes as many as a dozen a day, in which to record her feelings. Her poem, 'Peace Night', reflected a rare optimism that night, a survival of sorts, inspired by the child beside her.

> So I am 'like a gypsy' on the dark hill side
> In the weird reflection of a nation's pride.
> And *you* are like a pixie o my pretty child!
> And this hill our dixie, strange and dark and wild.
> When we are long forgotten in our mortal dress
> (I, with my red blanket, you, with your sweetness!)
> By the lonely ocean still will we abide
> Elfin boy and gypsy on the dark hill side!

But another poet, Thomas Hardy, now nearly eighty years of age, raged at the futility of it all, attacking the motives of a world that in its 'brute-like blindness' could have allowed this 'four years' dance of death'. In a poem written on Armistice Day, a day in which there was peace on earth and silence in the sky, he foresaw the legacy of the preceding years.

> Some could, some could not, shake off misery;
> The sinister spirit sneered 'It had to be!'
> And again the spirit of pity whispered 'Why?'

Virginia Woolf spent Armistice Day at the dentist, returning home to write her diary that night in a state of despair:

Every wounded soldier was kissed by women; nobody had any notion where to go or what to do; it poured steadily; crowds drifted up and down the pavements waving flags and jumping into omnibuses but in such a disorganised, half-hearted, sordid state that I felt more and more melancholy and hopeless of the human race. They make one doubt whether any decent life will ever be possible, or whether it matters if we are at war or at peace.

Private John Robinson was one of the lucky ones. He had received his demobilisation papers a week before the Armistice and on his arrival home had gathered his family, including his seven-year-old boy, in the front room. As they watched, the former soldier began to remove every article of the uniform he wore until he stood naked before them. Gathering up the muddy, bloody, ragged, sweat-soaked pile of clothes that lay on the floor Mrs Robinson threw the whole lot into the fire as the whole family, including their young son, watched the flames. They promised each other that War would never be mentioned in the Robinson family again.

Mrs Bullock, who had waved her son goodbye with such pain in her heart, had also been pleased that John had been sent home early despite the reason being prompted by the injuries he had received in the war. She consoled herself that at least he was alive and once again enjoying the park, as she watched from the window marvelling at his remarkable agility as he propelled himself forward with his crutches on his remaining leg.

Back in London, lurking in the shadows and far from the brightly lit entrances to hotels from where the party revellers were beginning to make their unsteady way home, were the men who could no longer attract the warmth of a woman's embrace, their faces unable to register relief, joy or any emotion at all. These were the war veterans, facially damaged beyond all recognition. Sometimes a mask was the only solution to any semblance of normality. But the mask itself, immobile, expressionless, resounded with a metallic ping should it encounter any hard object and had become a thing of revulsion.

Maude Onions found herself in a town ten miles from her stenographers' base near Boulogne. She had been visiting the wounded. A truck driver stopped and asked her if she wanted a lift back to Wilmereux. He cautioned her however that she might not like it, as there was a fellow passenger in the back of the truck. The 'passenger' had glimpsed his own face in a mirror and seeing it to be 'battered out of recognition' decided what he must do next. The driver told Maude that he 'did away with his identity disc first and himself afterwards'.

Trying to cheer up her driver as she sat up in front with him, the corpse with his shattered face lying in the back, Maude attempted to make conversation. 'So it's over at last,' she said. But the driver could not agree. 'I'd change places with him gladly,' he assured her, with a jerk of the head towards the corpse in the back. 'The war – for me – is only just beginning.'

Maude's chauffeur had heard that his wife had been sleeping with another man and the prospect of home as a place of refuge and warmth had been destroyed. The end of the war was, for this soldier at least, the end of the happiness he had known and the start of a life of uncertainty.

3

Denial

Christmas 1918

As women prepared for the homecoming of their men, shiny lip-stick and new teeth found their way into even the poorest homes. No matter what the expense, a 'mouthful of flashing pots' was the goal of many waiting for the return of their husbands. The poet T. S. Eliot lived above a pub and heard the discussions.

> Now Albert's coming back, make yourself a bit smart.
> He'll want to know what you done with that money he gave you
> To get yourself some teeth. He did, I was there.
> You have them all out, Lil, and get a nice set.

In the first months after the war the act of survival itself had been a cause for celebration and the peacetime silence brought with it a relief that people had long dreamt of. At the pre-Christmas general election on 14 December, when the wartime Coalition Government was seeking a return to office, Lloyd George had prom-ised that serving men would be returning to 'a Land fit for Heroes'. But the long anticipated reunions often met with bitter disap-pointment. Wives, mothers, fiancées, sisters, friends were reunited with men who had been changed irrevocably, both physically and mentally, by the horror and brutality they had been subjected to. These men neither looked nor sounded like heroes. Marriages con-ducted in haste during the war had often taken place in the fear that there would never be another chance. The prolonged absence of a husband gave time for reflection and often led both husband and wife to think again about their speedy commitment to one another.

The divorce rate began to rise so rapidly that in the twelve months after the war ended the courts processed three times as many divorces as they had in the year before the war began. Judges began to complain of 'congestion' in the system.

Gladys Cooper was considered the most beautiful woman on the London stage. Her audiences cared little about the content of the play. Nor indeed, to the actress's frustration, were they too bothered about the calibre of her acting. They were simply happy to sit in their seats and stare at her beautiful face. She and her husband Herbert Buckmaster had written to each other almost every day for three and half years during his absence at the front. They had promised each other that they would 'make up for all this hell of being parted when the war is over'. But on Buck's return he realised his wife 'had been accustomed to do without me and to manage her own life'. Gladys's earnings had shot up from £20 a week at the beginning of the war to £200 at its end. Her new friends were the Prince of Wales, Ivor Novello, Sybil Thorndike and Rudolph Valentino. His friends were men like him who had not been blown to pieces in the trenches. He planned to open a club in London where the military veterans could gather and talk about things that no one, especially wives, had experienced. Gladys and Buck realised they no longer had anything in common. Their marriage was over.

For some whose love lives had been disrupted by the war, there was a guarded anxiety that they might never recover their emotional stability. Violet Elliot-Murray-Kynynmound, daughter of the Earl of Minto, Viceroy of India, had been married in 1909 at the age of 20 to her father's aide-de-camp Charles Petty-Fitzmaurice, youngest son of the Marquess of Lansdowne. The marriage was a love match. People remarked on the beauty and devotion of the young couple. They had two children. A shell unleashed high into the air at Ypres in 1914 and the death of her father in the same year wrecked Violet's happiness. Her friends wondered how she and her two children would manage, now she was not only widowed but fatherless.

Two years later, however, Violet had married again. Nothing unseemly or hasty was attributed to this fact. The omnipresence of death and grief was seen as a reason for behaviour that out of the context of war might have been considered inappropriate, particularly among the upper classes. People understood that isolation, particularly in youth, could paralyse a life. A new husband would provide comfort for Violet and a father figure for her children.

Many friends, men and women, had written letters of congratulation on the marriage and almost all mentioned the blessed news that Violet's loneliness was at an end. Ettie Desborough, familiar herself with war's cruel blows, sent her 'one line of <u>great</u> love and every happy wish that I can think of in the whole world'. The Duchess of Devonshire expressed her 'delighted' wishes, while a particularly loving note arrived on Irish Guards stationery from Kerry, from Henry Petty-Fitzmaurice, Violet's former brother-in-law. John Renton, the much-adored factor at the estate office at Meikleour, the family house of Violet's former husband near Perth, wrote of 'the high esteem in which your Ladyship and the little children have always been held by the tenants' and hoped that she would continue to come and visit them all there. Only one letter referred to the 'agony of decision' and only two confronted and dismissed the concept of 'disloyalty'. Violet had collected up the large bundle of letters, several of them banded by the black margin of personal mourning, and folded a blank sheet of paper around them. She had written on the paper the words 'Congratulations. June 1916' in black ink and put the letters safely away.

Violet's new husband was John Jacob Astor, a member of the vastly rich American family who had made their money in the last century in fur trading and real estate. John's father, William Waldorf, owned the *Observer* newspaper. A cousin, John Jacob IV, had drowned in the *Titanic*. A brother, Waldorf, was a Member of Parliament and lived with his wife Nancy at Cliveden in Berkshire, a hub for the most distinguished political and social gatherings of the war.

Violet did not object when John, a reticent and complicated man, asked his wife to pack away all Charlie's photographs and possessions. A short while after the wedding John Jacob returned to the war and had his right leg blown off. Back home again, John suffered a continuous and dreadful pain in the remaining part of the limb, and retreated to his rooms, occupying himself with his passion for painting. One day his new wife walked into the bedroom to find a beautiful young model posing for the latest canvas while her husband lay stark naked on the bed.

Moving to open the window, Violet remarked, 'Yes, darling, I do agree, it *is* hot in here', and left the room, making no further comment. A woman of impressive resilience, Violet considered silence to be the most prudent response. But deep within the silent recesses of her private sitting room at Hever Castle in Kent was a secret. Here in the place where Anne Boleyn had loved and lost Henry VIII, the lovely and romantic place that her new husband had inherited on his father's death, Violet had prised open a brick or two and within the cavity behind had placed her favourite photographs, a lock of hair, the cufflinks and the medals that had belonged to the man she would always love best. After the war was over, being with their two children and holding these precious things lessened the loneliness that still gripped her.

In the weeks leading up to the first peaceful Christmas for four years, advertisements began to appear suggesting presents that would not have found a place in leisure magazines before the war. In many houses that Christmas, furniture was moved out of the way to make room for spanking new cane wheelchairs. The *Illustrated London News* recommended an ingenious gadget for individuals who had lost their arms. By the manipulation of a flat lever with two stockinged feet, a plate balanced on top of the lever could be made to rise towards the armless diner's mouth. Forks and spoons could be made to levitate towards the mouth in a similar way. On 13 December the same magazine was promoting an intriguing choice of gift in the Ellieson Carrier Electric Invalid's Carriage, a contraption that 'heralds a new era'. The Ellieson, capable of speeds of up to five miles per hour, afforded the disabled person the freedom from nurse, attendant or bath-chair man as well as an opportunity to breathe in fresh air. These self-propelling invalid chairs were in plentiful supply from Garrould's, the medical supplies store, and a photograph in the *Daily Sketch* on 17 December showed a charming model well wrapped up, but smiling broadly as she demonstrated the benefits of the machine.

But the soldier's disability pension was not enough to keep a family in rent, food and clothing, let alone allowing anything over for Christmas presents. For the one and a half million men who emerged from the war with severe physical injury, there was a clear financial demarcation in the rate of official compensation offered by the Government. Since the beginning of the war over 41,000 men had lost at least one limb. The severest bodily war wounds, the loss of a full right arm from the shoulder downwards, was worth sixteen shillings a week. Fourteen shillings were awarded if the arm was missing from below the shoulder but above the elbow, and then the rate dropped to eleven shillings and sixpence for limbs missing from below the elbow. The left arm however merited a shilling less with each specific affected joint. Allowances stopped at anything above the neckline.

Priority was given to the wounded men for whom surgical help could be provided. The Princess Louise Scottish Hospital for Homeless Soldiers and Sailors at Erskine in Renfrewshire treated one in five of the disabled veterans. The demand was so high that workers from the Clyde-side shipyards with their knowledge of steel and joints were recruited to make false arms and legs. Civilians had to wait their turn. Emily Brooker, mother of ten children, and stretched beyond both her means and energy, developed a terrible cyst in her eye, which caused so much pain that her entire eye had to be removed. The black patch that she wore over the Samson-like hole in her face was itself unsightly but the waiting list for artificial eyes was confined to wounded soldiers. As a temporary measure Emily was advised to place a white shell in the socket that drew more gasps than the black patch. When the hospital finally loaned her a replacement eye for the sum of £3, it did not fit properly. On the bus journey back home to Brighton, with the sightless bauble in position, Emily suddenly sneezed and out popped the new eye to the consternation of the conductor. Within a day Emily had dropped and smashed the precious but useless egg-shaped pebble. She did not have a further £3 to spare. The black patch was returned to its former position concealing the unsightliness beneath.

A poster produced by the Young Men's Christian Association showed a collection of fearful, damaged men, one holding his crutches, another with empty suit sleeve pinned up to his lapel, armless and shrinking back from the viewer. 'Don't Pity a Disabled Man,' the message pleaded. 'Find him a job.' But the eight million disabled veterans had arrived home anxious to find work only to discover that many were unable or forbidden to return to pre-war jobs in offices and factories because of their physical disabilities. Instead they took up positions on street corners, smartly dressed in suit and bowler hat, clinging to their pride, their trays held out in front of them tied on with a ribbon laced around their neck, and packed with newspapers, bootlaces and matchboxes. Some of those with missing limbs would turn their disability to advantage, appearing on stage in variety revues, demonstrating how to type or to play a piano with some skill by means of their toes.

Casualties of the war were everywhere. And drunkenness was often a means of release from the humiliation of poverty. Small children placed under the care of a disabled father while the mother went to work would be perched on windowsills outside pubs while the parent sat inside sluicing away his distress. Outside Hoxton's pubs in London's East End rows of neatly parked prams were a familiar sight, the abandoned occupants bellowing their heads off. Drinking went with manhood, it was said, and pride in their manhood was one of the things the wounded missed most.

Away from the city, the wounded were often less obvious, absorbed into kinder communities and able to escape to the open places of the countryside. Three-year-old Mary Beale lived at Bettenham in the Weald of Kent near the village of Biddenden where her father Os kept the farm. Up the lane lived Tom Noakes who owned two of the fields. Mary begged her mother Dorothy never to take her near Tom Noakes's fields for fear of bumping into the owner. The section of his arm from elbow to hand was entirely missing, shot off in the war. In its place was an enormous hook with which Tom pushed back trailing shoots that got in his way as he surveyed his small estate. *Chop chop*, he would go with his full right arm, and then *hoik, hoik* with his left hook to clear the branches of trees. Mary was terrified that one day Tom would hoik her.

Pam Parish, aged three, knew she should be sad for all the soldiers who had not returned to her village of Sidcup but she could not help dreading the visits of one of the neighbours. Stuart Lloyd had lived most of his life in Pam's village except for the four years when he had been away serving as a Captain while 'protecting the country', as Pam's mother told her. Nowadays he was always popping in for a chat with her mother, his brilliantly polished medals, including the cross and bar for distinguished service, pinned on to his tweed coat, shiny and clattery against one another as he moved. Stuart Lloyd was enough of a local hero to be regarded with awe in the town of Sidcup but the Parish sisters did not look forward to his visits.

'Now whenever poor Mr Lloyd comes to see us I want you to give him a nice hallo kiss,' Ethel Parish would urge Pam and her elder sister Stella.

'But he looks all upside down and strange,' they objected.

Their mother was adamant. 'Now, now, I will hear no such nonsense. I know you find it difficult but just think of poor Mr Lloyd.'

And when Mr Lloyd came through the door the pyjama-wearing sisters tried to unscrew their expressions of revulsion and force themselves to kiss his cheek as far away as possible from his mouth before running upstairs and making audible sick noises as soon as they reached their bedroom door. Before going to bed, the children were asked to include Mr Lloyd in their prayers. 'Please God make Mr Lloyd quite quite well,' they would dutifully ask, running the sentence on without a break as they asked God for forgiveness 'for anything I have done wrong today'. But there was little hope of God intervening. When Mr Lloyd stayed for supper the children would turn their faces away, dreading the reappearance of his food through his nose. Half of Stuart Lloyd's face was gone, his palate missing, blown off at the Somme.

According to Siegfried Sassoon, the noise of a shell passing overhead was like the sound of 'water trickling into a can'. The impact of bullet on skull was described by one American soldier, himself with a missing face, 'like someone had dropped a glass bottle into a porcelain bathtub'. Perhaps that was the sound Stuart Lloyd had heard a few years earlier. Or maybe the noise of whistling that preceded the appearance of the shell was all that remained in his memory of that day.

Many of the most extreme of war wounded cases had not come back to their own homes at all. They were hidden away in institutions, allowed out occasionally to take the air, objects of fascination and pity, to be stared at and then hastily ignored by the able-minded going about their business. 'Don't look,' John Leigh Pemberton's mother would caution her young son as they walked along the front at Westgate-on-Sea, passing the gas-blinded soldiers. But John was captivated by the old soldiers as they walked in an orderly line from the nearby Home for the Blind, their hands on the shoulder of the man in front for guidance. Safely seated in deck chairs they took pleasure from feeling the warmth of the sun on their faces. 'They are the Debris of War,' his mother told him.

There were people in Pam Parish's village of Sidcup who seemed to the children to have something wrong with themselves, something not easily identifiable, just people who kept to themselves, who wished to be left alone. The children never approached them, nor spoke to those whom the family referred to as 'Les Invalides'. In Burnham-on-Crouch in Essex where a big convalescent home housed hundreds of men with smashed up faces, the locals wrote to the matron asking her to keep the inmates inside, as it gave them 'the shivers' to see these horrifying casualties of war walking about, open to the public gaze.

Better protection for the head had replaced the cloth and leather caps that soldiers had worn at the outbreak of war but they provided no covering for the face. Emergence from a trench into the enemy line began with one quick glance. The unprotected face appeared first, in preparation for the scramble over the top. Dr Frederick Albee, a surgeon working on the front line, was amazed that soldiers failed to understand 'the menace of the machine gun'; he was incredulous that 'they seemed to think they could pop their heads up over a trench and move quickly enough to dodge the hail of bullets'.

At least 60,000 men were estimated to have been shot directly in the head or eye, vulnerable not only to a direct hit but also to the lacerating wounds caused by flying fragments of shell. Lookout sentries were advised to stand with their head and shoulders fully above the parapet for the chance of a statistically less damaging hit to the body. If a bullet itself did not make a direct hit, catastrophic burns from explosives could all but obliterate a man's face. Burns were likewise the chief hazard for airmen, due to the exposed petrol tank sited directly behind the flimsy wicker flying seat which could explode at any moment. Gun-turret fires on board ship were hard to extinguish too, and faces rarely escaped the flames. With unvaryingly poor nutrition, the weakened men offered little resistance to the infection that festered in the wounds.

Before the war Anna Coleman Ladd, an American sculptor working in Paris, had concentrated on decorative fountains featuring nymphs and sprites. But during the war, after a stint at the American Red Cross office in Paris, she became determined to use her creative gift to help servicemen who had been badly damaged in action. Patients would walk through the statue-populated courtyard and climb the stairs to consult Mrs Ladd in her flower-filled studio above. She listened carefully to men often with barely recognisable features, who explained to her that they wanted her to make them look exactly the same as they had before the shell had hit. If there was a way to pretend that the wounding had never happened, they could perhaps get on with their lives.

In England Francis Derwent Wood, a professor of sculpture at the Royal Academy of Art, had worked for the architect Sir Edwin Lutyens but was too old to enlist at the outbreak of war. He had begun voluntary work in London's hospitals and in 1917 found himself profoundly affected by the extent of the physical damage confronting him. Wood was further disturbed by the frightening suicide rate among returning soldiers and by the distress of families unable to come to terms with the shell-shattered appearances of their menfolk. Mirrors were forbidden in the wards but occasionally a visitor smuggled one in, anxious to please a relation consumed with curiosity about his own appearance. Stories went around that people had fainted with shock at the face in the mirror that looked back at them. Wood set up a department in the Third London General Hospital in Wandsworth devoted to covering up facial disfigurement. Patients and their families called the department the Tin Noses Shop.

With the combined help of pre-injury photographs and artistic guesswork, Coleman Ladd in Paris and Derwent Wood in London spent hours in discreet workshops putting together complete facial masks made of galvanised copper which would hide the effects of damage. Concealment, it seemed, rather than repair was the only option for those who no longer had noses, eyes, jawbones, cheekbones, chins, ears or much of a face at all.

Requirements varied. Some simply needed a screen for a missing eye; others wanted something that gave greater covering, extending from the chin upwards across the entire face. Sometimes a patient would produce a photograph that he hoped might be an improvement on his pre-war appearance. Rupert Brooke's image was sometimes chosen as an alternative. At Rugby, the public school attended by Brooke, there were plans to commission a portrait of their most famous old boy based on an already famous photograph by Sherrill Schell, taken in 1913. The unblemished face bore no resemblance to the broken men who had come back alive from the front but it represented something to aspire to.

Derwent Wood promoted his work to the sceptical by explaining that 'the patient acquires his old self-respect, self-assurance, self-reliance, takes once more a pride in his personal appearance. His presence is no longer a source of melancholy to himself nor of sadness to his relatives and friends.' Usually all the patient wanted was to become a face indistinguishable in the crowd.

After the mutilated face had been surgically patched up and given time to heal, Derwent Wood's work began. Once 'the surgeon has done all he can to heal wounds, to support fleshy tissue by bone grafting', he explained, he would try and restore the missing parts with his sculpting skills. The face would be smothered in wet clay. After a ghastly claustrophobic interlude, the cast would be dried and removed before a working model was produced from plasticine. From this model the basic copper mask would be made and the prosthetic pieces such as nose or chin would then be grafted on to fit. Eyebrows and eyelashes, glass eyes that had an impressively lifelike glint, hair made from copper wire and moustaches were all then added and glasses were usually used to hold the mask in place. When an eye socket was missing and there was no place into which a glass eye might be slipped, the paintbrush worked its magic, waking up the mask to the illusion of sightfulness.

The copper absorbed the painted facial characteristics with ease and these were added in enamel while the mask was in place in order to match the skin tone of the wearer more accurately. Sometimes a tell-tale sign of chipped paint or rust became visible to the observer and a touch-up visit to the artist was arranged. Enormous trouble was taken to find the right colour of paint that would look natural when exposed to bright sunshine, dull weather, or to electric light. A balance was sought between a newly shaved shine with a trace of blue-tone and the faint stubble of later in the day. Sometimes electric light would catch the glint of the paint, the unnatural gleam on the face giving away the artificiality of the skin.

The mask weighed between four and nine ounces, the equivalent of anything from a half to a full cup of butter, and measured one thirty-second of an inch thick, or in the estimation of one society lady, the width of a visiting card. For most of the wearers the masks were horribly uncomfortable as the tin rubbed against the ravaged face beneath producing a nearly intolerable sensation. Anything that touched the acutely sensitive and delicate new skin was an irritant. However one grateful patient told Mrs Ladd in her Paris workshop that his emotional life had been totally restored. 'The woman I love no longer finds me repulsive,' he wrote, admitting, 'as she had a right to do'.

In her French studio Anna Coleman Ladd was delighted that this newfound confidence encouraged her patients to 'twirl their artificial mustachios with all the verve and aplomb so characteristic of your true Gaul'. Some men were so delighted with the chance to live a near normal life that they allowed the fitting to be filmed. The process demanded the frequent removal of the mask while the smallest adjustments were made and the camera closed in on the contrasting faces, the one destroyed, the other resurrected.

The mask was incapable of ageing, a gift not bestowed on other parts of the body, leading in later years to an incongruous mismatch. And all the ingenuity of the artist was defeated by the challenge of making the mask smile, laugh, frown, look surprised or even happy. The face was completely and eerily immobile. Unlike a living face, with its infinite variety of response, the tin mask remained capable only of the one expression imposed by the artist. The masks were as alive as the effigies on tombs in churches up and down the country, the effigies of the dead. And unresponsiveness, fragility and strange physical sensations were not the only drawbacks. The device for concealing a face, initially convincingly real but on closer examination absolutely *unreal*, forced the imagination to concentrate on the truth of the dreadful Stygian picture beneath the mask.

Ladd and Wood expected their masks to have a lifespan of just a few years before wear and tear would cause them to rust and crumble. Some masks remained unworn in their boxes. The young plastic surgeon, Harold Gillies, was not surprised. At his own plastic surgery hospital in Sidcup, one of Gillies's convalescent patients was halfway through a sequence of operations, recovering from one as the healing process took place before his damaged skin was well enough for the next session under Gillies's restorative hand. This particular patient had been given a temporary leather mask to wear on a day's visit to London. The patient would leave the reception desk with a jaunty wave, and make for the railway station. At the end of the day the front door would swing open to reveal a fearful sight. The man had long grown tired of being stared at in the railway carriage and it had become his habit and little private game with himself to whip the mask off when the maximum number of pale-faced ladies had gathered in his carriage. Returning to the hospital he would hold up the appropriate amount of fingers to indicate the number of victims he had succeeded in terrorising.

Denial of the truth did not suit every temperament. Nor was it always conducive to romance. Gillies sympathised. 'One can appreciate a sweetheart's repugnance at being expected to kiss shapely but unresponsive lips composed of enamelled phosphor-bronze,' he remarked.

Covering up the damage did not always bring lasting satisfaction. Gillies believed he could find another solution by acknowledging the problem rather than denying it. He was convinced that there was a different way in which to bring new life and hope to these shattered men as well as to those who loved them.

4

Acknowledgement

Winter 1918

A week after the Armistice the well-known Australian violinist, Miss Daisy Kennedy, had sat next to an exceptionally good-looking young man at a lunch party in London. Chatting about heroes she had mentioned her pride at being a country kinswoman of the brilliant surgeon Harold Gillies. Looking straight at her the young man said, 'You couldn't pay me a greater compliment.'

Daisy Kennedy was puzzled. Might she indeed be speaking to the great man himself, she enquired? But she was mistaken. 'I am one of his patients,' the young man told her. And looking still closer, Daisy was amazed to see that there was not a mark on his beautiful face. He was perfect.

The young New Zealand surgeon Harold Gillies had seen for himself the extent of the severity of face wounds while out working at the 83rd Stationary Hospital in the town of Wilmereux, just outside Boulogne. He became determined to help men whose lives had been ruined in the second it took for the shell or bullet or piece of death-dealing shrapnel to do its frightful damage. He persuaded the head of army surgery, Sir William Arbuthnot Lane, to give him a ward at the Cambridge Military Hospital in Aldershot so that he could develop a small specialist unit. To ensure facial patients came directly to Aldershot, he arranged for casualty labels, printed at his own expense and bearing the hospital address, to be tied to the arm of the worst cases and sent directly to him from the field hospitals. Back in England Gillies began experimenting with all the resources and imagination he could muster to mend the faces of these shattered men.

Word soon got about of this remarkable surgeon and his expert team who offered hope where there had once been only despair.

Gillies's meticulous use of new surgical procedures succeeded in filling in vacant sockets that had once contained an eye, and replacing missing ears, noses and jaws. For some it was as if the Creator himself had returned to restore an old job. Before long Gillies had found the bed capacity at Aldershot wholly inadequate for the extensive demand and contacted the Chief of the Army Medical Staff, Sir Alfred Keogh. Both he and Sir William Arbuthnot Lane were initially distrustful of 'this new-fangled plastic surgery', but Gillies convincingly argued that by correcting physical disability, time-consuming claims against the Government for compensation would decrease. The proposition was an attractive one to a government that made no financial allowance for facial injury on the premise that such injury did not prevent manual productivity in the same way that a lost limb did. It seemed the psychological effects of damaged faces were impossible to quantify in cash terms.

Gillies hoped that he could eventually help enlighten the Government in their insensitive approach to such distress and his charm and exceptional surgical skills were hard to resist. The massively built Arbuthnot Lane, his disconcertingly 'shrill little voice' at variance with his bulk, was won over. He persuaded the Government to join the Red Cross in raising funds to build a special hospital in the grounds of a small estate near Sidcup in Kent.

The Queen's Hospital opened in August 1917 with one thousand beds, especially designated for treatment of the face. As the patients often stayed at the hospital for the many months that it took Gillies to complete each individual's series of operations, proper convalescent facilities were provided. These included a chapel, a cinema and a substantial canteen. A number of private houses and a large children's home were requisitioned to fill the growing need for beds. Queen Mary, who had contributed generously to the cost of establishing the hospital, had visited Gillies's new premises when they opened and saw for herself 'the marvellous results of the treatment'.

Gillies was the clinical director of the hospital, heading a team of some thirty surgeons from America, Australia, Canada and New Zealand who all brought their international experience to Kent to help with the huge number of face cases. But Gillies himself handled as many operations as a hard-working day would allow, not permitting his managerial responsibilities to get in the way of what mattered to him most.

Despite their lengthy, painful and often humiliating ordeal, the patients trusted this delightful man who called everyone, man or woman, either 'my dear' or 'honey'. He was an original, his scientific gift enhanced by an enquiring mind and a talent for painting. Before an operation Gillies would sometimes take a pencil and draw the potential reconstruction on a photograph of a damaged face. Art became an integral part of the surgical procedure, and in time Gillies persuaded several artists to join him at Sidcup as part of his unusual team of professionals.

Gillies was acutely conscious of the importance of the aesthetic as well as the practical success of his work. Private Horace Sewell, known to his friends as Paddy, was apprehensive about the nature of post-war life without his own nose. The day before his operation, Gillies arrived in the ward, carrying with him a sketchbook. 'Well Paddy, your big day is here,' he said to Sewell who was immediately reassured by 'the friendly smile that gave us all so much confidence'. Taking out his pens Gillies asked him, 'What sort of nose do you think we ought to give you?' Paddy insisted he was not fussy, but Gillies was determined to construct the very best nose he could, drafting several choices on to his pad, before deciding that a fine Roman model would best complement Paddy's rather round face.

Henry Tonks had originally trained as a surgeon, and with his thorough knowledge of the skeletal structure of the human body had been a professor of drawing at the Slade since 1892. Before the war, Professor Tonks's students had included not only Augustus John, his sister Gwen and the popular artist Ambrose McEvoy, but the society pin-up Diana Manners and a shy, sublimely beautiful 14-year-old girl, Edna Clarke Hall.

During the war Tonks had volunteered for service in the Royal Army Medical Corps and his presence at Aldershot was brought to Gillies's attention. Tonks came into the operating theatre and watched Gillies working, while making lightning sketches and pastels of the pre-operative faces. These pictures were invaluable to Gillies in helping him visualise the outcome of his proposed reconstructions. Tonks became one of Gillies's closest working colleagues.

Next to Tonks was another studio for the sculptor John Edwards, who made three-dimensional plaster casts to give another perspective to Tonks's drawings. Archie Lane, a dental technician, re-created whole missing jaws, and because he understood better than anyone the bone structure beneath a face, was able to make up small masks for eyes and noses.

Kathleen Scott, a talented sculptor and another former Slade student, also joined the team. The widow of Captain Scott, the explorer who in 1912 had frozen to death in the Antarctic, Mrs Scott had no sense of squeamishness and on the contrary found that 'men without noses are very beautiful, like antique marbles'. Mrs Scott was honoured to be invited by Gillies to use her creative gift to sculpt missing noses, ears, cheeks and chins on to a model of the shattered face.

Without anaesthetic the operations would have been intolerable and pain-relief systems were not wholly reliable. But Rubens Wade worked out a way of delivering anaesthesia to a patient in the sitting position, reducing the risk of the airways becoming obstructed. Wade's colleage, Ivan Magill, an Irishman originally in charge of the medical welfare of demobilised troops, enhanced the effectiveness of pain relief further with his technique of inserting the vapour directly into the windpipe.

Surgeons as well as patients benefited from these innovations. Chloroform pads often either fell off or obscured the operation site, while ether involuntarily exhaled by a patient could sometimes send a surgeon to sleep in the middle of the job. Occasionally the anaesthetic failed to obliterate the extraordinary pain of having a new face sewn on to the remaining flesh and bone, and it was sometimes necessary to hold the man down, so excruciating was the experience.

Corporal Ward Muir at the Third London General Hospital described the distress involved in talking 'to a lad who six months ago was probably a wholesome and pleasing specimen of English youth and is now a gargoyle and a broken gargoyle at that'. Conversing was 'an ordeal'. But the staff of the plastic surgery unit learned not to betray the horrors that confronted them. Accompanied by his hand-picked professionals, Gillies would enter the operating theatre 'head thrust forward from his slightly stooping shoulders, with the air of an artist who aspires to produce a masterpiece'. An assistant noticed that 'all the actions of his hands were consistently gentle, accurate and deft'.

In his efforts to 'restore beauty to the human form', Gillies asked a good deal of his patients. The experimental and improvised surgical risks which these battered men were prepared to undertake were courageous, but the hope of having some level of normality restored to their lives was enough to sustain them.

The most daring of the new surgical techniques involved the detaching of a healthy flap of skin from another part of the body, most commonly the shoulder or the chest. This flap would then be joined to the damaged area in the expectation that healthy new tissue would grow. A young naval rating, A. B. Vicarage, had been severely burned during the Battle of Jutland: the fire had scarred all of his exposed face, leaving him without much of a nose and tightening his eyelids so he could not close them. In addition his mouth had contracted so severely after the wounds had healed that he arrived at Sidcup unable to open or close it. The acid in his saliva that dribbled out in a constant uncontrollable steam was causing dreadful sores. Even the resilient Gillies considered Vicarage's injuries 'appalling'.

As Gillies lifted the skin flap from Vicarage's chest it rolled over and he had the idea to sew the grafted skin into a tube before fixing it on to the damaged part of the face. This procedure, which became known as the pedicle method, ensured that the underside of the healthy tissue was no longer open and exposed to possible infection. The tube embedded itself into the damaged skin and at the join, new tissue began to grow. Gradually Vicarage's new face began to form from the 'slender pink orchidaceous stalks'.

Some of Gillies's work involved repairing the hasty, unfeeling botched jobs made on prisoners of war by German surgeons. Gillies was appalled to find a nose full of hair growing in the centre of one unfortunate man's face because a graft on the nose had been taken from above his hairline.

Not every operation was successful. Herbert Lumley from the Royal Flying Corps, a jaunty pipe-smoking lad, was so badly wounded on his very first solo flight that although Gillies operated on him with particular urgency the skin graft would not settle and soon turned gangrenous. Survival was impossible. The terrifying ulcerous sight prompted the ever conscientious Gillies to remind himself, 'Never do today what can honourably be put off to tomorrow.'

The healing period between bouts of surgery meant the hospital corridors were full of hideous faces with slits instead of eyes, vacant bloody spaces which had once contained noses, skewed and distorted mouths with tongues lolling uncontrollably, huge and grotesque from a jawless chin. These were the patients, as Ward Muir observed, 'at whom you are afraid to gaze unflinchingly: not afraid for yourself but afraid for him'.

Often the convalescent men could not eat or drink and were given unlimited quantities of egg nog to provide the protein their bodies needed. Chickens were kept on the hospital estate, their eggs vital for the nourishing drink, while the huge demand for milk to make up the other component of the 'nog' was provided by the herds of cows that munched their way along the nearby grassy Sidcup fields.

Captain Jono Wilson had been sitting in front next to the tank driver in 1917 as they rolled towards Cambrai when for one moment he had raised his helmeted head over the top. His nose was the least protected part of the face. A German shell made a direct hit. The driver crumpled lifeless into his seat while Jono plastered his field dressing on to the hole in his own face and took a swig of rum. German prisoners carried him along the quayside at Boulogne and within the day he was 'happily ensconced in Major Harold Gillies's Face Hospital'. From there he was able to hear the bells of Sidcup ringing out to celebrate victory.

Although Captain Wilson acknowledged that 'a face hospital is perhaps one of the most depressing' of all such places, the atmosphere at Sidcup was often buoyant. The patients gave themselves the exclusive licence to describe each other as 'ugly'. There was laughter and music. A pilot strummed the piano with the burned bones of fleshless fingers and through lips that had been restored by Gillies, sang the refrain, 'And now I've got a mother-in-law from drinking whisky through a straw.' He had married his nurse.

Between operations men would leave the hospital grounds to go into Sidcup village wearing their distinguishing uniform of bright cornflower blue jackets and red ties, objects of curiosity and fear to almost all but themselves and those who cared for them. Blue benches were placed in strategic parts of the town, the colour a warning code that fearful sights might be seated on them. Publicans were forbidden to serve the patients alcoholic drinks for fear that tempers might suddenly fray. One man, Jocky Anderson, on celebrating the end of his fiftieth operation, managed to get hold of some alcohol and had returned to his ward, paralytic with drink, and smashed up everything in sight.

By the end of the war 11,572 major facial operations had been performed and gradually Gillies saw the number of cases before him diminishing. Men were returning to civilian life. Sydney Beldham, a new nose replacing the cobbled mash that had arrived in the operating theatre a year earlier, was employed in the proud job of chauffeuring his saviour. Infantryman Herbert Alfred Palmer had, in his enthusiasm to fight for his country, signed up at the beginning of the war at the age of 15, using his elder brother Edward's identity to mask his age. Five years later, with the broken structure of his face rebuilt, he founded the Bromley and Bickley Working Men's Club. Harry Reynolds met his wife at a hospital dance and trained as a radiographer. Mickey Shirlaw, a Motherwell miner, became fascinated by dental reconstruction and was trained by Archie Lane as a dental technician.

Another patient, Guardsman Maggs of the Welsh Guards, gave his surgeon such professional satisfaction that he was persuaded to make something of an exhibition of himself and his exemplary new nose in front of the British Medical Association. Invited to enter the room, Gillies spoke to him. But Guardsman Maggs did not recognise the French words that Gillies used and in his embarrassment flushed scarlet from neck to forehead. 'Look, look,' said a delighted Gillies as the blood travelled to all parts of the man's face, even reaching the tip of the guardsman's nose.

But some post-operative men did not have the self-confidence of Guardsman Maggs. Many continued to find it impossible to muster the courage to appear in daylight, seeking refuge in work as reel-to-reel operators in the screened-off booths of cinemas. Others were beginning to risk public reaction. Stanley Cohen had been injured two months before the end of the war, his face seared in a tank fire. Having survived the gruelling post-operative recovery period, Stanley Cohen remained fearful of testing public reaction to the still shocking sight of his face. With Gillies's help he had become the Sidcup nightwatchman, reassured that the cover of darkness would give him the protection he craved. And yet his friends were perplexed when Cohen started teaching at the local Sunday school. Where had he found the courage to expose his face to the judgment of other human beings? The explanation was simple. While adults showed revulsion, children merely greeted Cohen with curiosity. With children he was safe.

Devastating as the physical scarring could be, damage to the mind was sometimes even more catastrophic and those outwardly blemish-free suffered just as deeply. The wounded and limbless were obvious to those who came across them in almost every town and village in the country. Those scarred in mind were not. Men collapsed under the strain of an inability to tolerate or escape the memory of their war experience – Freud's 'unendurable realities' of the physical world. In the trenches the men had whispered to one another, 'He's a bit rocky upstairs', or 'He's gone a bit barmy' – a misleadingly anodyne term, from a pre-war abbreviation for the Barming Hospital at Maidstone. Flesh on shell-shocked faces shook with fear, and teeth continually chattered. 'A thousand-yard stare' was often used to describe the dazed vacancy in the eyes of a severely damaged soldier. Some doctors thought the condition was a result of extreme disturbance of the fluid around the brain caused by long-term exposure to gunfire.

Robert Graves had heard the lasting mental trauma of war explained as 'a morbid condition of the blood due to the stimulation of the thyroid gland by noise and fear'. But a correspondent in November 1919 in the *Illustrated London News* went deeper, attributing the signs of hysteria to 'aboulie or will-less-ness. The patient, worn out by the struggle against external circumstances, abandons the exercise of his own will and drifts with the stream of things, unaware of where he is going.'

The chief outward signs, easily recognisable, included the dropping of the corners of the mouth, a lolling tongue and a lack of movement in the eyes, with the lids partially closed. In addition an irritation to the sole of the foot made many of those who suffered from shell shock spread their toes apart. Some could barely stand upright, and walked with a jerky movement that was termed 'the hysterical gait'. Many adopted a stoop and a shuffle that resembled the tentative steps of a nervous skater. Seizures and shuddering fits were frequent. Many lived in a silent world. The effect of the guns had made them completely deaf. Sometimes the behaviour of a shell-shocked victim was fitful, unpredictable, miserable, embittered, sometimes physically violent, and sometimes – and for the wives, fiancées, daughters, lovers, aunts and grandmothers, perhaps worst of all – these men were simply silent. The Italian term for the apathy induced by shell shock was 'depressive-soporose amentia' – the last word denoting 'absence of mind'.

Dr W. R. Houston, a professor of medicine from the University of Georgia who had looked after many shell-shocked patients at the front, noted that some had emerged from battle with their vocal cords destroyed and their tongues paralysed, making them incapable of talking. Not only was speech denied them, but they had also become incapable of making 'the slightest sound, to whistle or to blow, or even to imitate the movements of the lip in speech'. Silence had become an absolute way of life. Sight was often affected and memory weakened, and yet the intensity of hallucination brought the sufferer into a world filled with fire and battle that became a constant torture. It was *the agitation of the mind*, according to Dr Houston, that demonstrated the most acute form of this 'wreckage of men's souls' and he was profoundly shaken by the time he spent with what had once been 'the flower and vigour of youth,' now become 'doddering palsied wrecks, quivering at a sound, dreading the visions of the night'.

Robert Graves had recovered quickly enough from the physical symptoms of the flu but in the refuge of his bedroom, shells continued to explode with such ferocity on his bedclothes that the sound of his own screams woke him. Strangers suddenly assumed the faces of those friends he had last seen rotting in the trenches.

Graves made some effort to check his 'unrestrainedly foul language' picked up in the trenches, but the telephone became an instrument of terror to him, and he would relieve himself by the side of the road with no attempt at discretion. The effort of seeing more than two people in one day prevented him from sleeping. Peaceful fields became tactical challenges for wartime defence strategies. Wives were baffled by husbands who complained they had been covered with lice since 1917.

The medical establishment was at a loss as to how to deal with this mental plague. Sir Anthony Bowlby, Surgeon in Ordinary to the King, wrote in the *Lancet* that he had always been convinced that the remedy for shock was warmth and that the physical wounds should be given the greatest attention. 'You can increase blood volume by fluids,' he wrote, adding that when soldiers are unable to keep the fluids down 'a rectal injection is most useful'.

C. S. Myers was one of the leading psychiatrists who tried to restore peace to troubled minds. Myers thought that if appropriate ideas were suggested to anaesthetised patients, memory might return. But when the words, 'German shells', were shouted into a soldier's ear it took the strength of five men to restrain him. Another neurologist, the Canadian Louis Yealland who worked at the National Hospital in Queen's Square in London, used a mixture of electrical therapy and chastisement. 'Remember you must behave as the hero I expect you to be,' he would tell his patients. 'A man who has gone through so many battles should have better control of himself.' Other 'cures' included the introduction of 'galvanic currents' as electricity was pumped into the patient, often 'until the deaf hear, the dumb speak or those who believe themselves incapable of moving certain groups of muscles are moving them freely'.

A product called 'Tabloid' had been promoted in the pages of the *British Medical Journal* during the war as an antidote for 'a vital war-time problem'. This codeine-based effervescent tablet was recommended as helping with 'nervous disorder attributable to shock and acute tension'. Daily warm baths, a month in the country and the therapeutic exercise of basket weaving were also proposed as help for the condition. But a suspicion that cowardice lurked behind some of this mental distress prompted certain doctors to treat the

suffering men with impatience. Those reluctant to return to the
trenches after being invalided home were suspected of deliberately
affecting the shuddering and shaking common to shell-shock cases,
and doubters would mutter cynically under their breath, in the col-
loquialism for a shirker, 'He's swinging the lead.' Doctors saw dreadful
self-inflicted wounds, cut inches deep into the hands, indicating the
desperate lengths to which men would go not to be sent back to
battle. There was little sympathy for those who stated simply that
the prospect of returning to the front was intolerable. Cowardice
and subsequent desertion was an offence punishable by death.

Shell shock was suspected of being open to calculated abuse. On
3 January 1919 an officer, Lieutenant Charles Robert Melsomm, was
court-martialled for drunkenness at his mess in Peckham. Lieutenant
Melsomm however denied the charges, alleging that he had been
sent home from France suffering from neurasthenia and that his
behaviour in the mess was caused by no more than a few alcoholic
'appetisers' that had an impact on a nervous state that was outside
his control. *The Times* had reported the imaginative testimony given
by James Kendall during his prosecution by Kent Police. The suspect
milk that Kendall had been found to be selling had, he claimed,
come straight from innocent cows, but as the poor animals had been
milked shortly after an air raid, the milk had emerged tainted as a
result of bovine shell shock.

Invaluable psychoanalytical work had been done under the super-
vision of the neurologist, Dr William Rivers, at Craiglockhart War
Hospital near Edinburgh. In 1917 Siegfried Sassoon had come under
Rivers's care when suffering a mental breakdown after refusing to
return to his regiment. At the hospital that Sassoon called 'Dottyville'
he discovered a physician who recognised that fear was not a failure
of courage, but an emotion that outweighed patriotism and hatred
of the enemy. Rivers believed in the effectiveness of talking about
the trauma in the open, and in him Sassoon found a clever, kindly
man with 'peace in the pools of his spectacled eyes and a wisely
omnipotent grin'. Wilfred Owen was at Craiglockhart at the same
time under the care of another doctor, Arthur J. Brock, who encouraged Owen to translate his experiences into his poetry.

But after the war ended, and after Wilfred Owen's death in action, both Rivers and Brock left Craiglockhart. No official governmental provision was made for looking after the thousands of shell-shocked soldiers. A group of individuals, concerned that sufferers would be sent to asylums run by the Ministry of Health, applied to register the Ex-Services Mental Welfare Society for charitable status. The aim was to look after 'cases of acute nervous and mental breakdown as would otherwise be sent to asylums including those cases known as GPI or General Paralysis of the Insane'. The public response to appeals for donations was heartening, but the association was not large enough to make a difference to the many thousands of sufferers who were venturing unprotected into the post-war world.

Those seeking work were compelled to humiliating shifts. Match-sellers on street corners tried to hold on to their dignity, dressed in their best suits, hats firmly in place on their heads. A friend of the reporter Philip Gibbs, an officer from a good family, well educated and accustomed to the highest standards, accepted an offer to sell magazine subscriptions by cold calling on private houses. He told Gibbs that the work took more courage than facing shellfire and that he felt relief each time the maid returned his card telling him the lady of the house was not at home.

Some men had given up trying altogether, unable to find the energy to address the next day. Philip Gibbs recognised the attitude. '"That can wait," they said, "I've done my bit. The country can keep me for a while. I helped to save it. Let's go to the movies."' Some-times involuntary anger forced its way through the apathy. 'Here and there an elderly officer blew out his brains. Another sucked a rubber tube fastened to the gas jet.' Newspapers and commentators speculated on the lack of stability in returning troops after such long exposure to battle and the brutalization of war. Would there be a resulting outbreak of uncontrollable violence?

E. P. Osborne, an historian writing about fallen soldiers, con-cluded that: 'A great war is invariably followed by efforts to dissolve the existing social order and by an increase in the number of offences against the law, which is the backbone so to speak of the national organism.' But the fears were not well founded. Post-war figures soon began to show that crimes involving murder or attempted murder had barely increased since before the war, whilst the numbers for aggravated assault had decreased by half. Only the figures for burglary and assault on women remained the same, demonstrating that covetousness and lust, two biblical prohibitions, were unaffected by global turmoil.

Men were not the only lustful offenders. A laundress, Ellen Henson, had become pregnant three times during her husband's absence at the front. Mr Henson stopped giving his adulterous wife any money and removed the children from her custody. In retaliation Mrs Henson locked herself and the three children in a room with the gas jet open. They all somehow survived. But fear and suspicion of potential violence continued to seep into silent crevices of insecurity, abetted by alarmist newspaper speculations. The *News of the World* described the court appearance of one defendant, Lieutenant Colonel Norman Rutherford, accused of shooting dead a man who had apparently developed a special relationship with Rutherford's wife. According to the newspaper, the defendant 'stood straight and tall, eyes to the front', whilst it noticed with a direful lick of the lips that Rutherford's prosecutor had throughout the trial held 'his lithe, perfect body motionless' as if poised for revenge.

Many criminal cases turned out to be comparatively innocent. After five years in the RAF, Second Lieutenant John Trinder was charged with exposing himself to a young married woman in a railway carriage of a Great Eastern train, although drink, not a warlike lack of control, was said by the defendant to be the cause. Bigamy was on the increase, but the Recorder at the Central Criminal Court put the new figures down to 'considerable carelessness' on the part of girls entering into marriages without making enquiries into the past history of the men. There was an occasional disturbing story of unaccountable brutality. On 9 January *The Times* reported that John Meaton, aged six, from Maidstone in Kent had been found 'in a dying condition' under a hedge on the outskirts of the town, his throat slit apparently by a razor blade. 'A young man named Philpot, said to be mentally deficient', was detained on suspicion.

While little evidence emerged from most crimes to suggest an uncontrollable appetite for violence unleashed by the war, there was a growing restlessness among those who had survived the fight relatively unscathed. They were eager to inhabit that 'Land fit for

Heroes' promised by Lloyd George. But hundreds of thousands of men were still officially part of a now redundant British Army. All they could think of was the return home and of a new, rewarding and productive life ahead. But the demobilisation process was becoming increasingly chaotic and the men who had fought for their country were beginning to despair.

5

Anger

New Year 1919

On the last day of 1918 most of the population of the island of Lewis in the Scottish Hebrides gathered at the little port of Stornoway waiting to greet five hundred returning soldiers and sailors. There was a particular sense of jubilation in being demobbed in time for the New Year. Over six thousand men from Lewis had volunteered to serve in the war, a fifth of the island's total population. More than a thousand had been killed, so this was a homecoming that was filled with a particular longing.

The small mail-boat, SS *Sheila*, was not big enough to accommodate all five hundred men, so while the soldiers and some civilians crowded on to her decks, HM *Iolaire* came across the Minch from Stornoway to the Kyle of Lochalsh to help bring the two hundred and sixty naval ratings across the final stretch of sea. The *Iolaire* set off from Kyle first. It was already late in the evening but the cold mid-winter darkness did nothing to suppress the exuberance of the men's spirits.

Forty miles away the mood was matched by the families waiting on the Stornoway quayside. A few miles from home, the strong wind intensified, whipping huge waves across the *Iolaire*'s deck, drenching the sailors. But nothing mattered that evening except the promise of reunion. As the waves grew larger and fiercer the *Iolaire* struggled to stay on course, plunging and rising between the huge walls of water. Then within wading distance of the shore, the boat overshot the entrance to the harbour. This dreadful 'error of judgement' baffled the islanders, who knew that the captain of the *Iolaire* was familiar with that stretch of water and with the dangers of the rocks. Later on, rumours of drunkenness among the crew were denied but never fully quashed.

The ship no longer responded to the Captain's direction and smashed into the Beasts of Holm, a mass of deadly rocks that jutted from the surrounding cliffs into the harbour's mouth. Fifty men leapt into the thundering icy sea and were drowned instantly, only twenty feet from land. Not long afterwards the whole ship went under, one man clinging to the mast that remained protruding just above the water.

Because of the night-time darkness the waiting families were unaware of the dreadful tragedy unfolding in front of them. Over two hundred men were lost that night but only when daylight came did the desperate truth become clear. The dangers of war had been overcome only for these young men to die on the very shore of their childhood home. The *Scotsman* wrote of 'a grief that cannot be comforted'.

As the first full year of peace began, the Scottish tragedy seemed to compound a growing despair generated by broken promises and false hopes. First the long-delayed demobilisation process was being handled with appalling bureaucratic inefficiency. Secondly, the end-of-year general election had left many sceptical of Lloyd George's promise to provide a 'land fit for heroes'. There was also a strong desire for revenge on an enemy who had killed and maimed so many men. And there was growing sympathy and support for the escalating power of Russia's Bolshevik revolution. Unemployment, anger and disappointment all combined to destabilise a despairing country.

An incident had taken place just after the Armistice that warned of the incipient anger among the troops, only barely contained beneath the surface. Fifteen thousand recently demobilised but disabled soldiers had assembled in Hyde Park. Special dispensation had been given for even lightly wounded soldiers to be brought home in advance of the others. A never-ending line of special trains made their way through Kent from Dover, curling through the countryside towards the yawning mouth of Charing Cross Station, carrying the wounded home. Many were still covered in trench mud, and many were destined for hospitals where desperately cheerful nurses would tell visitors to 'Keep it bright. Keep it light.'

The men who had assembled in the park that winter day were now out of uniform but most wore the silver badge indicating an honourable discharge for disabilities. Some displayed a series of stripes reflecting the number of wounds received. The War Office, aware of the men's obvious restlessness at delays over pension payments and lack of job opportunities, had alerted George V of their mood but hoped that the sight of their King might somehow calm them.

The King arrived in the park on horseback wearing army uniform, accompanied by his two elder sons, the Prince of Wales and the Duke of York. His mother Queen Alexandra and his wife Queen Mary followed in an open carriage. Barely two weeks had elapsed since the brief and sporadic elation surrounding the ceasefire. The troops stood to attention, army bands played and the Prince of Wales detected that while at first 'everything appeared in order' a sinister sort of mood soon became apparent, 'a sullen unresponsiveness'.

The King held his nerve in the tense atmosphere, riding his horse down the front rank, until suddenly from the back came a commotion and loud cries of 'Where *is* this land fit for heroes?' With no warning the orderly line of men dissolved as the disabled soldiers rushed at the King, pushing at each other and crowding round the King's horse and threatening to topple him to the ground. They approached, however, not in anger but in a simple spirit of appeal to the King to listen to their distress.

Queen Alexandra found herself badly jostled in her landau as her mounted police escort forced his horse firmly up against the door of her carriage in an attempt to protect her. But the excited and confused horse suddenly thrust its huge head right into the Queen Mother's regal lap. Sensing the nervousness of the frightened creature, Alexandra, always a lover of animals, began to stroke the horse's nose, holding it gently between her white-gloved hands until the animal quietened. At the same time Alexandra continued to smile at the crowd as if she were delighted to see them and not in the least disturbed by the chaotic scenes around her.

'Those men were in a funny temper', the King shrugged afterwards as the royal procession trotted back down Constitution Hill and through the gates of Buckingham Palace into the inner courtyard. But unlike the King, who shook his head 'as if to rid himself of an unpleasant memory' before striding inside for lunch, the Prince of Wales was prepared to acknowledge that something more disturbing had just taken place. 'It dawned on me that the country was discontented and disillusioned,' he wrote.

The official process of demobilisation had begun only on 9 December, four weeks after Armistice Day, and huge numbers of soldiers and their families were becoming incensed with the delays. Demobilisation camps had been intended as holding points for a maximum of twenty-four hours, after which soldiers were expected to be released, and provided with railway coupons, a ration book, a clothes allowance and a weekly pension of 38 shillings calculated to last twenty weeks. But the administrative process was slow and unfair. Men who had jobs to return to were usually dismissed quickly, while the jobless found themselves held in camps for weeks rather than days.

Miners had been exempt from conscription but more than 40 per cent of them had signed up. Given the volatile mood of the remaining workforce it was essential to return as many as possible as soon as possible to the pits. But no one had found the time to start addressing the relevant administrative paperwork until a full month after the Armistice. The *Daily Herald*, a newspaper sympathetic to the Labour party, had reported on the growing frustration. On 7 December it demanded to know

> Why in the world the delay? Munitions making has stopped; motorists can joy ride; the king has had a drink; society has had its victory ball and is settling down to its old job of pleasure making . . . Danger of too rapid demobilisation? Bunkum! Why not let them go home at once?

The disbanding of the armed forces remained the most pressing issue of the election due to take place that month. The Prime Minister tried to explain the need to keep Britain's defences in place until the Peace Treaty was actually signed. Armistice meant 'short truce' and there was no guarantee that the volatile German army, which itself had not yet been dispersed, did not still present a threat. In addition the Government protested that a peacetime transport system could not tolerate such a huge and sudden increase in numbers. At the end of the war there had been 3,500,000 men in the British Army. The Government had decided that all but 900,000 were to be released; the rest were now on their way home from the numerous theatres of war.

The general election of December 1918 straddled the first peacetime Christmas, with polling on the 14th and the count made on the 28th. The election was known as 'The Coupon Election' after the Liberal Lloyd George and the Conservative Bonar Law had made an agreement (or issued a 'coupon') with all the Liberals who had been part of the wartime Coalition Government. One hundred and fifty-nine Liberal candidates were assured that no Conservative would challenge their seats and that the arrangement should be reciprocal. There was therefore no chance of one Coalition candidate competing against another. In effect the election was rigged.

The Coupon election carried with it a new and powerful significance. The revolutionary circumstances brought about by the war, in particular the employment of women in the war effort, had nudged the country towards something like democratic equality. Previously marginalised sections of society were gaining an unprecedented self-confidence through their newly acquired voices. The Government recognised that returning soldiers, many of whom had not previously qualified for the vote, would feel the urgency in voting for a new government of a country they had fought to save. The Representation of the People Act passed in February 1918 thus abolished several of the restrictive property-owning conditions and millions of men aged 21 and women aged 30 and over, as well as graduates of British universities, were now eligible to vote for the first time. The electorate had trebled from 7.7 million to 21.4 million.

The Labour party had put up 350 candidates, and several women were proposed as potential members, including the suffragette Miss Christabel Pankhurst and a leader of the Women's Trade Union League, Miss Mary Macarthur.

Lloyd George had outlined his five campaign points. It would be the Government's main business to get the soldier home as quickly as possible; to give fair treatment to the returned serviceman; to conduct the trial and punishment of the Kaiser; to punish those individuals and countries found guilty of atrocities; and to secure better social and working conditions for the people of Britain. Four of these points were retrospective and dealt with the war; only one examined the circumstances of a new post-war Britain.

The count of 28 December had returned the Coalition Government to power with the Liberal Lloyd George remaining as Prime Minster and Andrew Bonar Law as the Conservative coalition leader with a combined vote of under five million. Between them they won 478 of the 707 seats. Herbert Asquith, the former prime minister who had led a breakaway group of Liberals, found himself out of Parliament altogether. One woman was elected, Constance Markievicz, who was returned for the seat of St Patrick's, Dublin. On the extreme wing of Irish politics, representing Sinn Fein, the Irish Republican party, she refused to take the parliamentary oath of loyalty to the Crown, and was thus denied her place on the green benches. But the other seventy-two Irish seats had also been won by Sinn Fein, proving that 47 per cent of the Irish electorate had made clear their wish for Ireland's independence from Great Britain. One of the new Members of Parliament was a romantic idealist called Michael Collins. He had voiced his determination to see through the establishment of Ireland as a republic and his powerful popularity was of growing concern to the British Government who feared a further interruption to the hard-won peace.

The Labour party under the leadership of William Adamson, a former Scottish miner from Fife, had increased its vote from half a million to two and a half million, netting the party sixty-three seats and making them the official party of opposition. This new level of support for the Labour party showed the increasing strength of socialist sympathies. After the war the party had met in an emergency conference, pulling its members out from the unity of the Coalition back into its own party-political group. At the same time the party called for 'the fullest recognition and utmost extension of trade unionism' and gave its full support to the Trades Union Congress whose membership now numbered four and a half million – almost double that of five years earlier.

Labour's goals included the immediate nationalisation and democratic control of vital public services, including mining, shipping, armaments, the railways and the electricity industry. The party made clear its support for the unions by outlining plans to deal with unemployment, the universal right to work, factory conditions, working hours, safety, and women's remuneration and compensation.

On 5 January the deepening anger at not being allowed home broke through disciplinary restraint. Eighteen thousand military men marching from army camps at Shoreham and Southwick in West Sussex arrived at the town hall in Brighton at 11.00 a.m. A spokesman for the group, a man wearing two wound stripes, voiced the frustration felt by so many men with nothing to do. What sort of a world tolerated a position in which the men who had fought to save their country filled their time 'doing physical jerks'? Did it make sense for soldiers to be employed 'washing up pans and dishes and generally doing women's work'? Surely, he argued, they would be more useful at home. In order to press the point a handful of demobbed soldiers dressed up in crinolines and feathered bonnets, bringing a music hall atmosphere to the otherwise grim scenes in the streets.

Some demobs were kept waiting for other reasons. Ten thousand soldiers being held at Folkestone had refused to embark on ships reserved to take them to swell the numbers of British troops supporting the White Army in Russia. They marched to the town hall demanding the immediate issue of release papers. The Chief of the Imperial General Staff, Sir Henry Wilson, was fearful. 'We are sitting on top of a mine which may go up at any minute.' Mutiny, legally terminated by the death penalty, was rife and going unpunished.

On 7 January Lloyd George stepped into Whitehall to be confronted in person by three thousand soldiers who had marched into the capital and gathered in Horse Guards Parade just outside the entrance to Downing Street, ready to protest at the chaotic ineptitude of the disbanding process. The Prime Minister knew he faced a potential threat from whole battalions. Once again he explained that it was necessary to keep an army in place on the Rhine and in France and for emergency purposes at home. He turned to Winston Churchill, newly appointed Secretary of State for War and Air, to devise a way out of this deadlock. Churchill came up with a solution. He suggested that the reserve army should be made up of those who had joined late in the war. Three men out of four would be released and the Government would pay the fourth man double wages, in Churchill's phrase, 'to finish the job'. The Government was relieved to find that most soldiers responded to Churchill's leadership with at least an outer show of calm.

But patience among demobbed servicemen had entirely evaporated. They returned home to find that pensions had collapsed and unemployment was already endemic in some communities. The cost of living had risen while for the poorest paid workers wages remained little higher than their pre-war level. Even then work was hard to come by, and a steady income never guaranteed. As Maude Onions had begun to conclude, it seemed that 'war cannot bring peace'.

In Ireland a separate parliament had been established by the Sinn Fein candidates who had been victorious in the 1918 election. The Dáil Éireann ignored the protests coming from Whitehall about its illegal status and began running the country's affairs as if its fully authorised independence had been won.

Within the mining community disaffection was widespread. During the war the Government had taken over management of the mines but after the Armistice ownership reverted to hundreds of individual landowners united in their opposition to nationalisation. The financial rewards of the industry were enormous: unless you were a miner. Discrepancies in wages and conditions were endemic.

Shorter hours, better working conditions and increased wages became the workers' main objectives. The noise at the bottom of the cramped lift shaft, where the cage thumped and crashed on to the pit floor as it reached the bottom, was thunderous. Dozens of hewers, stone men, putters and electricians streamed out into the cramped passages as they made their way to the engine room, the canteen and the ambulance office. The din only receded during what was sometimes a two- to three-hour underground walk into the claustrophobic centre of the hill to reach the coalface, where men might remain on anything up to a seven-hour shift. The many dangers underground, including poisonous gas and collapsing walls, had resulted in 1918 in the deaths of 1,300 miners and injury to a further 160,000. If mine owners would not listen to the desperate outcry and the Government also failed to respond, the miners had no option but to take action themselves.

In the second week of January 1919 there were eighteen separate coalminers' strikes, and a week later a further twenty as heavy snow began to fall in the north of the country. A total of 34,969 days were lost in strikes as compared with just under six thousand the year before. During these strikes the canaries, whose song would only be interrupted by the presence of methane and would thus alert the miners to the presence of poisonous gas, were brought to the top of the pit. Suddenly they were able to sing freely in the open air. The much loved pit ponies who pulled the coal wagons along the restricted corridors between the face and the lift shaft, whose eyes had not seen unrestrained daylight for many months, were likewise brought up to the outside world during the strikes. But instead of finding comfort in the experience of sun on their faces as many soldiers blinded by gas had done, they were confused and frightened by the intensity of light and eye shields were rapidly wrapped round their eyes by their masters to calm them.

But the consideration given to the welfare of the ponies was not extended to the coordination of strike action itself, and pits were closed on an ad hoc basis, diffusing the potential power of centralised action. Striking members of the dockers' and railwaymen's unions, who together with the miners formed the sometimes erratically managed Triple Alliance, failed to make their solidarity evident. A strike in the Clyde shipyards in Glasgow that lasted from 27 January to 11 February, when the Red Flag was raised, took place in a vacuum.

Amid this confusion consumers' needs and the financial stability of the country remained, in the view of the right-wing press, more of a priority than the welfare of the miners. An editorial in the *Spectator* magazine of 25 January emphasised that over 99 per cent of British industry relied on coal, including the exporting of cotton, iron and steel. The magazine had spoken to a Professor Cobb of Leeds University who 'gives good reasons for discounting the popular faith in electricity' as a possible alternative to coal, based on the wastage level of heat. Gas might be preferable, the magazine argued, but the capital cost of transferring the running of industries to that alternative source of energy would come to 'a very large amount'. The miners, the magazine insisted, must be made to go back to work.

Plaster casts at the Paris studio of sculptor Anna Coleman Ladd were taken from injured faces. The 'restored' face masks were painted to match skin tone to give a convincing reality to the mask. Most recipients were eventually buried in the masks, wary of revealing their injuries to the world, even in death

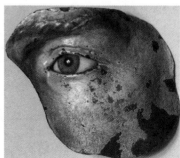

No: on Register 434.
2627 Private Carey S.   1st S.African Inf: Age 22.
Wounded 14.7.16.   Admitted 27.7.16.

2.11.16. Operation (Captain Gillies).
Excision of scar tissue reproduced flaps as shewn in original photo-
-graph.
The central chin flap marked A in diagram, was elongated by two inci-
-sions which enabled it to form the central part of the new lip.
Mucous membrane flaps were brought out on each side and made to meet
in the middle. Part of this sloughed.

Operation 7.5.17. (Captain Aymard).
In this case the scar tissue was removed as indicated in the diagram
and the deficiency in the mucous membrane between B and C supplied by
a flap brought down from the upper lip on its inner side and sutured
in place and the base of attachment left uncut.

Operation 16.5.17. (Captain Aymard).
The base of the mucous membrane flap was
cut through and the flap secured by sutures
so as to form a mucous membrane covering
for the lower lip.

Discharged permanently unfit for Service.
1.10.17   B 179

Above left: Chinese workers were brought in to clear up the devastated battlefields of France in preparation for visits from those anxious to see where their loved ones had fallen

Above right: Full or partial prosthetics made of galvanised tin were used to cover up some of the more horrific facial scarring of trench warfare

Left: Harold Gillies, leading plastic surgeon at the Queen's Hospital at Sidcup, Kent, made detailed drawings of facially damaged men before operating on their injuries

Soldiers at Roehampton Hospital in London, centre for prosthetic limbs. Over 41,000 men lost at least one limb during the war. Government compensation for loss of a full limb was worth sixteen shillings a week. Allowances stopped at anything above the neckline

Disabled and unemployed veterans selling bootlaces and matches were a common sight in city streets after the First World War

The 'thousand-yard stare' into vacancy was a familiar sight in victims of shell shock

London buses were sprayed against infection during the great flu epidemic of 1918–19, which turned its victims' skin the colour of polished amethyst. Fifty million people worldwide are estimated to have died of the virus, three times as many as were killed in the First World War

Junior diplomat Harold Nicolson (second left, front), in one of the sessions at the Paris Peace Conference in the summer of 1919, which he described in every detail to Marcel Proust, being careful not to forget the macaroons

Queen Mary, Queen Alexandra and King George V walking across the Buckingham Palace courtyard on 19 July 1919. They were on the way to watch the London Peace Parade that celebrated the signing of the Treaty of Versailles which ended the Great War

Left: In 1919 a cunningly concealed bath chair and a hovering helper allowed the newly wed Lady Diana Cooper to attend the grandest winter balls despite a badly broken leg

Below left: Picasso and his wife Olga spent the summer of 1919 in London where he was painting the vast backdrops for Serge Diaghilev's production of the new ballet *The Three-Cornered Hat*

Below right: Crowds came to see a spectacular show celebrating the achievements of the wartime hero Lawrence of Arabia, packing the seats of the Albert Hall during the summer of 1919

Right: Sir Edwin Lutyens dashed off an early sketch for his friend Lady Sackville to show her his idea for a temporary memorial to the dead of the Great War

Below: The Great Silence: Piccadilly Circus, 11 November 1919. Families huddled at the edge of the pavement, poised to dash across the street, a window cleaner steadied his ladder and the violet-seller fell silent. Over them all, the elegant stone wings of Eros were as ever frozen in motion. The only sound was the splash of the fountain

Above: Pam Parish aged three with her mother Ethel in 1919. On 11 November 1919 she fell to her knees to observe the first two-minute silence in tribute to those who had died in the war

Above left: Tommy Atkins and his fiancée Kitty were reunited after the war when he became a meter reader for Hackney Electric, disillusioned with his pre-war work as an under-chauffeur and disappointed by the lack of adventure and 'ooh la la' that he had hoped to find in France

Left: Doris Scovell, cook, and Will Titley, footman, had fallen in love 'below stairs' and treasured their days off together at the Brighton seaside

Below: The six sisters of an only brother Tom Mitford (here shown as a schoolboy at Lockers Park Prep School) found it impossible to refuse him anything

Soon strikes began to damage the industrial muscle of the country, stretching productivity in other coal-reliant industries to snapping point. The Prime Minister, ever an advocate of conciliation rather than confrontation, was anxious to contain the spread of the strikes and prevent a national coal stoppage. Officials from the collieries stepped in as volunteers, and naval ratings recently returned from the war were drafted in to help keep the coalface operating.

The Cabinet was nervous that the strikes might be the prelude to something more lasting and profound. In Glasgow the city was brought to a standstill on 27 January and troops rather than policemen were sent in to restore order. The army had been playing the domestic peacekeeping role for several months and Lloyd George was determined that there should not be a repetition of the policemen's strikes of the preceding August. A policeman was often paid less than a munitions factory worker and the same fixed rate as a street sweeper. Almost the entire Metropolitan force of 12,000 men had marched down Whitehall demanding pay increases and a war pension for policemen's widows.

By the end of February the cumulative effect of the miners' stoppages had reduced London to its final three days' supply of coal. And the disruption was beginning to be infectious. In February operators of the London underground stopped working and drivers of the Metropolitan Railway joined them. And the railway workers' union leader, James Thomas, angrily addressed a conference of industrialists demanding a share of the profit from a post-war boom that he felt confident was on the way. He threatened strike action unless something was done.

The potential for a national crisis suddenly become acute as the miners' union at last began coordinating its efforts with the railway and transport unions. *The Spectator* of 22 February remained unsympatheric. The magazine asked how miners themselves would feel if 'the doctors would not attend them or their families if they were ill, if the chemists would not supply them with drugs, if the tobacconists would not sell them tobacco, the publicans beer, the butchers meat, or the farmers milk and eggs and vegetables?'

Lloyd George made a proposition to the President of the Miners' Federation. Robert Smillie was a tough 62-year-old ex-coalminer with a passion for the writing of Robert Burns and Ruskin, and, so a colleague observed, 'a face and voice so terribly full of conviction'. The Prime Minister told Smillie that he would listen to his men's grievances if they would return to work. If they would not, the Government would send in the troops. The fear of bloodshed on top of so much bloodshed, and the threat of the authorised use of weapons against an exhausted volunteer army recently demobbed, was enough to get Smillie to back down. Knowing the volatile and unpredictable mood of the ex-soldiers, Smillie could not be certain of preventing retaliation. Within a month all the miners and their ponies went back to the darkness of the pits.

But these grievances still remained unresolved while others began to make themselves felt. Lloyd George had promised those who elected him to a new term of government that he would 'secure better social conditions'. The consequences of irregular employment went beyond the failure to bring home a dependable wage. The shortage of housing and the quantity of unreliable tenants prompted landlords to ask for references, but with no workplace to supply the references many house hunters were blocked from solving the problem of where to live.

As early as 1917 the Government had received a comprehensive report by the joint committee formed to address labour problems after the war. A committee was formed to look into the housing problem. Made up of members of the Trades Union Congress and representatives of the Labour party, it emphasised the 'extreme urgency' with which the shortage of housing should be addressed. The most deprived areas were in London, Liverpool, Newcastle and Glasgow. In Glasgow half the population were already living two to a room and a further third were crammed into a room shared by three adults. Three quarters of the mining and metal workers in the town of Coatbridge in Lanarkshire were living in one- and two-roomed houses. No new building had taken place during the war because of the combined shortage of materials and manpower. Landlords were getting ready to raise their rents immediately after the Armistice.

The committee urged the Government to put in hand the funding for 'the absolutely necessary' building of at least a further million homes, planned for completion within four years of the release from the army and navy of bricklayers, masons, carpenters, plasterers and plumbers. This building plan would in turn provide work for hundreds of thousands of demobbed labourers. The new houses should be of 'up-to-date sanitary construction, each home to be self-contained; with rooms of adequate floor space, height and window lighting, properly equipped with kitchen range with hot water fittings, stoves, sinks and gas and water laid on'. The committee further recommended that 'every cottage must stand in its own garden of not less than one eighth of an acre'.

These 'Dwellings of the Great Peace' would provide a model for the next generation. The estimated cost was put at £250,000,000, the same cost as five weeks of war. The committee concluded that 'the nation cannot afford not to do it'. But although the new Housing and Town Planning Act of 1919 propelled local councils to start clearing slum housing, the housing problem remained acute. Meanwhile rent money was out of reach of the unemployed.

Even before the war entered its final year, in an effort to address the impending housing problem in the south-east, plans had been made for a new town of desirable dwellings to be built on the Sussex Downs. In an act of astonishing insensitivity the streets at Anzac-on-Sea were to be named after the initial battles of the war in which thousands had lost their lives. The proposed avenues of Mons, Loos, Salonica and Ypres failed to attract any buyers. Only when the name of the town was changed to the soothing 'Peacehaven' was any interest shown. New names like Sunview, Southdown and Seaview were placed at the edge of the new avenues and they suddenly felt English and reassuring.

But there was little financial help available for the building of the houses themselves, and gradually a motley collection of shanty towns began to emerge on the beautiful downland landscape that W. H. Hudson, the Victorian ornithologist and countryman, once described as 'the solemn slope of mighty limbs asleep'.

However not even a palace could have eased the anxiety felt by the British royal family at this time. The King was locked in a position of shame and guilt. His shame concerned the behaviour of his German relations, and in particular his first cousin, the Kaiser himself. The guilt over his own negligent treatment of another first cousin, the murdered Tsar of Russia, Nicholas II, continued to cause George immense pain. George had been particularly close to Nicky and their physical similarity, with their long pointed faces and matching beards, was so great that in photographs they had on occasion been confused for one another. George was anxious to lessen the guilt he felt at his failure to provide his close cousin with sanctuary when his life depended on it.

By the spring of 1919, nine months had elapsed since the Tsar and his wife and children had been shot in a scene of astonishing mass brutality, and a horse had been killed over the grave of Nicholas in violent emphasis of the hatred his assassin had felt for him. The Prince of Wales was aware that this multiple act of violence had shaken his father's confidence in 'the innate decency of mankind'.

Nicholas's mother, the Dowager Empress Maria Feodorovna, had escaped the serial murder of her family but had been stranded in Yalta, living in fear for her life. The Dowager Empress was the sister of George's mother, Queen Alexandra, and George felt he should offer his help. A British warship, HMS *Marlborough*, under the command of Captain Johnson, was sent to Yalta. Until then the Dowager Empress had resisted all offers to bring her to safety, but Captain Johnson had brought a letter from Alexandra urging her to come to England. The invitation from her sister finally induced the Dowager Empress to leave. Twenty members of the imperial family boarded the ship, together with their closest servants. On the high deck fifty passengers, thirty-eight of whom were women, watched their homeland recede as four hundred members of the Russian Imperial Guard slowly circled the *Marlborough* in a British sloop. First Lieutenant Francis Pridham listened as the Russian voices drifted, unaccompanied by music but in perfect harmony, across the water, singing the now redundant words of the Russian imperial anthem, 'God Save the Tsar'. Standing alone was the slight but still beautiful figure of the Dowager Empress, motionless and silent as she listened to the familiar words. Pridham realised that 'none other than that beautiful old tune rendered in such a manner could have poignantly reflected the sadness of that moment'.

Addressing his feelings about another first cousin, the King had begun to confess publicly to a loathing of all things German, telling Franklin D. Roosevelt on the Assistant Secretary of the Navy's visit to Britain in 1918, 'I have never seen a German gentleman.' He had written in his diary on the day of the Kaiser's abdication: 'I look upon him as the greatest criminal known for having plunged the world into this ghastly war.' In 1917 in order to distance the British royal family from his German cousins the King had changed the family's surname from Saxe-Coburg-Gotha to Windsor. The new name, he felt, with its homely associations, would be infinitely more appealing to the British people. The Kaiser heard about the change while on his way to the theatre and jokingly announced that he was about to see a performance of 'The Merry Wives of Saxe-Coburg-Gotha'.

Up and down the country this loathing of all things German remained intense. After the war previously withheld stories about the dreadful things the enemy had done continued to filter out. Not only had the Germans been responsible for the deaths of husbands, fiancés, brothers and husbands but they had torpedoed hospital ships, and caused unbelievable suffering with chemical gas. They had, in Barbara Cartland's words, 'disregarded the accepted rules of war'. In the final days of the fighting Philip Gibbs was told by one officer: 'If I had a thousand Germans in a row I would cut all their throats and enjoy the job.' During the election campaign crowds had filled the streets yelling out 'Hang the Kaiser' and 'Get Rid of Enemy Aliens'. At the beginning of December 1918 a special meeting was held in Hackney to discuss demands for all 'enemy aliens to be thrown out of the country on the conclusion of peace'. Lloyd George's suggestion that the Kaiser be tried at Dover Castle and if convicted be exiled to the Falkland Islands came to nothing. But the tone of the suggestion was in line with the British wish for recrimination.

On 5 January, a week-long Communist-inspired demonstration had taken place in Berlin and, running out of control, had resulted in a terrifying and violent battle and the loss of 1,200 lives. The appalling suffering of the German people both during and after the war made little impact on the general level of anger in England;

three quarters of a million Germans were estimated to have died from malnutrition between 1914 and 1919. A particularly gruesome and hugely popular film, *Behind the Door*, showed the skinning alive of a German submarine commander who had seized the wife of a German-American merchant marine captain.

Some found the prejudice directed at Germany distressing. They had not forgotten the pro-German sensibility that had existed in British society from Victorian times. Fifty-three thousand Germans had lived happily in Britain before the war. During Victoria's reign, under the influence of her German husband Albert, it was not uncommon at a grand dinner party for conversational exchanges to be made in three languages, the guests picking their way between English, French and German, even in one sentence. An enquiry about a trip abroad demanded an agile game of linguistic hopscotch, 'Vous êtes allés chercher a change of air among die schönste boulevards?' The streets of London were filled with itinerant German music makers and restaurants like Schmidt's in Charlotte Street were always fully booked at lunchtime.

But the virulence of feeling against the enemy intensified in 1915, when the *Lusitania*, the British passenger liner, was sunk by a German torpedo, and a thousand civilians were drowned. The act was viewed as unforgivable and unforgettable. Anyone with a German name was targeted. In Salford a jeering crowd including many women attacked a shop belonging to Mr Herman Pratt, a respected and popular pork butcher. Breaking down the door, they threw everything they could lay their hands on into the street. Out went pork joints, crockery, chairs and bedding and finally the piano, until the remaining wreck was set on fire. There was looted bacon for breakfast in many poor homes the following morning.

During the war the Kaiser was blamed for everything possible that went wrong. Victoria Sackville, enraged by reading in the newspaper of a price rise in milk, pushed the article from her in disgust. 'Ce sale Kaiser – voilà qu'il a upset the milk.' Even after the war, everyone from the King downwards remained vocal in hatred of the Germans. Cinemas and newspapers disseminated the prejudice. An advertisement in *Vogue* asked its readers, 'Why drink German Hocks or Moselles when France our ally offers us the produce of her choicest vineyards at the Moseloro estate, superior in quality to German Hocks and Moselles shipped to this country before the war?' Nicknames in frequent use by both ex-soldiers and civilians for the German people included Squarehead and Boche, from the French word *Caboche*, meaning Cabbage Head. The British press ran headlines repeating Lloyd George's objective that the Germans should be squeezed until 'the pips squeak'. As the troops sat out the long wait for demobilisation papers, propaganda continued to strengthen the feeling against the defeated enemy. The film *Shoulder Arms* starred Charlie Chaplin, dressed in khaki instead of the more familiar tramp outfit, trying to capture the Kaiser while disguised as a tree. The film was shown in stables and village halls across France wherever a screen could be erected.

A story by Rudyard Kipling written in 1915 entitled 'Mary Postgate' continued to enjoy popularity. In the story a woman watches as a German airman dies of thirst in front of her as she refuses him water. Kipling's approval of her behaviour is left in no doubt. But one curious anomaly in this hostile view of all things German was found in the post-war passion for breeds of German dog. *The Times* noticed that it was 'as easy to buy an Alsatian as to rent a house or flat in London'. Some of the best-trained dogs had been looted from German prisoners, and their vigilance, fidelity and suspiciousness towards strangers were attributes highly prized by lonely widows and people of a nervous disposition.

Most people, including the King, looked forward to the restrictions and conditions that the Peace Conference would impose on the country they had been fighting for the last four years. By the end of the war, as a result of harassment and deportation, the number of Germans left in Britain had dropped to 22,000, under half the pre-war figure.

The feelings shared by the King and his subjects on the future fate of Germany did not extend to Russia, the country so recently ruled by George's cousin Nicholas. The powerful influence of the revolutionary movement was growing by the week. British grievances were undercut by an incipient sympathy with the men whom many thought of as their Russian 'comrades'. Talk of the Bolshevik threat was known in the popular press as the Red Scare, while Communist sympathies were referred to in the army and in hospitals as going 'Bolo'.

The red threat (red was the colour of the Communist flag) was on the increase in America too. In December a bomb had exploded in the New York apartment of the Acting Superintendent of Police while the oblivious owner was asleep. Captain W. B. Mills woke up amazed to find himself ten foot from his bed, and sprawled in the corridor of the apartment where he had been hurled by the explosion. A few months later a maid at the home of a Senator in Seattle opened a package addressed to her employer. The bomb that was contained inside blew off both her hands.

Back in England the Bishop of Durham was convinced that England was already 'making its first advance towards the dictatorship of the proletariat'. The remaining monarchies of Europe, and in particular the murdered Tsar's English cousin, continued to shudder at the thought of what might happen next.

6

Hopelessness

Spring 1919

Queen Mary was distressed to notice that her hair had begun to turn grey. The first few months after the end of the war had been difficult. Unlike almost every family in the country, she had been spared the death of a close relation but she had an instinctive fear of suffering and of illness. The appearance of so many of the wounded men that she had visited in hospital during the 'single long dark winter' of the last four years had filled her with sadness. And the tip of her husband's beard, she also noticed, but withholding comment, was starting to gleam white.

Mary was conscious of her tendency to withdraw from any engagement with life and, when under the strain of events she was persuaded to go to bed for the day, she was liable to refuse all food and to lose her voice. This was a dangerous state of mind for Mary who tried to ensure that she was constantly occupied, whether with charity work or reorganising and shopping for additions to the collections of furniture, paintings, silver and porcelain that had been stored at Windsor during the war. Her fascination with and passion for the acquisition of 'things', and her much praised eye for unusual and lovely decorative objects, helped physically and symbolically to fill spaces in her life. She began to discover that if she lived in the present and concentrated on 'things' while blotting out the past she had a better chance of getting through the day.

Friends or even complete strangers were wary of the Queen's visits to their houses and her propensity to covet their possessions. In advance of her arrival they would hide anything that suggested itself as remotely enviable or indeed small enough to be carried away. The Queen would stand in front of an object that had caught her attention. 'I am caressing that little jug with my eyes,' she would say to her host in a voice that with years of practice now succeeded in being both factual and full of yearning.

Mary continued to defer to her husband's preference that she should dress as she always had, in the fashions set at the end of the last century by his own mother. An experimental phase of wearing wide-brimmed hats instead of the tight-fitting affairs she had made her own received a cursory look of disapproval from her husband and was swiftly abandoned. And although she had started taking dancing lessons from a master of movement, Sir Frederick Ponsonby, who was also Keeper of the Privy Purse, this innocently rebellious gesture of interest in the new rage for dance came to a halt when one day the King walked in on the lessons, the displeasure on his face unmistakable. Only with her close friend Lady Airlie did Mary feel able to have fun, laughing with her over cartoons in *Punch*, and sending her slightly risqué comic postcards concealed in an envelope, and posted to Ashley Gardens, Lady Airlie's Westminster flat. If Mary's eldest son had come into the drawing room at Windsor to find these two middle-aged women singing 'Yes We Have No Bananas' at the top of their voices, or seen his mother, dressed in green and white brocade, assuming momentarily the character of a grasshopper while jumping round the room playing the rhyming and guessing game of Dumb Crambo, he would have been astonished.

On Saturday 18 January 1919, the day on which the world's politicians and heads of state sat down to start negotiations for the Peace Treaty at Versailles, death burst in upon the very core of Mary's life. The Queen had spent the early days of the month happily at York House in Sandringham with her family around her as relaxed as the royal family had ever been. She had even transformed the ballroom into a temporary cinema. Noting the state of the weather, as she unfailingly did at the beginning of her daily diary entry, she remarked that Saturday had been a lovely day and that she had walked over to see her new tenants at the Mill House, a local vicar and his wife, before being driven back by her daughter to York House for lunch. At half past five, just after tea, the telephone rang. Mary answered. Lalla Bill, the nanny who cared for her youngest son Prince John, was calling in a state of terrible distress.

'Our poor darling little Johnnie had passed away suddenly after one of his attacks,' Mary wrote in her diary in her firm hand that evening. 'The news gave me a great shock.'

Johnnie, an epileptic, was thirteen and a half. As a very young child he had been known as the mischievous one, the family jester, whose behaviour endeared him to many but exasperated his disciplinarian father. Johnnie was in the habit of putting glue on door handles and pins on chairs. He would daub himself like a Red Indian with paint from his paint box. He loved to go shopping and relished an outing to see a Punch and Judy show. But his ebullience had given way to concern as his academic progress slowed down and the unpredictable fits increased in frequency. For the first few years of his life he had always been included in family photographs, grinning impishly in a sailor suit, but since the outbreak of war Johnnie had been kept out of the public eye. The shame of having a sick child was compounded by George V's view that illness was an inappropriate state for a member of the royal family.

Johnnie went to live near Sandringham House in Norfolk, under the care of his nanny, Charlotte Bill, whom he called Lalla. She cherished the small boy, encouraging him in his love of music and drawing, and taking him out for long walks, although she made sure that the other end of the long rope that he wore round his waist was firmly attached to her hand, in case he should fall into a sudden fit. And although Mary visited her youngest child whenever she could, wartime demands meant that neither of Johnnie's parents saw him very often and the violence of his fits distressed his brothers and sister so much that they kept away from him. But the devotion of Lalla, and the quiet companionship of his lonely, widowed grandmother Queen Alexandra, had sustained him. On the afternoon of Johnnie's death his mother found Lalla 'very resigned but heartbroken'.

The British press, from whom the true nature of Johnnie's illness had been kept since its diagnosis nearly ten years earlier, were full of sympathy for their Queen when the news of his sudden death was broken to them. Queen Mary's energy and dedication to the injured and bereaved during the war years had been consistently noted and appreciated. Monday's edition of the *Daily Mirror* devoted its entire front page to the death of the Prince.

Johnnie was buried in the graveyard at Sandringham three days later. Years of restraint even in her private diary meant that Mary only allowed herself to write that the funeral was 'awfully sad and touching'; she 'missed the dear child very much indeed . . .' A suppression of the natural instinct to weep at the loss of life during the past few years and now even at the loss of her own son had become instinctive. As the country's figurehead she had adopted the national way of dealing with grief – life must go on. To register more would be to unleash the restraint that made it possible to go on. And this national restraint, this setting an example, was also her own particular private habit. She had learned to suppress.

Death had not yet finished with the survivors. An influenza virus more deadly even than the war itself was on the loose. It attacked and killed within the day.

When the virus first appeared in the summer of 1918, it produced only the old familiar indicators of flu, including sweats, headaches, pain in the eyes, back and limbs. But unusually these signs were followed by a sense of immense depression and at this stage the flu became unrecognisable from previous incarnations. When the virus entered the body it was transformed into something almost invariably fatal. The drama of the sickness was reflected in an explosion of colour. First the skin turned a vivid and almost beautiful purple, reminiscent of the heliotrope flower or of polished amethyst. Then the lungs and all the other major organs became filled with a thick scarlet jelly that choked the afflicted. Death occurred as the victims drowned in their own blood and bodily fluids. Even if a sufferer recovered, the illness could leave behind a lingering sense of misery and hopelessness.

The massive operation of sending the Allied forces home meant that millions of young men were dispersing all over the world. Thousands were carrying the flu virus picked up in the fatal incubating grounds of the trenches. Spain was the first country to report massive casualties of the epidemic. In the very act of welcoming a soldier home from abroad, a family was often unknowingly embracing the bearer of a new kind of fatality. Although troop movement was the main agent of the spread of the disease, the huge crowds that gathered together in celebration at the end of the war had undoubtedly encouraged the infection.

No one knew how long the epidemic would continue. The newspapers, worn out with sustained stories of death over the last four years, seemed barely able to acknowledge what was happening. Reports of the advance of the disease appeared well down the page and deep within the body of the newspapers. On 3 January 1919 Mrs Susannah Jones, wife of 'Stoker' Jones, an officer in the Royal Navy, died from influenza in her eighteenth year. Mr and Mrs Jones had been married for one day. There was an air of resignation in the reports. *The Times* suggested that the swift spread of the epidemic might have been a result of 'the general weakness of nerve-power known as war-weariness'.

James Shaw of Worcester Road, Manor Park, a crane driver at the docks, recognised the flu symptoms while going to work. Without his wage there would be no money to look after his two daughters, Lucy aged seven and Edith May aged two and a half. So he took his safety razor and cut Edith May's throat. Lucy wriggled from under him as he was halfway through the job and ran bleeding from him. Exhausted by a war that he had thought would never end and with all hope for a happy future destroyed by an illness that had almost certainly come to claim him, he put the razor to his own throat. The poor suffered no more than the rich. The mortality rate in Chelsea and Westminster was 6.1 per thousand and 5.2 per thousand, while in Bermondsey and Bethnal Green it was 5.6 and 5.1. No one was exempt.

Sudden death was not unfamiliar to the English, accustomed as they were to the alarming rate of infant mortality. Scarlet fever, pneumonia, tuberculosis, diphtheria, appendicitis and septicaemia carried children off with accepted regularity. Nor were flu epidemics an unusual occurrence. There had been serious and fatal outbreaks in 1900, 1908 and 1915, and the very familiarity of the condition meant that the eruption of the illness that began in 1918 was all but ignored at the beginning.

The origins of the 1918 strain of flu were unclear. It was thought that animals or perhaps chickens or birds had passed the virus through to pigs before it had emerged in its final dreadful mutation in humans. Occasionally both adult and child managed to survive the infection. In March 1919 Winston Churchill, the newly appointed Secretary of State for War and Air, was in Paris for the Peace Conference. His wife Clemmie had given birth to Marigold, their fourth child, four days after the Armistice and Churchill was content to think of his family back in England, the baby under the dedicated care of their Scottish nanny Isabelle.

But Isabelle had come down with the flu, and in her delirious state had taken the four-month-old baby into her bed. Clemmie found nanny and child tucked up together with the Scottish woman talking 'fast and loud in an unearthly voice like a chant for several hours'. There were still few doctors available. Many of them had not returned from their war duties and Clemmie's own attempts to nurse Isabelle failed. The nanny died at 5.30 the following morning after catching the disease. Clemmie was terrified. Her own temperature hovered at a dangerous 102 degrees. 'I long to see you,' she wrote to her husband, 'I am unhappy.'

While Marigold and Clemmie began to recover, another anxious mother in Sidcup, Ethel Parish, began to feel the extremes of hot and cold. She went shivering and alone to her bed but when her own child, Pam, began showing signs of the illness, the three-year-old baby of the family was carried in the arms of her aunt into the darkened room to join her mother. Delighted to be reunited with her adored mother they were left alone. Against the odds they both survived.

Joanna Selby-Bigge was a year older than Pam and less fortunate. At the age of four she was not as robust as Pam. Joanna was the adored child of her parents, Rachel and John, both former students at the Slade. After serving in the ranks in the Macedonian Mule Corps, John had begun a new life as a chicken farmer at King's Sutton in Northamptonshire. When Joanna died shortly after her fourth birthday, the use of superlatives seemed to be the only way to remember her by. On the beautifully carved headstone her parents chose the few and the best words they knew to describe their daughter.

Joanna Annabella Lewis Selby-Bigge
Jocundissima
Dilectissima
Amantissima
Born May 1915
Died July 1919

Two days after Maude Onions had sent out her signal, the British
Medical Council held a conference to discuss how to respond to
public anxiety about this new threat. The conference's conclusion
was that 'carrying on' was the best possible course. The medical establishment could offer little alternative, except the customary
recommended salvation for everything, including fear: a good tot of
whisky. Doctors were not the only scarce medical resource. An
estimated three fully trained nurses (as distinct from volunteers) were
available to help treat every million people in England and nurses
themselves were not immune to the disease. Six nurses at Great
Ormond Street Hospital alone had died of the virus in the last few
months. And as the influenza victims took second place to the 10,000
wounded and shell-shocked men still lying in hospital six months
after the ceasefire, the suffering public felt themselves to be very
much reliant on their own resources at home.

The depleted medical team did their best to try and contain the
crisis. The Government's Chief Medical Officer issued some pre-
cautions. People were advised to wear a small gauze mask across
their mouth, to eat well and to try drinking half a bottle of light
wine or taking a glass of port after dinner. Hot baths were thought
to help and a decrease in the use of tobacco seemed to have some
beneficial effect. Older people were accustomed to warding off illness
and used their own remedies. Opium, rhubarb, treacle, laudanum,
vinegar and quinine were all thought to have their own special
curative powers.

In February 1919 Robert Graves was finally given his demobilisation papers. Aware that he was going down with the new killer
flu he went as soon as he could to join his new wife and baby at
Hove in Sussex where the Welsh maid was enjoying noticeably
robust health, due she swore to the leg of a lizard tied in a little

bag round her neck. The nurse who looked after Graves during the worst of his infection spent much of her time staring at the waves crying, 'Sea, sea, give my husband back to me', even though the missing husband had not been shot or even drowned, but simply unfaithful.

Oxo spent millions on advertising their meaty drink supplement as a good way of increasing nutrition and 'fortifying the system'. Healthy sceptics thought the illness psychosomatic. Fear itself was felt to be a possible predisposing agent of infection, so doctors discouraged people from dwelling on the subject, or even using the word 'pandemic' which itself might induce panic.

For the first time since records began, the death rate had been overtaking that of births. Just before the 1918 Armistice one third of the police force had become ill simultaneously. Sober-suited council employees took off their ties and became gravediggers. Coffins that had been stockpiled during the war, as there were no bodies to put in them, were suddenly in short supply. The Leicester railway workshops turned to coffin manufacturing and Red Cross ambulances were employed as hearses.

The Savoy Hotel had announced that it also was in the grip of the euphemistically named 'Big Sneeze', reporting that at a recent lunch party of five millionaires only two had turned up. The chemist in the Strand opposite the hotel had sold more quinine in one day than their total sale of the last three years. The barman at the hotel, always up for a challenge, invented a cheery new cocktail based on whisky and rum combined called a Corpse Reviver. Children began to sing a song in the playground,

> I had a little bird
> Its name was Enza
> I opened the window
> And in-flew Enza

Across the world reports spread of the methods adopted in different countries for tackling this new plague. The killer bug made its silent way through North America, Asia, Africa, South America and the South Pacific. Arizona made handshaking illegal; in France you were arrested for spitting. The cruellest aspect of the disease was its targeting of young adults who were neither old enough to have built up a resistance during earlier epidemics, nor young enough to benefit from the introduction of improved school meals for children. The most vulnerable were those very men who had survived the war. And young women, having endured rationing and a recent cold winter, seemed to be at even higher risk, prompting the *Hackney Gazette* to comment in January 1919: 'This adds a new danger to life. One is never safe in this world.'

Cinemas provided a place to take the mind off death. People remained inside the building watching reel after reel, never leaving their seats and breathing the unventilated contaminated air. Kensington Borough Council insisted that cinemas should be emptied every four hours to allow windows to be opened and the bugs let out. The manager of the Coronet at Notting Hill refused to disturb his customers, claiming that he had an effective aerating machine that worked while the audience remained in their seats, twirling the air and neatly redistributing the infection around the auditorium.

The epidemic had several national identities. In Britain it was known as 'Flanders Grippe'; the Spanish called it 'Naples Soldier'; in Persia it was referred to in almost lyrical terms as 'The Disease of the Wind'. But most people talked about the Spanish flu.

As early as 2 January 1919 *The Times* was reporting somewhat optimistically that 'the influenza scourge seems to have run its course' and that the death rate had dropped by almost half since the preceding week, with only 581 casualties recorded. But in the late spring of 1919 as the epidemic gradually slackened, the appalling casualty rate became clear. Four per cent of the population of India had died; in the United States five times as many lost their lives to it as had perished in the Great War, and in Europe a further two million joined the dreadful statistics. It was estimated that in total forty to fifty million people had died. Although the infection lingered on until the summer, taking Joanna Selby-Bigge with it, the cases had at last become less frequent.

The flu epidemic had contributed to a dwindling lapse of confidence in any all-powerful Divinity that might claim to nurture and protect mankind. Organised Christianity in particular had suffered a slump in popularity. The three cornerstones that anchored a churchgoer to his church had been eroded and in some cases had disappeared altogether. With no funerals to put the official marker down at the end of a life, fewer marriages owing to the scarcity of men to marry, and a related drop in the number of christenings, the frequency of church rituals had been significantly reduced. The local *Gazette* in Bakewell, Derbyshire, ran an angry editorial three days before the anniversary of the ceasefire. Churches were never full. Part of the reason, said the *Gazette*, was because they were 'cold, draughty, unclean and poorly lit'. What is more, it continued, hungry parishioners felt Matins took place too late to cook lunch and Evensong interrupted tea.

But deprivation of warmth in body and stomach was not all. There was a further reason. People felt that the Church, and by association God, had let them down. During the course of the preceding five years, 'when every family in the land has known suffering, pain and death, our churches even in remote villages became recruiting agencies, our pulpits were used as political booths'. People began to stay at home rather than go to church, let down by the holy men themselves who clearly 'do not believe what they preach'. One woman told the *Gazette*: 'I went for a walk last night instead of going to church: I felt it would do me more good,' she explained, frustrated at the way the clergy seemed so out of touch. 'I often think if they'd let me get up in the pulpit I could tell 'em something to help 'em.' A conspiracy not to speak the truth about the terrible reality of war had grown up even within the Church and people had stopped listening. Words from the pulpit floated down on silent, empty pews.

Instead a growing belief in the power of the self was taking hold. Spiritualist societies, already popular before the war, doubled in number. The relaying of comforting messages of reassurance from loved ones reaching out to their families from beyond the grave were seized on in particular by the middle and upper classes who could afford the expensive connections to the spirit world. 'Mysticism' became a household word in salons of grand houses. But as in the Ancient Greek kingdom of death, the Hades of Homer's poetry, the spirits had no substance and a reaching out to their elusive nothingness simply increased the hopelessness of the mourner.

An obsession grew for physical proof of the paranormal. Sir Arthur Conan Doyle, popular creator of Sherlock Holmes, had developed a growing fascination for the occult. The death of his first wife Louisa in 1906 was followed during the war by that of a brother, two brothers-in-law and two nephews. The final blow came when his son Kingsley contracted an infection from war wounds and died of the Spanish flu in 1918, triggering Conan Doyle's fixation with the spirit world. He would lecture to packed theatres in his authoritative and rhythmical Scottish accent about how he now regarded communication with the dead as more important than his writing. For a brief time the famous contortionist Houdini came under Conan Doyle's influence. But after the novelist-turned-spiritualist took Houdini to see Eva, a bosomy blonde clairvoyant apparently capable of bringing the dead to life, the magician returned to America unconvinced. Eva had managed to produce nothing more lifelike than a huge inflatable rubber doll.

An ingenious artist working on the beach at Brighton between the town's eastern boundary, Black Rock, and the Palace Pier had hit upon a clever way of giving substance back to the missing soldier. Abandoning his pre-war speciality of drawing likenesses of stately homes, the sand artist would fashion from the grains an alarmingly lifelike relief form of a wounded soldier lying down. Every morning in the balmy springtime sun, he would make repairs to the damage caused in the night by wind and wave, and sitting beside his empty cap he would wait for his appreciative audience to pass by. Beside the soldier he scratched the words 'Some carve their name in stone, I carve mine in sand/And I hope to carve my dinner with the aid of a generous hand'. His cap was full and his stomach grew rounder by the day.

Faith was tested and stretched as equally imaginative mediums went to great lengths and disgraceful strategies to persuade their audiences of the human reality of the spirit world. Barbara Cartland was less than convinced by a medium who announced that she was an incarnation of an Egyptian princess and arrived dressed in a chiffon scarf wrapped round her breasts demanding a large flask of brandy before beginning work.

If tangible evidence of the presence of the dead was difficult to find, reminders of their existence became important. One young woman would sprinkle Ajax, a man's hairwash, on to her pillow each night. Another dressed a tailor's dummy in the full uniform of her dead Grenadier Guards husband and slept with it every night beside her bed. The clothes carried his smell and for a brief waking moment she could imagine her husband had returned. The widowed Lady Ailesbury would only allow herself to be kissed on the left cheek, the other remaining 'sacred to the memory of my dear Lord Ailesbury'.

The sense of free-falling chaos prompted by uncontrollable and persistent grief could sometimes be steadied by a determined control of the mind, and the practice of the highly fashionable mind-training programme of Pelmanism came to be adopted as a solution by some. Pelmanism was a purely secular philosophical activity whose popularity had spread quickly at the end of the preceding century. The idea for Pelmanism had come from William Joseph Ennever, a 29-year-old British journalist, son of a piano manufacturer. Its advocates claimed that it could 'soundly strengthen and develop a person's mind and character while removing those barriers that led to inefficiencies and no growth as an individual'.

The Times wrote of the potential benefits the programme could offer to thousands of people who felt themselves overcome by mental lethargy. A suggested schedule of reading and physical exercise before breakfast would set in motion a habit for the day that discouraged the temptations of inertia, over-indulgence and excessive consumption of alcohol. The former prime minister Herbert Asquith, still suffering from the death of his son Raymond, had recommended the practice of Pelmanism as a way of holding emotions in check. Other well-known individuals including Sir Robert Baden-Powell, founder of the Boy Scout movement, the novelist Sir Rider Haggard, playwright Jerome K. Jerome and the composer Ethel Smyth were devotees of the movement, along with thousands of bankers, journalists, doctors and – interestingly – a large number of clergymen. A change in outlook on life, the growth of optimism and self-belief came as a relief to those who followed the guidelines. A clarity of purpose came to Pelmanists, they claimed, as well as an increased ability to see things more brightly, and 'to hear meaningful sounds where there had only been a rumble'.

There were other ways to raise oneself from the stupor induced by the ending of the war. Long before the war was over an urgent need had developed to establish the precise manner and exact place of death of those lost on the battlefields of France. Many wished to see these alien, other-worldly sights before they were covered over. Personal columns ran advertisements offering photographs of individual war graves in France and Flanders costing thirty shillings for three prints. Enterprising companies accepted commissions for placing flowers and wreaths on graves. The French Government announced that widows, children and parents of French soldiers who had given their life for their country would be offered a day's free excursion to visit the graves of those they loved. Pilgrimage trains left Paris each morning for Albert, Arras and Rheims.

In England newspapers carried advertisements for guided tours to the battlefields much as pre-war tourists had been enticed by special deals to seaside towns. Prices for package trips to the 'Devastated Areas' included hotels and cars and even an officer guide, if so desired, promoting an eerie holiday atmosphere. Visitors were recommended to bring their own food and to ensure they were dressed for the cold, while ammunition boxes that lay discarded everywhere conveniently suggested themselves as picnic tables, upended and laid with sandwiches, in the middle of this silent wasteland.

The Michelin Tyre Company began publishing illustrated guide-books to the battlefields even before the end of the war. Climbing to the town ramparts at the entrance gate to Lille, so the volume dealing with the Battlefields of the Somme enthused, afforded 'a magnificent panorama' of the city, a city that essentially was no longer there. After a trip to see the hamlet of Marquelise where 'the old chateau opposite the Church is in ruins', and taking the footpath opposite the church from which 'a fine panoramic view may be had of the battlefield on both sides of the Amiens–Compiègne road . . . the scene of desperate fighting during the German offensive of June 9–11 1918', the tourist was advised to return to the car, turn it round and take the first road to the left towards the rubble and broken-pew filled church of Margny-sur-Mer which is illustrated with a photograph in the state described. The photographs were profoundly shocking. For the first time people saw abandoned overturned tanks looking like huge animals that had lost their way. A French journalist, M. H. Thierry, compared the landscape to a sea 'whose waves are formed by the rise and fall of shell-holes'.

There were almost daily casualties among the visitors from unexploded bombs as if the ghostly enemy was taking revenge from beneath the soil. The Michelin volume that covered the Second Battle of the Marne described the area of land that had been host to the fighting:

> The ruined villages are as the shells and bombs left them. Everywhere are branchless trees and stumps, shell craters roughly filled in, trenches, barbed wire entanglements and shelters for men and ammunition. Thousands of shells, shell casings, rifles and machine guns lie scattered about. Corpses are occasionally seen.

While unexploded shells made it a dangerous place to be, unburied bodies made it a distressing place to visit even for the ghoulish. C. Day Lewis compared it to the imagined surface of the moon, a place lacking in any beauty, any hope, any comfort, any godliness. One of these first tourists, William Johnson, 'could barely conceive how thoroughly the agents of death levelled the ground, leaving nothing emerging more than a foot or two above the surface except for a few former tree trunks bowled over sideways and shattered and splintered until they mimicked ghoulish stalagmites'.

Women searching for a trace of comfort in the devastated landscape were seen plunging their bare hands into the earth and rummaging in the soil looking for any little token of evidence, however macabre. Raymond Asquith had described the sight of 'limbs and bowels resting in hedges'. But flesh had rotted over the months and another visitor, William Ewart's sister, who had lost her husband, failed to find him in the mud at Bapaume. However, the experience of looking at the precise landscape, the very trees and mounds of mud that her husband had seen in his last moments, brought her an unexpected and welcome relief. William Ewart reported that his sister left that place transfigured and that she 'went laughing into the world again . . . nor has the dancing light ever left her gay blue eyes. Her ear responds; she loves; she lives.'

The shock of witnessing such extensive devastation both of natural and man-made beauty could be intense and enraging. Charles Whibley on his return from Louvain wrote in despair in *Blackwoods* magazine at the obliteration of the library there. 'To gaze upon the wanton ruin and to think of the treasures within the shattered walls is to condemn to eternal obloquy the Kaiser and all his works . . . the pitiless annihilation of books and manuscripts is a crime from which all but Huns and Vandals shrink in horror.'

Even before the war was over, huge parties of hired workers, including at one time an estimated 92,000 labourers, had been sent to tidy up the mess of the battlefields. Many of these were the Chinese recruits who had originally helped in the building of British military infrastructures in France. They were still at work in 1919, wearing their traditional jackets, closed at the front by frogging clasps, and the flat wide-brimmed hats designed as protection from the heat of the paddy field – an incongruous sight among the grey sodden meadows of France. An atmosphere of distrust had grown up around them, particularly among women. Official reports told of members of '*le péril jaune*' breaking rules by smoking with the foreman; there were accusations of stealing and reports of several incidents of violence, even one of a suspected murder.

Plans to repatriate the Chinese had been delayed, although a substantial contingent of Poles, considered to be less volatile, were brought in to help with the battlefield clearances. Gradually the reels of barbed wire, which had been coiled on the backs of soldiers, were now cleared away; trenches were filled in, shell holes covered over, and shattered shapes like stick men, the now leafless and branchless trees, were removed. While a number of graves and headstones had already been built, and the kissing of a name engraved on a stone brought comfort, many graves still consisted of a few feet of earth hastily covering the dead, and bodies were frequently trampled over and unearthed.

Back in England, a chocolate shop on Richmond Bridge run by a Belgian lady had been closed for the duration of the war, but one day Leonard Woolf, who described himself with no apology as 'an addict of chocolate cream bars', walked past the door with his wife Virginia and noticed to his pleasure that the shop was open once again. He and Virginia each bought three bars, carried them home and ate them 'silently almost reverently'. For Leonard this was the moment when 'The Great War was at last over'. Rationing of gas and electricity had now been abolished and *The Times* announced that 'a cargo of Canary bananas' had been unloaded at Liverpool and that a further shipment from Jamaica was expected the following week.

When the 1919 Easter celebrations began, the congregation in Canterbury Cathedral were delighted once again to see the light streaming through the ancient stained glass. The precious windows, including some fragments of those dedicated to Thomas à Becket just ten years after his death, had been kept in safe storage since 1914 and had now been returned to their rightful place. As the parishioners sang the hymns of the Resurrection, they looked for the country likewise to be miraculously restored to life.

7

Performing

Early Summer 1919

Dame Nellie Melba was a little apprehensive. The opera singer whose glorious voice and extended trills had delighted pre-war audiences at Covent Garden was remembering her final visit to England before the war. In May 1914 she had celebrated her fifty-third birthday in style. All her friends had been at the party, among them the beautiful Gladys Ripon, indefatigable promoter of the Ballets Russes, the irrepressible fun-loving socialite Mrs Hwfa Williams, and the ebullient Portuguese Ambassador the Marquis de Soveral. Ten of the sixteen men who had toasted her birthday that day were now dead. Nearly five years later, arriving from the warmth of Australia to the unwelcome cold of the English spring, Dame Nellie found herself in 'this new haphazard metropolis, so grey and so strange'.

At lunch with Adeline, Duchess of Bedford, Nellie was amazed to see her widowed friend produce from her bag two little gold-lidded pots with a flourish of obvious pleasure. Inside one pot was a tiny pat of butter and in the other a few teaspoonsful of sugar. The expression on the Dowager Duchess's face was triumphant. Rationing of food was still in place and no exceptions were made, even for the smartest establishments.

As the evenings began to lengthen there was a renewed determination that something of the gaiety of the capital should be restored. On 4 May a new season of opera was announced by Covent Garden which since July 1914 had been used as a furniture repository by the Ministry of Works. Dame Nellie had readily accepted the invitation to perform the opening ceremony although on the night itself she was disconcerted to see how standards had slipped since the war. Despite the enthusiastic atmosphere, Melba found little of the familiar 'old brilliance'. She spotted men sitting in the stalls wearing shabby tweed coats. 'Who were these people', she wondered, 'who could afford the price of stalls tickets' but at the same time apparently 'could not also afford to wear the proper clothes'? She was not, she insisted to friends, thinking so much of the standard of material things, but rather of the 'question of spirit'.

May turned out to be a deliciously warm month and in many parts of the country no rainfall was recorded for three weeks. Despite the lack of rain, the Meteorological Office reported that 'the countryside looks prosperous'. Even the funeral of the martyred Nurse Edith Cavell that took place at Westminster Abbey on 15 May was treated as an occasion of national pride. Nurse Cavell had helped two hundred Allied soldiers to freedom in Belgium and was caught and executed in 1915. Now with the written permission of the German minister of war, her body had been exhumed from its Belgian grave in March and returned to England. Large crowds had waited all along the route to see the train that carried her coffin as it passed by on its way to Norwich, Nurse Cavell's birthplace. As her body was gently placed in a grave at the east end of Norwich Cathedral, the choir sang the hymn 'Abide With Me', reiterating the words, 'I fear no foe with Thee at hand to bless', that Nurse Cavell had spoken aloud to her executioners immediately before being put to death.

Life was beginning to move forward. Or back. Society appeared to carry on as if the war had not even taken place. Dowagers unpacked their dusty jewels from tissue-wrapped velvet cases and concealed their double chins with strands of pearls tightly wound round their throats. Queen Mary appeared at a court ball, her impressive chest laden with full jewelled regalia, looking – according to the diary of a young American socialite, Chips Channon – like 'the Jungfrau white and sparkling in the sun'. Channon was less taken with the Queen of Romania in her 'green sea foam crêpe de chine saut de lit spotted with goldfish' that she had painted on herself.

Debutantes slightly past the age at which they would usually make their debut, suntanned and worldly-wise after years of working on the land or driving ambulances in France, put on their dancing frocks. The June weather continued to reflect May's sunny mood. Garden parties were held at Buckingham Palace for war-workers, and the odd bowler hat made its appearance among the silken seal-bobbing sea of toppers. One socially ambitious Minister's wife was enjoying herself thoroughly until she realised 'me shoes is tight, me corset is tight, me 'usband is tight, time to go home'.

A 19-year-old French girl, Suzanne Lenglen, with a first name that was to become synonymous with sporting prowess, won the Wimbledon tennis singles tournament. Much attention was given to her tennis dress, sleeveless on the top and so short at the hem that it barely reached the ankle. The County Cricket Championships had resumed again after their suspension in 1914. Gaggles of geese that had been given a wartime playground no longer honked their way across the grassy stretches of Lord's, and Old Trafford's temporary Red Cross enacampment had been disbanded. Although many excellent cricketers had been killed in the conflict and the greatest star of them all, W. G. Grace, had died of a stroke in 1915, bats were once more taken out and oiled.

John Alcock, a charming, extrovert 26 year old, shared a passion for flying with his friend Arthur Brown, a shy Mancunian. Both men had been part of the Royal Naval Flying Corps during the war, although Alcock had spent the final year in a Turkish prison camp. On 14 June 1919 the two men had accepted the *Daily Mail* challenge to be the first to fly the Atlantic in seventy-two consecutive hours. The newspaper, a publication always first to associate itself with mankind's scientific advances, put up a reward of £10,000.

Alcock pronounced his Vimy IV twin-engined plane 'absolutely top-hole' but the journey was terrifying. When the exhaust pipe burst at the beginning of the flight, noise was their first problem. The roar of the engine accompanied them throughout the 1,890 miles from Newfoundland. Cold was the second obstacle as the batteries in the pilots' flying suits ran out and the two men shivered and shuddered their way through storms of snow, sleet, rain and hail, losing all radio contact when ice froze the gauges in front of them. A bottle of whisky and another of beer warmed them briefly before the empty bottles were thrown over the side. Sandwiches that had helped stay their hunger were soon finished. Thanks to Brown's death-flirting crawl from the cockpit to the wing to clear the air filters of snow, they managed to maintain an average speed of 118.5 mph. Fog was another hazard and once, barely able to see where their machine was taking them, they tasted the salt of the waves on their lips. Alcock estimated that they were flying just sixteen feet above the surface of the freezing waters of the Atlantic. Having come through polar extremes of weather, they eventually landed in a bog in Clifden in Ireland, 16 hours and 27 minutes after their departure and well within the *Daily Mail* deadline.

The victorious pilots were presented with the winning cheque of £10,000 by the Secretary of State, Winston Churchill, at a celebratory lunch on midsummer's day at the Savoy Hotel. The menu included *oeufs pochés* Alcock, *suprême de sole* Brown and *gâteau* Grand Succès.

A painting by Ambrose McEvoy shows Alcock pink cheeked and proud, dressed in his flying clothes of high-waisted boiler suit, with a tight-fitting flying cap wrapped round his head, covering his ears and meeting beneath his chin. The fur on his huge gauntlets stretches up his arms to his elbows and his thick flying goggles are pushed back from his face. Alcock had made flying irresistibly glamorous. General Seely, President of the Air Council, was among a growing number of private individuals who owned a plane; he was even known on occasion to hand the controls over to the care of his wife.

Speed in the air, agility on the sports field and glamour in the gardens of royal palaces combined to prove that all the pleasures of an English summer had resumed after four years of interruption.

The delegates in Paris had been working on the Peace Treaty for five months while the rest of the world had been waiting for the outcome, anxious for the protracted proceedings to be at end. Europe still did not feel a safe place. Continuing violence was not confined to Germany. Communist demonstrations in Berlin and Munich were matched in Hungary and in Austria. In Italy, a 200-strong Fascist party had been founded by Benito Mussolini, the son of a blacksmith and a school teacher. A month earlier, an anarchist had succeeded in wounding the French Prime Minister, Georges Clemenceau.

But Germany remained the focus of punishment and recrimination. Behind what the 33-year-old British delegate Harold Nicolson called 'the sham cordiality of it all' plans for revenge on Germany were being slowly worked out. One evening Nicolson dined at the

Paris Ritz with Marcel Proust. The writer had arrived looking dishevelled, 'white, unshaven, grubby, slip-faced' but avid for detail. Imploring Nicolson not to hurry over his description of what was happening behind the closed doors of Versailles – 'Précisez, mon cher, n'allez pas trop vite!' – Proust listened 'enthralled' as his companion fleshed out the minutiae of a day in the negotiating chamber, careful to omit nothing, 'the handshakes; the maps; the rustle of papers; the tea in the next room; the macaroons'.

The proposed conditions had been agreed upon by the four main delegates, President Woodrow Wilson of the United States, Lloyd George of the United Kingdom, Georges Clemenceau of France and Vittorio Orlando of Italy. Germany would no longer be allowed a navy or air force. The army was to be confined to 100,000 soldiers. Territories that had provided the country with revenue from coal, iron and steel were to be removed from her ownership. And onerous financial penalties were to be imposed, amounting to a bill for over £6½ million to meet the cost of reparations to France and the provision of pensions to war widows in England. In addition the victorious powers planned to insist on an Allied peacekeeping occupation of the Ruhr, the centre of German industry.

On 28 June, the day the Treaty was to be signed, the muted clatter of conversation filled the Galerie des Glaces at Versailles 'like water running into a tin bath'. The ushers motioned for the packed room to fall silent and for a moment nothing happened at all. The Allies were all waiting for the German delegates. They were the last to enter, appearing 'isolated and pitiable'. As they were guided towards their seats, 'the silence was terrifying'. Harold Nicolson was watching carefully.

> Their feet upon a strip of parquet between the savonnerie carpets echo hollow and duplicate. They keep their eyes fixed away from those two thousand staring eyes, fixed upon the ceiling. They are deathly pale. They do not appear as representatives of a brutal militarism. The one is thin and pink eye-lidded: the second fiddle in a Brunswick orchestra. The other is moon-faced and suffering: a privat-dozent. It is most painful.

One by one the delegates signed the Treaty. It was 28 June, the fifth anniversary of the assassination of the Archduke Franz Ferdinand in Sarajevo, the catalyst for the war.

Suddenly through the open windows Nicolson heard the sound of a gun salute followed by cheering and he remembered some wise words that he had once heard: 'Success is beastly.' Later he drank some 'very bad' champagne at the taxpayers' expense. The whole procedure was over. The war was won; the peace agreement had been signed. Meanwhile, in Berlin the economic crisis was becoming desperate. Butchers were selling crows, squirrels and woodpeckers from counters that before the war had held juicy joints of beef and succulent legs of lamb.

Maynard Keynes, the chief British economic adviser at the conference, resigned immediately in disgust at the terms. He knew the proposals, in sapping the German economy, would lead to disaster. A forced reduction of military power and a rearrangement of German-owned territory would have been enough. In agreement, Nicolson went to bed that evening 'sick of life'. A letter was brought across the Channel by aeroplane to Buckingham Palace announcing that the peace was signed. The King wrote in his diary: 'Today is a great one in history and please God this dear old Country will now settle down and work in unity.'

The Treaty concluded, the Prime Minister suggested that a Peace Parade, in the form of a colourful pageant and victorious march-past, would be a fitting way to mark an end to the recent horrors. Reminders of the war were, he hoped, decreasing as brilliant green leaves unfurled on London's trees and the grey days of the previous November began to recede. Now was the time for celebration, and in the mid-summer, with London looking its most vital and optimistic, such a performance would be an uplifting event. Not everyone welcomed the idea. Virginia Woolf dismissed the very notion of the parade. 'A servants' festival,' she pronounced it, 'something got up to placate and pacify the people.' But the Prime Minister remained convinced of the worth of his suggestion. And in addition to the march, he felt that participants and onlookers would need a central object, something physical on which to focus their attention, which would form the symbolic heart of the march-past and the twenty-mile parade route.

On a sunny morning at the beginning of July, the architect Sir Edwin Lutyens had a meeting with Sir Alfred Mond, the Commissioner of the Board of Works in charge of the building of monuments that would ensure the sacrifice of the war would never be forgotten. After their conversation, Lutyens left Sir Alfred Mond's office, the sun still high in the sky behind him. He was on his way to an early dinner in Mayfair and while not wanting to be late for his date, his mind was already concentrating on this most important of commissions.

'I am thinking of something a bit like this,' he explained to his great friend, the ebullient society hostess Lady Sackville, as they sat in her dining room at 34 Hill Street. And immediately, the architect – 'that most delightful, good-natured, irresponsible, imaginative jester of genius' as Lady Sackville's daughter, Vita Sackville-West, described him – retrieved from his pockets a pad of paper and the blue, red and charcoal pencils he always carried with him. He drew what at first sight looked like an upended box but on reflection resembled an upended coffin. Lady Sackville thought the design to be just the thing, and with characteristic presumption born of a woman rarely refused a favour, she asked him if she might keep the sketch. Lutyens already had in mind a name for his monument. 'The Cenotaph' combined the two Greek words, *kenos*, meaning 'empty', and *taphos*, denoting 'tomb'.

A couple of days later, Lutyens received an invitation to come to Downing Street. Lloyd George apologised for the short notice, but explained his urgent proposal that Lutyens should design 'a point of homage to stand as a symbol of remembrance worthy of the reverent salute of an Empire mourning for its million dead'. The memorial should be non-denominational and carry no cross or any Christian symbol that might alienate soldiers of other religious beliefs, and it would have to be in position within the next two weeks in time for the parade on 19 July. Unaware of Lutyens's earlier conversation with Mond, the Prime Minister was impressed by the swiftness of the architect's response. The design was delivered to the Prime Minister's office that afternoon. It was identical to the one already hanging on the green silk wall of Lady Sackville's Mayfair bedroom.

A few days before the parade *The Times* pointed out the danger that the intoxication of victory might derail the message of sacrifice and sorrow that the parade was surely intended to convey. While the soldiers would be seen to be 'marching in the full consciousness of triumph' these same men will with only a few minutes' interval also be saluting the temporary memorial 'with tear-filled eyes'. The obligation felt by the Government to deploy jazz bands, rockets and merry-go-rounds might unsettle the day of quiet memory that many mourners craved.

Saturday 19 July was a dark, damp day in London and at lunchtime it had even started to rain, but the parade had gone off beautifully. People had started to line the streets overnight on the Friday and Trafalgar Square was once again jammed with crowds. The numbers exceeded those who had turned out for Queen Victoria's Diamond Jubilee and for the Coronation of Edward VII, and hotels and board-ing houses in central London were so booked up that visitors were looking for accommodation as far north as Harrow and Watford. Troops had gathered in Kensington Gardens and in Hyde Park, sleep-ing under canvas the night before. Despite the rain, an open-air programme of folk dancing and the enactment of the fairy scenes from *A Midsummer Night's Dream* were due to take place in Hyde Park later in the day.

As the parade passed the new memorial and saluted the dead, many of the parading soldiers were in tears. It was estimated that if, instead of the living, the British dead had been assembled to march, three and a half days would have elapsed before all those who had died would have been able to file past the monument.

Eventually the parade arrived at Buckingham Palace where the King and Queen were waiting, seated near the Members of Parliament, under the imperial and imperious gaze of George's white marble grandmother splendid in her position at the top of the Mall. The spe-cially built terraces opposite the royal party were filled with wounded men and officers, and the brilliant scarlet-coated uniforms of Chelsea Pensioners. There was a small and touching stand on the west side of Constitution Hill for the Service Orphans Home while opposite them were the dark dresses and hats of widows and mothers, sitting together in specially reserved seats at the suggestion of the Queen herself.

Every corner of London was determinedly *en fête*. As the procession marched through Vauxhall the sound of cheering came from the windows of tenement buildings, from the floors of huge warehouses, from those pushing wheelbarrows, and those standing on packing cases, from the narrow streets, from the crammed corner shops, from the crowded pavements. The sound seemed to enliven the whole city. One elderly observer believed the reception was comparable to the welcome given to Wellington on his return from Waterloo, witnessed by the old gentleman's father. The soldiers sometimes had to duck the potentially dangerous hail of biscuits and apples that was showered on their heads from the windows above, while girls with Union Jacks wound turban-style around their hair ran into the crowd with handfuls of cigarettes.

Later in the evening Londoners waited with excitement for the fireworks. Lady Diana Cooper rose from her host's Mayfair dinner table, as 'eager as a child' according to her new husband, and led the other guests up the attic ladder on to the open roof in order for them all to get a better view of Constitution Arch in Hyde Park where 10,000 rockets were to be fired. The 24-year-old beauty had once been assumed by many in Society, among them her own mother the Duchess of Rutland, to be a natural choice of bride for the Prince of Wales. But nothing could have been further from Diana's own independent mind. She had fallen in love with the young diplomat Duff Cooper and against her parents' wishes had married him.

Once up in the open air Diana did not notice the glass skylight obscured by the chimney pots, and missed her footing. Duff was still downstairs finishing off a last glass of port and at first heard nothing beyond a sudden silence and then the sound of breaking glass followed by 'the terrible thud of a falling body'. Diana herself felt just like Alice passing through time, the wonderland shelves whizzing by her until she landed twenty-five feet below on the floor of a large linen cupboard. Looking up she saw that her wide-brimmed hat had been too broad to go through the hole made by her slim body and Alice-like was still sitting out of reach on the skylight several floors above her.

★

Six weeks earlier Duff Cooper had held his final bachelor dinner party in the Savoy's Pinafore Room overlooking the river. The night was as lovely and fine and full of hope as an early English summer evening can be, the windows flung open to the river below. The table was covered with red roses and there was a gardenia for each of the twelve guests' buttonholes. But the beauty of the room, the delectable food and the prospect of marrying one of the loveliest girls in the land had not been able to dispel Duff's gloom, and the next day at lunch at the Hyde Park Hotel, with a sharp steel-brace of a hangover, he confided to Diana of how easily he could have 'replaced the eleven living with eleven dead all of whom − or at least eight of the eleven −' he had loved better.

Their wedding at St Margaret's, Westminster, on 2 June had been one of the spectacular social events of the summer. Sir John Lavery gave them a picture he had made of Duff, Lord Beaverbrook had presented them with a gleaming new car, and Ellen Terry arrived on the wedding day at Diana's home in Arlington Street carrying a rose that she had picked that morning from her garden at Small Hythe in Kent.

The preceding four years had swallowed up nearly all of Diana's greatest friends, during what she called 'the nightmare years of tragic hysteria'. Diana's war had been a strange and schizophrenic experience. During the day she had been immersed in the demanding occupation of nursing, at first in the converted ballroom of her own family house in Piccadilly and later at St Bartholomew's Hospital in the City. But by night she went to parties as lavish as any held before the war. The best of them had been at the house of the philosopher G. E. Moore where there had been 'wine in plenty − it was said too much', the atmosphere ever undercut by the diminishing attendance of the young men who had never missed a party in their lives. Diana was haunted by the sense that she had not spent enough time with those she loved. 'If only one happened to know Death's plans,' she lamented. Whenever a close friend had returned to London on leave there were exotic drinks like vodka and absinthe and the dinner menu would be 'composed of far-fetched American delicacies − avocado, terrapin and soft shell crabs'.

There had sometimes been three bands, one of white musicians, one of black and one Hawaiian. Flowers would be replaced even in the course of one evening, the orchids of earlier exchanged for the wild flowers that accompanied the equally wild music that played on till dawn. And then when they eventually went to bed, they wept in secret into their pillows, half dreading the next time when they would again 'brace ourselves to the sad revelry'.

One Sunday during the fourth year of the war, on a precious day off from her hospital duties, Diana had taken particular care to pack a delicious picnic that she had planned to share with Duff at a lake not far from London, near Cobham. Into the basket went eggs in jelly, chicken breasts, butter, bread, strawberries and cream from Belvoir, the Rutland family estate in Leicestershire, and a bottle of hock to be chilled in the lake. But Diana tripped on her way to meet Duff, dropped the basket and spilled the valuable contents in a sticky mess all over the pavement. She rushed to Duff in tears. 'Who will comfort me when Duff is killed?' she wondered. 'Who will comfort me for *his* loss? Who will keep me sane?'

In the final few months of the war Duff was sent to the front. Diana wrote to him constantly. One evening crossing Westminster Bridge, which appeared 'wonderful in the pale dead crepuscule light', she spotted a half-built building. 'Great straight aspiring pillars cut off at the same time before they bore the weight they were built for – too lovely an edifice to be half-built, but so beautiful in its abrupt cessation'. The building seemed to her to symbolise her own generation.

Absent from the gaiety of Diana's life were her brother-in-law, Ivo Charteris (Diana's sister Violet had put his uniform in a glass case and his framed photograph was placed next to her pillow as she slept), Billy and Julian Grenfell (whose beauty had brought tears to the eyes of his master at Eton), George Vernon, Edward Horner, Patrick Shaw Stewart and Raymond Asquith. All had been casualties of the war. All were Diana's dearest friends.

The remaining bachelors in London all longed to be loved by the woman who Duff Cooper said 'intensified all colours, heightened all beauty, deepened all delight'. But she had long been more than half in love with Duff, although people were baffled by her choice. Lady Sackville thought him 'a wretched looking little specimen'. Duff himself was not sure he was quite up to the standards required for such a husband. Not only was he poor, but he knew that his reputation as 'a wild young man who played too high and drank too deep' would hardly endear him to the Rutlands. But Diana's parents finally agreed to the engagement and the *Daily Sketch* went to town filling its front page with pictures of the wedding.

On 20 July, the day after Diana's accident, the rain came down even harder and London had a bedraggled, neglected air about it. Duff Cooper walked through the wet streets, on his way to visit his injured wife, passing the sad-looking bunting and flags, and noticing the silence of yesterday's procession route. 'There was no sign of life,' he noted, 'except in Piccadilly', where he was passed by several lorries packed with cheerful-looking German soldiers. 'I suppose they were going home.' He wondered how long it would be before Diana was back on her feet.

But the theatrical urge behind the parades of the summer of 1919 was not yet exhausted. Uninspired by the moustachioed, red-faced, over-fed grandees of the military and sceptical of the handling of the war, the public fastened on a previously little known war hero. T. E. Lawrence filled the required role perfectly.

Born in Wales in 1888, Lawrence of Arabia was the third of five illegitimate sons of Thomas Chapman, an Anglo-Irish landowner, and his lover, a children's governess. At university Lawrence had become obsessed with physical fitness and constantly tested his bodily endurance, taking a thousand-mile walking tour of crusader castles in Syria in the summer of 1909, and training himself up for demanding military tactics. Working in Cairo as a military intelligence officer, Lawrence was soon trusted enough to be sent as liaison officer to meet Emir Feisal, the Arab military leader. In Lawrence, and the British Army he represented, Feisal found an ally to join him in his battle against Turkish control of Arabian lands. The beardless, ruddy-cheeked Lawrence, who had never before seen action, became acknowledged as the unofficial leader of the Arabian army. His understanding of the Arab sensibility, their language and way of life was unrivalled. As he criss-crossed the endless sand plains of the desert at some speed, riding on a camel, carrying 'a large treasure of gold', often alone and unprotected, he succeeded in uniting the rival chieftains. With a fighting force that had swelled under his leadership, from 10,000 to twenty times that size, he displayed all the qualities of an outstanding General. It was an astonishing story.

Lowell Thomas, a 27-year-old American lecturer at Princeton University with a background in journalism, had been commissioned by the US Government to find stories that celebrated successes of the war. In May 1917 conscription had been introduced in America as a result of the country's lack of enthusiasm at entering a European war and the Government was looking for a means to ignite 'the people's righteous wrath' against the Germans. The unremitting gloom of trench warfare held no appeal to an American population remote from the conflict and with a taste for the romantic.

Thomas had arrived in Jerusalem in the autumn of 1918, as a war correspondent attached to General Allenby's army, a position made available to him by John Buchan, writer and also Director of Intelligence in the British Ministry of Information. Thomas wandered through the dusty streets of the recently captured Holy City wearing Arab head-dress, the folds of fabric bunched at his neck or sometimes raised to his mouth as a shield from the dust. One day Thomas spotted a slim, small (at five foot five) but beautiful, blond young man with a high domed forehead and flashing blue eyes. Lawrence was 'arrayed', as Lowell put it, in Bedouin robes with a curved golden sword tucked firmly into his waisted sash. The British Governor, Ronald Storrs, introduced Thomas to 'the Uncrowned King of Arabia'.

Working with Thomas was Harry Chase, in Thomas's words 'an unusually able cameraman', and together he and Thomas began to make a film about the liberation of Jerusalem and the emancipation of the Arab, Jewish and Armenian communities. At the centre of the proposed film would be a new star.

In the spring Lawrence had been invited by the British Government, fully aware of the extraordinary power he wielded among his Arab associates, to attend the Paris Peace Conference. But Lawrence found his support of the Arab community at variance with Anglo-French feelings. The Allies wanted to divide the Turkish territories between them rather than handing them over to the Arabs as promised at the end of the war. Lawrence did not hide his dissatisfaction

and Harold Nicolson watched Lawrence 'glide along the corridors
. . . the lines of resentment hardening around his boyish lips: an
undergraduate with a chin'. On occasion Lawrence's bad temper
reduced the admittedly lachrymose acting Foreign Secretary, Lord
Curzon, to tears. At an introductory dinner with the hero of the
desert Winston Churchill was deeply shocked by the latest example
of Lawrence's arrogance. During a private investiture Lawrence had
informed George V that he would rather the King returned the
medal stamped with the honour of Commander of the Bath to its
velvet cushion than pin it to his tunic. Lawrence had explained to
the King that he felt Britain was not honouring her wartime pledge
to the Arabs. The King was obviously displeased but Lawrence was
intransigent, bowed and left the room. Ignoring the discomfort of
the other dinner party guests listening to Lawrence tell the story,
Churchill could not restrain himself from openly rebuking Lawrence
for his rudeness.

Despite his heroic qualities there was something enigmatic and
disconcerting about Lawrence. He would squat on the floor in the
position that had become instinctive to him during his time in Arabia.
People felt uncomfortable in his presence. In April 1919 Lawrence
had been offered a seven-year fellowship at All Souls College, a position for which he felt himself unqualified, as someone incapable of
being 'a good dresser . . . adept at small conversation and . . . a good
judge of port'. But flattered by the academic accolade from his old
university, he accepted.

There Robert Graves was unsettled by Lawrence's constantly flickering eyes 'as if he were taking an inventory of clothes and limbs'.
In his rooms there were three prayer rugs and a four thousand-year-
old clay soldier that he had brought back from a child's grave at
Carchemish where he had dug before the war. Graves and Lawrence
discussed poetry, never the war, and when they went out together
into Oxford to have tea in Fuller's teashop Lawrence would clap his
hands high in the air together in oriental style to attract the waiter's
attention. He had a plan, he confided to Graves, to plant mushrooms
in the All Souls quad.

But no hint of such disconcerting eccentricity emerged in Lowell
Thomas's film-lecture. He first took his production to New York in

the spring of 1919, where he put up his own money to rent the Century Theatre in Central Park West. As Thomas took the stage to invite his audience to 'Come with me to lands of history, mystery and romance' he described 'the young shereef' as 'the new Richard Lionheart' while standing in front of an incongruous but magical image of a young man with an Anglo-Saxon face, gorgeous head-dress and ornately belted robes. The first film, *With Allenby in Palestine*, included cavalry charges, motorcycle chases amid palm groves, and camels racing across the horizon, their riders holding their rifles up high against the sky. For an adventure-loving audience searching for a few hours of escape this glamorous and colourful story compared favourably with the dull, grey muddiness of the Western Front.

The second film, *With Lawrence in Arabia*, centred on Thomas's irresistible mix of what he listed as 'biblical places, camels, veiled women, palm trees, Jerusalem, Bethlehem, deserts, Arabs, cavalry charges and the story of a mysterious young hero'. In Chase's footage the humanity of the Arabian world was never missing. Arabs stared gravely into Chase's camera lens, as British soldiers, less composed, self-conscious and prone to nervous giggling, posed as if for the still photograph they were more familiar with. Thomas himself, wearing his American army uniform and scarf-swathed headdress, occasion-ally ambled into the scene.

Soon the show transferred to the larger setting of Madison Square Garden, a performance space the equivalent to London's Olympia and one of the largest theatres on the North American continent. After that Thomas took his show to Canada and an unprepared and amazed audience heard the astonishing tale at the Massey Hall in Toronto on 6 June. The following morning readers of the *Toronto Star* marvelled at descriptions of this 'Uncrowned King' and Lowell Thomas's 'astounding' story about a 'British Boy who united the Arabs'. The tale, the paper said, seemed to belong more properly in the fictional pages of Rider Haggard or Kipling.

Returning to New York the final performance at Madison Square Garden was once again a sell-out. An influential Briton had slipped into his place in the stalls. Mr Percy Burton, impresario and manager of such stars as Sarah Bernhardt and Sir Herbert Beerbohm Tree, rushed backstage as soon as the show was over and managed to detain Thomas long enough to tell him of his passionate insistence on a transfer to London. Thomas said it would be quite impossible. The show was already booked in theatres along the length and across the breadth of the United States. Burton was determined and persuasive. Thomas weakened. He might be able to manage a brief trip over the Atlantic, during the hottest period of the American summer, when the atmosphere in theatres there was so stifling that performances became impossible. But Thomas, sensing the upper hand was his, made two extraordinary conditions for the proposed trip. First, he asked that the most famous theatre of all, Drury Lane, should be booked for the showing, and secondly he required the King himself to issue a personal invitation to Thomas to bring the production to England. Burton was not easily beaten. Returning to London he pulled strings, made telephone calls and sent a cable to Thomas. Drury Lane was unavailable but would the stage of the Royal Opera House at Covent Garden be acceptable? And yes, King George V was delighted to extend a personal invitation to Thomas to visit England with his show that summer.

By the time Thomas arrived in London on 14 August the two features had been merged into one with the new title *With Allenby in Palestine and the Liberation of Holy Arabia.* The film of General Allenby's cavalry was a revelation to the British audience. The reviewer in the *Sphere* listed the human elements under the General's command: 'Hunting yeomen from the "shires" and the "provinces", Anzacs who were bred in the saddle, Sikhs, Punjabis, Pathans, Gurkhas from the Salt Range, natural horsemen and above all horse-masters'. The audience for the opening night at the Royal Opera House was a hand-picked crowd of Very Distinguished People. The Prime Minister Lloyd George and most of the Cabinet came to hear the talk as well as several Generals. A publicity puff from Lloyd George himself was printed prominently on the handouts. 'In my opinion Lawrence is one of the most remarkable and romantic figures of modern times.'

The borrowed background set had originally been designed for the Moonlight-on-the-Nile scene from Handel's oratorio *Joseph and His Brethren.* In front of the painted palm trees stood the band of the Welsh Guards in their scarlet uniform. As a tribute to Lawrence's birthplace the band had been asked by Thomas to provide 'half an hour of atmospheric music' to put the audience in the right mood. Several skimpily dressed young women with undulating midriffs followed the choir and performed the dance of the Seven Veils with remarkable authenticity. The audience, especially the men among them, were mesmerised. From behind the scenes came the distinctive sound of the Arab call to prayer, a new arrangement written by Thomas's wife and sung by an Irish tenor.

As Thomas appeared on stage, a musky incense filled the theatre, billowing from several braziers positioned up and down the aisles. 'Come with me to lands of history, mystery and romance . . .' he again began as the Welsh bandsmen struck up their musical accompaniment, amplifying the tale of danger, colour and courage. Every grunt of a camel and each rumbling sound that preceded a charge of the cavalry was given its own peculiar musical effect.

Lawrence himself never appeared on stage although at least five times that year he crept into the Albert Hall after the lights were dimmed to watch in anonymity. Thomas's wife would sometimes spot him and Lawrence would blush crimson at being discovered and rush away into the dark. To some who knew him though, his figure was unmissable, looking out into the darkness as if he were 'looking out from under a tent' and standing, according to the war artist Eric Kennington, 'as if he were floating – like a fish'.

In an unprecedented move, newspaper editors cleared the front pages of advertisements and ran the reviews for Thomas's show in their place. Allenby came. Feisal came. Sir Ernest Shackleton came and tried unsuccessfully to persuade the cameraman Harry Chase to jump ship, to work on some technical adaptations to Shackleton's own footage of the Antarctic. General 'Fighting Charlie' Cox came, the Australian Brigadier General, and was so impressed by what he saw that at the end of the performance he mounted the platform to congratulate Thomas and in his enthusiasm lost his balance, toppling into the orchestra pit below and breaking a leg. Winston Churchill should have been at a late-night sitting in the House of Commons; he was nowhere to be seen. Someone let slip that despite his personal reservations about the 'King' of Arabia, Churchill had been unable to resist scuttling off to see the show that everyone was talking about.

More publicity ensued. Hundreds of people desperate for a ticket would bring portable stools and sit all day outside the box office in the hope of a seat. The King requested a special performance at Balmoral in Scotland where he and Queen Mary were spending the summer. The Royal Opera itself remained conveniently outside London, playing to a surprised but delighted provincial audience who had expected them to move back to their home in the capital. As the summer came to an end, however, Sir Thomas Beecham could stay away no longer even though he was benefiting from the profits of Thomas's full houses. There was a new operatic season to launch and Beecham had no choice but to return.

Thomas cancelled the American tour as Burton took yet another brave step. The Royal Albert Hall had a capacity of six thousand. He booked it. To the astonishment of his family, but most of all himself, by the end of the summer Lawrence had become one of the most celebrated of all wartime heroes. His patriotism was ranked with that of Rupert Brooke. Indeed, by surviving the war he had even eclipsed Brooke's previously unchallenged position.

Lawrence was ambivalent about his fame. He felt that the war years had taken him 'to the top of the tree without the fun of swarming about the middle branches'. War seemed to have interrupted a natural maturing and peace seemed to trap rather than liberate his character. A new but increasingly close American friend, a fellow literary enthusiast, Ralph Isham, observed that summer how Lawrence's 'hatred for his body was a boy's hatred; his fear of women was a boy's fear; his terror of being noticed was a boy's terror'. Isham wondered if this idolisation would one day topple him and urged his friend to return to 'the infinity, the silence' of the desert. Lawrence himself wrote to another friend, Nancy Astor, that 'everything bodily is hateful to me . . . this sort of thing must be madness and sometimes I wonder how far mad I am.' He compared his fame to a 'tin can attached to a cat's tail'.

Lowell Thomas, by now comparing Lawrence to Francis Drake and Walter Raleigh, capitalised on the diffidence of his hero, introducing his show with words suggesting that Lawrence was at that very moment 'somewhere in London, hiding from a host of feminine admirers, book publishers, autograph fiends and every species of hero worshipper'.

Not everyone believed Lawrence's protests that he was not entirely enjoying his sudden celebrity The eminent playwright George Bernard Shaw thought he was making a mistake by trying to disguise 'his genius for backing into the limelight'. However, Lawrence had abandoned the Arab headdress that for a few months after the war he had continued to wear, and instead adopted clothes that were as anonymous as possible, a trilby or untidy tam o'shanter helping to shield him from intrusive fans.

Lloyd George had been delighted with London's grand parade of thanks, but not far from the official ceremonies, in Luton in Bedfordshire, there was an indication that marching bands and an upturned catafalque would not be enough to restore England to a state of contentment. That day, driven to despair over the levels of unemployment, a group of cap-wearing ex-servicemen torched the Luton town hall where the Mayor was holding a celebratory lunch. After raiding a music shop, the rioters dragged pianos into the street, pounding on to the keys the rousing tune of 'Keep the Home Fires Burning' with appropriate irony. Further disturbances in Wolverhampton, Salisbury, Epsom, Coventry and Swindon had also interrupted the day of peace. Reporting these events the *Daily Herald* detected a country-wide 'epidemic of violence and atrocious murder'.

But the centrepiece of the Peace Parade remained in people's minds. On the following Monday *The Times* had printed a letter suggesting that it would be a pity to consider the Cenotaph 'an ephemeral erection', given the simple dignity that it evoked. It wondered whether 'a design so grave, severe and beautiful' might be refashioned into stone and kept on permanent display.

Ten days after the Peace Parade a smaller ceremony took place in one of the poorest parts of London's East End. In June 1917 a new form of enemy warfare had overtaken the Zeppelin airships. To children the glinting light of the approaching Gotha bombers made them appear as 'huge silver dragonflies'. Eighteen children, an entire class of five and six year olds at the Upper North Street School, had been killed by a bomb dropped from the sky in the first ever daylight raid. After a joint funeral in which the East End came to a halt while the coffins placed on eighteen horse-drawn hearses had been smothered under eiderdowns of white flowers, the children had been buried in a mass grave.

Life in Poplar had not improved much since the war. Unemployment and poverty was so acute that after disturbing reports of starvation, the borough's counsellors devised a scheme by which the rates would be diverted towards a food voucher scheme. And no one had forgotten Poplar's worst day. On 23 June 1919 a statue was unveiled in Poplar Recreation Grounds just off the East India Dock Road. The occasion was heartbreaking for the memories it revived. Friends of the dead children gathered around the marble and granite monument, their faces as white as the stone figure of the angel that surmounted the memorial, with wings spread wide and high to the sky and hands clasped in prayer. One child, Jack Brown, now aged eight, could not get the memory of the smell that morning two years earlier out of his mind. He had thought at first it was roast rabbit. Now he knew it was the burning flesh of his friends. The Mayor of Poplar, the Reverend William Lax, paid tribute to the children who he said had 'suffered for the country as any men who have perished in the trenches, or on the high seas or in the air'.

Despite the harsh penalties of the Peace Treaty, anti-German feeling remained unconfined. Condolence cards had been handed out among the crowd that day with the words 'In memory of the victims of the Hun death-dealers'. The Peace Parade and the cult of heroes like Lawrence diverted attention from the restlessness that loitered in the lives of the general population.

8

Honesty

Late Summer 1919

A new phrase was hovering over the candle-lit dining tables of intellectual society. People were talking of a tendency to *avoir le cafard*, a lingering dissatisfaction with life, a sense of being down in the dumps for no identifiable reason. The phrase had also crossed the Atlantic where Lucy Duff Gordon was anxious about the future of her couture business. People did their best to forget: the older generation moved house, the well-off travelled, and Lucy watched the young people who 'went to victory balls, danced all night, got hilariously drunk and went to bed in somebody else's house'.

And yet happiness was elusive. With an honesty rarely expressed at the time, Lucy saw that 'those who were not under the spell of hectic gaiety were bored and listless'. The recent past was an inescapable fact and even the combined amnesiacs of drink, drugs and sex could not effect a permanent reprieve. Previously unspoken of subjects were bursting through taboos.

Just before the end of the war, Marie Stopes, a clear-eyed and handsome 37-year-old academic, had published a book that brought the advantages of contraception into the open. Her own marriage had never been consummated and she had divorced her husband as *virgo intacta*. Motivated by her own personal 'misery, humiliation and frustration' she pledged to help other women. Astonishingly, her own lack of sexual experience did not diminish her understanding of the importance of sexual love. At first her book was turned down by a publisher who told her 'there are few enough men for girls to marry and I think this would frighten off the few'. But in 1918 she was able to put her own advice into practice when she married for a second time. Humphrey Roe was a wealthy and generous manufacturing magnate and it was Stopes's new husband who provided the funding to get her book into print.

Married Love was addressed to the vast majority of women who were neither simply maternal nor unashamedly 'loose'. During the war soldiers had returned on leave to the open arms of their sweethearts, the limited time making many unmarried couples less cautious than they would have been in peacetime. Thousands of illegitimate births might have been avoided if contraceptive advice had been available. Instead a conspiratorial silence surrounded the origins of many new babies. Gladys Wearing's husband and her son had both been killed in the early days at the front. To the puzzlement and delight of Gladys's goddaughter, Pam Parish, and Stella her sister, Gladys arrived one day at their house pushing a pram out of which peered a baby girl. The baby they were told was called Zaidee. There was then a lot of grown-up talk and an assumption that curious young ears were not listening. But after being begged for an explanation, Mrs Parish confided to her astonished children that Gladys had adopted the child born to her elder brother's sweetheart. Conceived on one of his leaves home, the stigma of illegitimacy had been too powerful to ignore. A solution had been found in pretending that Gladys's illegitimate niece was her own adopted child. To Pam and Stella's further consternation they heard that Gladys had fallen in love with their neighbour, Stuart Lloyd. Gladys did not seem to mind that half of Mr Lloyd's mouth was missing and to the horror of the Parish sisters Gladys seemed positively to enjoy kissing Mr Lloyd's poor bashed-in face.

A central part of Marie Stopes's message was the use of proper contraception rather than the chancy rhythm and withdrawal methods. She spoke to the poor on whom unwanted pregnancies had the greatest financial impact. Childbirth itself was a dangerous process. Although anaesthetic was available to the rich, the poor made do with gripping on to a knotted towel as the primary form of pain relief. If the mother was lucky enough to have a hospital birth, there were no facilities available for staunching a haemorrhage except perhaps with the ward curtains, hastily ripped down. Infection was uncontrollable.

Contraception was the better way and abstinence and withdrawal were the cheapest and most popular methods. And when they failed, abortion was the alternative and final resort. Condoms were only used in special cases. They were expensive, and their frequent reuse after thorough washing with soap and water meant that holes often developed in these thick, de-sensitising sleeves. Dutch caps were also available and, according to one disillusioned user, were 'thick rubber things made from something like car tyres'.

The medical establishment was sceptical about contraceptive devices. The Royal Society of Medicine warned that the use of all forms of contraception was 'deleterious and dangerous'. The Society also believed that a popular paste, called Volpar, the shorthand for Voluntary Parenthood Paste, carried the risk of producing deformed children. Pessaries made of lard, or margarine combined with flour, or even coconut butter mixed with quinine, were thought to have some success. Marie Stopes herself recommended the use of a large flat sponge soaked in olive oil which was 'an absolutely safe domestic condiment found in most homes'.

Purges made of pennyroyal, a herb that contained a uterine stimulant, compounds of aloe and iron, scalding baths, gin and excessive exercise were all popular methods of ending a pregnancy. The most determined even swallowed a thimbleful of gunpowder hoping for a satisfyingly explosive effect. The death of the unborn, unwanted child often included the death of the mother as well.

Marie Stopes, however, was determined to establish her belief that the use of contraceptives removed the anxiety of unwanted pregnancy and therefore made sexual intercourse all the more enjoyable. A second book, *Wise Parenthood*, was published in the same month as the Armistice, in time for returning soldiers to take notice. A rhyme, as familiar as the household copy of the book that now lived on the top shelf of thousands of wardrobes, soon reached children's playgrounds.

> Jeanie, Jeanie full of hopes
> Read a book by Marie Stopes,
> But to judge from her condition,
> She must have read the wrong edition.

After the war many widowed or sorrowing, or indeed jilted women craved the warmth and sexual companionship of a man. But there were many whose reunion with their husbands had been disappointing, particularly when the dreadful experiences of war had caused so many men to retreat into silence and despair. Even previously happy relationships became a casualty of the conflict. Marie Stopes's books brought honesty and hope to thousands of these women. But Stopes was unequivocal in addressing *Married Love* to both sexes, dedicating that book to 'young husbands and all those who are betrothed in love'. The book was in part made up of practical information, including the answers to such questions as 'In what position should the act be consummated?' ('Looking into each other's eyes, kissing tenderly on the mouth, with their arms round each other.') Marie Stopes also addressed the psychological difficulties that sexually active men and women of all ages encountered. Her supreme law for husbands was to 'remember that each act of union must be tenderly wooed for and won'.

In one gentlemen's club, where men professed themselves wholly uninterested in buying the book, the demand for the library copy was so huge that members were restricted to one hour of reading before being asked to hand the book on. Marie Stopes received five hundred letters a day consulting her on all sorts of personal problems: just under half of them were from men. The open language she used when discussing the pleasure of a healthy sexual relationship was successful in its intention to 'electrify'. *Married Love* sold two thousand copies in the first two weeks after publication and was reprinted seven times that year.

Michael Arlen, an Armenian Jew, was beginning to write a novel, *The Green Hat*. He too was interested in the restlessness of the postwar world and the idea that in order to overcome numbness and to feel truly alive you needed to live to excess. Writing about the desire for the unidentifiable, endlessly elusive answer to satisfaction he listed what would *not* provide the answer. 'It is not chocolate, it is not cigarettes, it is not cocaine, nor opium nor sex. It is not eating, drinking, flying, fighting, loving.' But Arlen was unable to offer an alternative. 'Life's best gift, hasn't someone said,' he concluded unsatisfactorily, 'is the ability to dream of a better life.'

The Marquis of Londonderry, Under-Secretary of State for Air in the House of Lords, found that the experience of being at the controls of his own aeroplane 'smothers or partially smothers things I won't let myself worry about. Literally and metaphorically it is very beneficial.'

Philip Gibbs was also frightened that a lasting sense of calm would remain out of reach. Censored for so long over the truth of what he had seen at the Western Front, he wrote these words in his book *Realities of War* in August 1919:

> Five years after another August this England of ours, this England which I love because its history is in my soul and its blood is in my body and I have seen the glory of its spirit, is sick nigh unto death . . . Those boys, lovely in their youth, will have been betrayed if the agony they suffered is forgotten and 'the war to end war' leads to preparations for new, more monstrous conflict.

As early as 1915 there had been some question about how the war would be referred to by future generations. As usual *The Times* provided the platform for discussion, printing a letter from the editor of *Burke's Landed Gentry* who considered inadequate the 1915 term 'The European War' as it 'ignores a very important part of the fighting in which this country is concerned in China, South Africa, Asiatic Turkey and elsewhere'. Another correspondent suggested using the phrase 'The Great War', although in 1918 an American professor about to embark on writing a history of the conflict had settled on 'The First World War', a title that was accused of cynicism, but was chosen 'in order to prevent the millennium folk from forgetting that the history of the world was the history of war'.

The poet T. S. Eliot was struggling with his own form of *cafard*. The migraines suffered by his wife Vivien had been getting worse and Eliot himself had been suffering from bronchitis. He felt overwhelmed with 'a weariness and emptiness' when left alone with Vivien. His father had died at the beginning of the year and the death had nearly broken Eliot. He had begun wearing a family ring as a reminder of what he had lost. Virginia and Leonard Woolf had published his *Poems* in June, an emotional and intellectual mix of comedy, bitterness and regret and astonishing originality of phrase and rhythm. Leonard Woolf saw something of this clashing juxtaposition of language reflected in Eliot's own physical appearance that was 'Rather like a sculpted face – no upper lip; formidable, powerful, pale.

Then those hazel eyes seeming to escape from the rest of him.' Eliot was pouring his disenchantment with life into the writing of a new, much longer poem, *The Waste Land*.

The *cafard* was seeping into every pore of society. Soon after the Prince of Wales had received his demobilisation papers from the army the question had arisen as to what he was going to do with himself. The Prince himself wanted to stay in the army. Life as a Grenadier Guard appealed to him. After spending several months on the Western Front, he had been profoundly shaken by the 'relentless slugging match contested with savagery and in animal-like congestion'. He had become popular among his men, 'a sort of cobber of ours' as one soldier put it, and there was open affection for the young man with the 'boyishly self-conscious slightly retiring face'.

After the Armistice he had visited Harold Gillies's hospital in Sidcup. Leaving one of the wards that the patients themselves called 'The Chamber of Horrors' he came out 'looking white and shaken'. But there was something beyond the life of the trench that put this particular soldier further apart from his family: first-hand experience of life as a commoner. This experience had widened the imaginative gulf that already existed between himself and his father, who wanted David to continue preparing for his eventual kingly duties: opening new roads, planting trees, and launching hospitals and ships. The Prince had his own word for these activities. He called them 'princing'.

Lloyd George had come to the rescue that spring, proposing that the Prince should become a roving ambassador for Britain, travelling abroad to thank the countries of the Empire and other parts of the world for their enormous contribution to the war effort. He would be the supreme public relations representative who, with his youth, good looks, energy and charm, would broadcast to the world the value of Britain under a modern monarchy in a post-war world.

The King had agreed with Lloyd George's suggestion but not without issuing a caution to the 25-year-old prince, who already seemed to be developing a disturbing propensity for enjoying himself. He told his son, 'The war has made it possible for you to mix with all manner of people in a way I was never able to do. But don't think that this means you can now act like other people. You must always remember your position and who you are.' But the Prince of Wales had found himself 'in unconscious rebellion against my position'. He was not at ease during that first strange year of silence and detected in himself a growing sense of false gaiety as he found himself dancing through ballrooms that had only recently been full of wounded soldiers. It felt like a betrayal.

The heir to the throne was not alone in expressing his disillusionment with life. While the Prime Minister had hoped that the joyful scenes in the capital that had greeted the conclusion of peace negotiations would spread throughout the country, the impossible reality of post-war life continued to make itself evident in public demonstrations against the Government. Disillusionment had spread from the intellectual confines of London to the claustrophobic alleys of Cardiff's 'nigger town'. Here unemployment among the thousands of West Indian, Arab and Somali seamen remained particularly acute and in June had prompted an outburst. Racial tensions had interrupted national unity throughout the war, especially in places where colonial conscripts had taken up temporary residence in British military, air force and naval quarters. Now in July the streets again exploded in violence. Policemen were slashed in the face with razor blades, guns were fired and iron crossbars torn from lampposts were deployed as vicious weapons. The riots showed no sign of letting up throughout the summer.

By the end of July nearly two and a half million British workers were estimated to be on strike as bakers nationwide slammed shut their ovens and miners from Scotland, Northumberland, Durham, Lancashire, Wales, Nottinghamshire, Derbyshire, Yorkshire and Kent once again abandoned their pits. In Liverpool the troops were called in to put a stop to looting that erupted from a combined dissatisfaction with unemployment and price rises and a deep sense of identification with the Bolshevik movement. One man was killed and 370 were arrested as filthy children, sons and daughters of dockers and casual labourers, ran through the streets in their ragged clothes, offering to carry luggage for a few coppers. The poor were making it clear that they had suffered enough.

And the capital itself was not immune. Two days later, at what became known as the Battle of Wood Green, the police were attacked by several hundred youths. Women became wary of answering the door, fearing they would find some angry, unwashed labourer waiting outside, begging for a cup of tea. In Lancashire 450,000 cotton workers left their factories for eighteen days, among them dozens of recently discharged and distressed soldiers unable to join the cotton workers' union and therefore unentitled to strike funds.

Then the Liverpool police force again went on strike in search of union recognition, setting off four days of rioting, torching, unrestrained burglary and hand-to-hand violence in the city. The fighting took place up and down the length of Scotland Road near the docks, the centre of Liverpool's working-class life. Children filled their pockets from the Mo-Go chewing gum factory while their parents tucked bottles of shop whisky into their bags. The Riot Act was read. Troops were sent in. The great bulks of a battleship and two destroyers moored in the Mersey; tanks powered their way down the streets of Liverpool against an arsenal of rocks until a bayonet-wielding charge forced a retreat. After the death of one man and the injury of hundreds, over two thousand striking policemen were dismissed with the pledge that they would never be reinstated. Demobbed soldiers took their place.

The energy behind the rioting evaporated when most of the Metropolitan police force chose to accept the Government's increased offers on pay and pensions. Those few who remained unhappy with the deal had to capitulate when the Police Act made it illegal for a policeman to join a trade union, and against the law to strike.

Over in Ireland, the increasingly passionate desire for independence had resulted in the growth of a brutal regime. The new Irish Republican Army had appointed Michael Collins, the Sinn Fein member for Cork, as Director of Intelligence. He had set up an assassination squad called the Twelve Apostles who were beginning to establish contacts that would lead to the assassination of British agents.

In one small pocket of Britain, however, an unprecedented harmony had existed between British sailors, soldiers and airmen and those from the West Indies. There had been so many volunteers from the Caribbean that it had not proved necessary to impose conscription, as had been the case in other countries. In many cases the enthusiasm to join the Allies had been so keen that men had paid for their own passage to Europe. In the cemetery at Seaford, on the East Sussex coast, nineteen gravestones carried the symbol of a sailing ship and the names of men who had formed part of the British West Indian Regiment. Not entrusted with officer responsibilities owing to the suspicion attaching to the colour of their skin, these men had continued to report to white men.

But the local inhabitants of Seaford found the men congenial and in December 1915 the *Eastbourne Chronicle* had reported that at a church service held by the Bishop of Lewes, fifty-three West Indian soldiers had come forward to be confirmed. 'It was inspiring to see the reverent attitude of the soldiers,' the paper observed, 'who being 4,000 miles from home, discharged their duty to the Empire and found a welcome in the mother church.' To make the occasion even more pleasurable, the Seaford branch of the Ancient Order of Foresters, discovering that some of the visiting soldiers were members of the same organisation, arranged for them all to pose together in a joint photograph.

One of the soldiers, Private 875 Eric Hughes, felt so at home with the local community that he took a chance on his romantic prospects with two sisters to whom he had taken a fancy, inviting them out to the cinema. But as the war came to an end and the flu epidemic cut into every town and village in the country, Seaford recorded its own casualty rate. Among those who died either from flu or a localised outbreak of mumps were seventeen members of the West Indian regiment. The town mourned these men in equal measure to their own people. A rare compassion and simple honest comradeship had overcome the prevailing prejudice.

Away from the drama of the Albert Hall, the summer fireworks and the explosions of unrest in the towns, rural England remained largely unaffected by the war. Up and down the country, from York-shire to Sussex, and just off the narrow village lanes that ran behind and through the backs of houses, brilliantly coloured cottage gardens were tended with the same loving attention they had always merited.

Chickens continued to run along the zinnia-filled flower beds with a timelessness undisturbed by war. In the peace and comparative silence of the countryside far from the capital, Leonard Woolf was reassured to see that farming practices endured with the 'quiet continuity' of centuries.

Here was an England, even after the Zeppelin bombardment of the later war years, that had been almost untouched physically. Children still swam in lakes, rivers and ponds, shot squirrels with home-made arrows, ate apples from the local orchard, and played marbles and, for ten-year-old Stephen Spender, it was a place where no one minded if you carried your innocent caterpillars around in a box with you.

Country people like the family of George Noakes in Lewes, East Sussex, continued to live off the land. One day his grandfather brought a basket of birds to the house in Bull Lane containing some sparrows and finches. That evening there was sparrow pie for dinner. Rook pie was another of George's mother's specialities and in the spring there was a further treat. 'At lambing time it was lamb's tail pie as all lambs' tails were docked for cleanliness, and also to improve the meat' so that, as George explained, 'the nourishment would all go into the body. When the tails were left on they got very fat.'

David Garnett, a London bookseller and conscientious objector, left the city to visit his friend Harold Hobson, an electrical engineer who lived in a caravan in Teesdale, some fifty miles from Newcastle. There he felt himself melting back into the pre-war summers. Together Hobson and Garnett swam in the freezing pools of the rocky Tees stream. They bought hunks of the local cheese that tasted like the best sort of Wensleydale but with the added richness of Stilton. Only once did the reality of the last four years bring Garnett forward with a jolt into the summer of 1919. On Peace Day itself he had spotted a demobilised soldier sitting beneath a tree, holding a gun, his face filled with an expression of desperate unhappiness.

The beaches all along Britain's coast were turning dark with the Sunday coat-wearing, sun-seeking crowds. Few had been able to afford to replace their dark wartime overcoats with something brighter or more summery, but standards and dignity were high especially among the poor and a day out required dressing in one's best.

As the summer months grew warmer fifty thousand holidaymakers left London for Yarmouth and another three hundred thousand visitors went to find inexpensive pleasure on the beaches of Blackpool. During most people's first holiday for five years, the local police station flung open the cells to provide floor place and somewhere to sleep for those who could not afford a room in the pricey and overcrowded boarding houses.

But the simple fun of the beach offered no solution to those mired in the *cafard* and who sought a more effective release from the truth of their feelings. Since before the war the press had been reporting a growing national concern over the increasing consumption of powerful and addictive drugs for pleasure. At the Victory Day Ball at the Albert Hall, Lady Diana Manners had led a procession of Society's most prominent women watched by four thousand ticketed guests. Dressed as Britannia, she had appeared resplendent in her theatrical role. But not far away a tragedy had been developing. Another guest was Miss Billie Carleton, a modestly gifted but much loved actress, one of the 'photo-portrait starlets' whose picture frequently appeared in the popular press. Privately, Billie was a smoker of opium and a lavish consumer of cocaine. On the afternoon following the ball she was found in her bed at Savoy Court Mansions, just a block or two behind the hotel, her pupils already enlarged as the skin beneath her fingernails turned an ever-deepening shade of blue. A doctor had treated her with injections of brandy and strychnine but had failed to revive her.

At the inquest Billie's maid confirmed that Miss Carleton had attended the Victory Ball, taking with her a golden jewel box full of white powder crammed into her evening bag. An actor friend told the court that it was 'rather public property' that Billie took drugs. The police confirmed that at the scene of death they found cocaine beside her bed and that the deceased's pupils were dilated.

Mr de Veulle, a chief witness at the proceedings, was a man sometimes engaged, the court heard, in 'the gentle art of dressmaking' and sometimes following a career as an actor on the West End stage. He was cross-examined and in defence of his character denied that he was 'a sort of young person' and that he had ever 'dressed as a girl in his life'. *The Times* reported that Ada Song Ping Yoo, aged 38, of Limehouse, an Asian community stronghold, had been charged with supplying cocaine and prepared opium to Mr and Mrs de Veulle for what the court called 'disgusting orgies' that went on from Saturday night until Sunday afternoon at 16 Dover Street.

Under oath Mr Ping Yoo's Scottish wife Ada admitted that she would sit in the middle of a circle of men in pyjamas and ladies in chiffon nightdresses who watched as she prepared the opium. Later the guests would grab cushions to put behind their heads and 'remained in a comatose state until the following afternoon'. Ada confirmed that one of the guests was Miss Billie Carleton. Humankind, those in court concluded, was not able to bear much reality.

Diana Cooper had remained confined to a tiny housemaid's room in the house in Green Street where her Peace Day fall had taken place. She lay in a muslin-curtained bed, topped off by a tricolour of ostrich feathers, surrounded by a flotilla of white-coated medical attendants. Some of Diana's friends wondered privately whether the accident might not have been entirely accidental. When Raymond Asquith had died Diana felt such pain that 'the near future seemed un-faceable'. People wondered whether this physical pain in her leg was perhaps preferable to that of suppressed misery, an emotion she felt to be 'squalid, low, devitalising'. The ready prescriptions for morphine as well as the constant attention she received deflected her thoughts from the void left by her absent friends.

Diana had long found morphine to be 'a staunch partner in times of stress'. In the early days of the war the drug been openly on sale at the chemist's. And Diana had always tucked a tube of quarter grains into the parcels sent from Arlington Street, adding to the other essentials Diana felt the boys at the front would need which included brandy, handkerchiefs, pencils and pocket classics. The chemists Savory & Moore in Mount Street, Mayfair, took advertisements in *The Times* praising their stock of gelatine sheets impregnated with morphine and cocaine and recommending them as 'useful presents for friends at the front'. Diana did not think of morphine as the least bit 'menacing' and instead of using it as a suppressant of pain she took it 'as a giver of Chinese courage and stimulus and ultimately dreamless sleep'.

Morphine also carried with it a classiness that could never be associated with whisky and soda, an alternative stimulant that held little attraction for Diana. Since the early years of the war Diana had never concealed from her close friends the delicious effects of release that she enjoyed from drug taking. Even a visit to the dentist where she knew she would be given gas to manage the extraction of a tooth was anticipated with immense pleasure. In a letter to her adored Raymond Asquith in 1915 she described one 'grand night' when she and Raymond's wife Katherine lay 'in ecstatic stillness', both of them 'drugged in very deed by my hand with morphia' – although she also confided to Raymond 'the grave difficulty of the actual injection, the sterilising in the dark and silence and the conflict of my hand and wish when it came to piercing our flesh'.

All through the summer Sister Manley, an Irish nurse who during the war had worked in the hospital in the Rutlands' converted ballroom at Arlington Street, had been looking after Diana, who lay with her broken leg up raised in the air attached to an 'erection like a gallows'. Presents of cold roast game appeared at the door, so there was no need for cooking, and twice a day, after lunchtime and after work, Diana would listen for the sound of Duff's arrival. Duff, like his wife, was a novice driver and through the open window Diana, at the sound of 'frenzied hooting and jams of brakes and gears', would claim her daily dose of morphine from Sister Manley – so she might be 'gay and stimulated'. On occasion Duff was early and the scene Diana made until she was given the overdue shot worried him. To appease him Diana invited a hypnotist to come to her bedroom and wean her off it.

But the drug's delicious effectiveness proved too seductive, and too addictive, and Diana was both reluctant and resistant to carrying out the hypnotic cure. Instead she would fake sleep and, leaving her breathing heavily, the hypnotist would tiptoe out of the room; whereupon Diana would summon the colluding Sister Manley and the morphine shot would be injected as usual. The chart for the professionally satisfied hypnotist read 'natural eight hour sleep'. The reality was different. The only consequence of morphine use that Diana feared was the loss of her looks and Duff reassured himself in private that 'her fear of ugliness is, I think, the best preventative'.

Drugs continued to be the substance Diana relied on to maintain the emotional as well as physical control of her body. 'Perhaps it will take me to a lovely grass-grown moat filled with irises and lilacs and put your hand in mine and sink all fears,' she wondered to Duff. But she found other ways of controlling her mood. Sometimes she and Duff dined alone off mineral water and Brand's Essence, a chicken-based consommé that unlike home-made chicken soup was fat free. Weight was important, or rather the lack of it, to young women. Girls who ate nothing much in order to arrive at the fashionably androgynous shape were accused of 'banting', the word for excessive slimming named after William Banting, the Victorian author of a slim-ming pamphlet called 'Letter on Corpulence addressed to the Public'. The verb had made him a household name. And if Diana was not concentrating on limiting her food intake, then alcohol was always a good additional prop as an appetite suppressant and mental stimulant.

As the summer came to an end Diana Cooper was still waiting for the fracture to heal. She had moved from the housemaid's room back to her own home in Arlington Street where her convalescence in her own gold silk sheeted bed was recorded on canvas by the leading artist, Sir John Lavery. Her injury had been treated by the celebrated Scottish surgeon, Sir William Arbuthnot Lane, supporter of Harold Gillies's pioneering plastic surgery hospital at Sidcup and much sought after for his successful new technique of mending frac-tures with internal plates and screws rather than the old-fashioned use of splints.

Diana was determined not to give in to her disability. After more than two months in bed, in September she left her bedroom for the first time and was wheeled by Duff to Hyde Park and then back to the Ritz for lunch. The pusher and the chair's occupant had soon become a novelty fixture in London society as she was trundled to and fro by Duff – both of them mackintoshed for the rain, beneath which Duff would dress in a black cloak-coat, white silk scarf and top hat, Diana in her 'trousseau best, diademed in seed pearls' – to dinner at the Ritz or for fresh air round the park, or to see the triumphant new season of the Russian ballet.

The chair would not fit into a taxi but it did not matter. There was a shortage of taxis, with many of the drivers either never to return to the wheel or still awaiting their demobilisation papers. Instead Duff would push Diana for miles round the city streets. On one occasion he felt a trip to a concert in Hampstead was a push too far from Mayfair, and anyway Duff was not much of a classical music fan. Arthur Rubinstein however came to Diana's rescue, thoughtfully hiring a hearse, the extra coffin-height neatly accommodating the chair so that her Ladyship could go to the concert after all.

The weather that autumn was gloriously sunny and as late as 11 September the green of the Oxfordshire fields near Lady Ottoline Morrell's house at Garsington still seemed as brilliant as it had in May. The temperature rose to 89 degrees Fahrenheit, the hottest day of the year. *The Times* reported that lidos up and down the country were once again packed with swimmers taking advantage of the unexpected sunshine. To Ottoline it was as if during the intense light of those days 'the sun was taking a last passionate embrace of the summer fields'. The Garsington guests wore their summer clothes.

But the English weather is fickle. On the following day the sun vanished and within days ponds up and down the country had frozen, as deep snow fell across the length and breadth of the country. As much as two inches were recorded as far south as Dartmoor. The unfinished harvests were ruined. A week or so later the beneficial mood of summery light-heartedness had evaporated. On Monday 22 September 50,000 foundry workers went on strike for better pay but the Government were even more alarmed by the next stoppage. On Friday 26 September the failure of the delivery of post and milk confirmed to Ottoline the effects of a bitter ten-day railway strike, held over from the preceding March. She wondered if 'it may be the beginning of a revolution'.

Lloyd George was aware that the railwaymen's action could develop into a national strike. The paralysis of the railway system meant that coal was piling up outside pits all over the country with no means to transport it. Discontent was infectious. The anniversary of the Armistice was approaching and there were no official plans to commemorate the day. The Peace Parade of the summer had been something of a public performance and the temporary memorial in Whitehall had evoked pride in everyone who saw it.

But Edward Honey, an Australian soldier and journalist living in London, had been unable to erase from his mind his uneasy response to the high spirits that he had witnessed on Armistice night. The exuberance of the day demonstrated to Honey a failure to understand and pay tribute to the fundamental horror of the past four years. He felt there should be some way of recognising the silent grief that so many of the bereaved were unable to express.

9

Silence

11 November 1919

The late November issue of the *Tatler* carried 'a camera study' by the fashionable photographer Hugh Cecil, known for the daring simplicity of his pictures. His latest photograph was of an unnamed woman in a sleeveless black chiffon evening dress, leaning so far forward that her head was resting on her enfolded arms, one hand hidden, the other visible yet almost lifeless on her knees, the draped folds of the sleeves falling down from her arms towards her waist. The fourth finger of the left hand, the one that traditionally carries the wedding ring, was out of sight but even though the woman's face was turned away from the camera and only the dark curly hair on the back of her head was visible, you could tell that she was beautiful. The picture was reminiscent of the looking-glass image of the romantic, fabric-draped paintings of Lord Leighton and Lawrence Alma Tadema; but it turned the optimism of the late nineteenth century on its head. Cecil's picture was entitled 'Grief'.

A year had elapsed since the guns had stopped firing and at first glance the country seemed drawn towards a determined gaiety. But the legacy of psychological wounds remained raw beneath the celebratory optimism. By the time the first anniversary of the Armistice arrived, many – particularly those in senior positions in government, and most particularly the King of England – had hoped that the memories of the war would have begun to recede. But the intervening year had proved that the effects of the war on the British people were not to be erased in so short a time. Indeed the first year of peace carried with it more national tumult than had been seen in several decades before the war.

As England prepared to enter the second year of peace many were doing their best to put that first unsteady year behind them, to be thankful that most of the soldiers who had survived had now returned to their families, that the deadly threat of influenza seemed to have passed, to hope that the economy would gather strength and that a new decade would usher in a new and peaceful way of life.

Right up until a few days before the first anniversary of the Armistice there had been no public announcement of any plans to mark the day itself. A letter to *The Times* on 4 November from a demobbed officer, a patriotic Mr Donald Howard, pointed out that 'beyond the advertisement of a big fancy dress ball – an excellent institution of itself but not one that embraces or affects all classes of the community', he was unaware how the occasion was to be recognised. 'To those of us who were at the front,' he gently pointed out, 'and to those who were at home, this was the day which more than any other of late filled our hearts with thanksgiving, pride and happiness.' Could there be a flag display, he wondered, or a gun salute, or most rousing of all 'the singing, not merely playing of the National Anthem in theatres, cinemas, restaurants and all possible public places'?

Edward Honey had written to the *London Evening News* with an alternative suggestion. Concentrating on the bereaved rather than those relishing victory, Honey's idea was less tangible than a monument, and all the more accessible because it did not require people to travel or involve any sense of pilgrimage. Honey proposed a moment of silence, an act of remembrance that would be open to every man, woman and child at any place they chose to be. 'Five little minutes only,' he proposed. 'Five silent minutes of national remembrance. A very sacred intercession.' He suggested not an obliterating of the past but a proper act of memory such as could only be retrieved in a state of silence. In those five minutes people would have a chance to find 'new strength, hope and faith in the morrow'. Church services could provide the framework within which such a pause could be staged but better still, 'in the street, the home, the theatre, anywhere, indeed where Englishmen and their women chance to be', this five minutes of 'bitter-sweet remembrance' would provide a moment to reflect.

The Prime Minister had been told of Honey's idea by Sir Percy Fitzpatrick, High Commissioner for South Africa. Sir Percy explained to Lloyd George how during every single day of the war at noon South Africa had observed a silence. The troops in South Africa had paused for three minutes because, they reasoned, 'when we are gone it may help bring home to those who will come after us, the meaning, the nobility and the unselfishness of the great sacrifice by which their freedom was assured'. During the silence, a chance would be given to salute the memory of the fallen, to recognise 'The Great Sacrifice' and to allow four groups of individuals to be acknowledged for the part they had played in the war. First should come women who had both lost and contributed so much, next children for whom future freedom had been won, then the men who had survived the war and finally of course those who had not.

Lloyd George was intrigued by the idea. But such a national event needed royal approval. Two weeks before the anniversary of the Armistice the Prime Minister and the King met to discuss the idea. George V was rather dubious about the practicality of imposing such a scheme on the normal day-to-day bustle of life. A fastidiously punctual man, he could not bear the idea that the concept could be destroyed by one careless individual failing to hold to the allotted time. Members of his own family did not seem able to keep their watches in line with his own and if anyone was tactless enough to mention his mother's 'rebellious unpunctuality', as the secretly amused Prince of Wales put it, they knew that trouble lay ahead. The King discounted the five or even three suggested minutes as far too long. Even to expect a whole nation to keep to the precision of a two-minute silence was, he thought, probably asking too much.

In November 1919 the King was behaving cautiously with good reason. Here was a man whose confidence had been severely undermined by the fear that the country might reassess a previously largely unquestioned belief in his royal birthright. He deliberated long over the reception that every important decision might receive. But Lloyd George, 'the man who won the war', remained enthusiastic about the idea and he wore down the King's resistance, reassuring him that maroons would be fired in London at the beginning and end of the designated time and that the rockets would alert everyone to the importance of observing the precise moment.

An announcement made directly from the King at Buckingham Palace to all his subjects throughout the land was carried in all the main newspapers on Friday 7 November. The statement read:

> Tuesday next, November 11, is the first anniversary of the Armistice which stayed the worldwide carnage of the four preceding years and marked the victory of Right and Freedom. I believe that my people in every part of the Empire fervently wish to perpetuate the memory of the Great Deliverance and of those who have laid down their lives to achieve it. To afford an opportunity for the universal expression of this feeling it is my desire and hope that at the hour when the Armistice came into force, the 11th hour of the 11th day of the 11th month, there may be for the brief space of two minutes a complete suspension of all our normal activities. No elaborate organisation appears to be required. At a given signal, which can be easily arranged to suit the circumstances of the locality, I believe that we shall inter-rupt our business and pleasure, whatever it may be, and unite in this simple service of Silence and Remembrance.

And so the relevance of the day that marked one year since the Armistice assumed its shape and the day of the Great Silence came into being. The Great Silence would commemorate the Great War, and would provide a time to remember the Glorious Dead and their Great Sacrifice, as well as to celebrate the Great Deliverance.

The King now embraced the idea of the silence with gusto, although not everyone was equally enthusiastic. A 16-year-old school-boy, Evelyn Waugh, was a pupil at Lancing College in West Sussex. His elder brother had been expelled from Sherborne for writing a homoerotic novel about the school and Evelyn by sibling associ-ation was forbidden to follow him there. But he was grateful to find that one of the refreshingly liberated aims of Lancing 'was to produce prose writers'. Making the most of his developing skill he responded to the idea of the Great Silence. 'A disgusting idea of artificial non-sense and sentimentality,' young Waugh wrote in his diary. 'If people have lost sons and fathers, they should think of them whenever the grass is green or Shaftesbury Avenue is brightly lighted, not for two minutes on the anniversary of a disgraceful day of national hysteria. No one thought of the dead last year. Why should they now?'

But a reason and an excuse to concentrate on that loss was exactly what millions of frustrated mourners had come to wish for. *The Times'* death announcements page on 11 November 1919 still carried a subdivision entitled 'Death by Wounds'.

That morning mist and gloom were hovering over Whitehall, and traces of the snow that had fallen two days earlier were still on the ground. Temperatures had dropped during the night to a level lower than any could remember for over fifty years. A dancing sparkle of frost covered the English countryside. Four-year-old Geoffrey Woolley was in the garden with his governess where the gardener was going about the winter business of repairing and sluicing down the tall rockeries. The first chimes of the drawing-room clock that marked the hour began to ring out from inside the house, and the governess suddenly burst into a run, racing towards the gardener, shouting that he must turn off the hose at once. The noise of the water threatened to destroy the imminent silence.

The day of the Silence fell in the middle of the school term and there was an unusual calm in the Parish household. Three-year-old Pam's brother and sisters had gone to school. Apart from the cook preparing lunch in the kitchen, the maid upstairs dusting the bedrooms, and the family's two pet badgers waiting patiently by the front door in the hall to be taken for their morning walk in the fields around Sidcup, all was quiet. Pam and her mother were alone in the house. Just as the grandfather clock began to strike, Pam's mother, her long thick chestnut hair flying behind her, rushed into the playroom and, gripping Pam by the hand, motioned to her not to speak, not to make a sound. Copying her mother Pam knelt beside her on the kitchen floor. Together they joined their hands together, fingertips touching, in the gesture of prayer. Pam, though still only three, knew she was being asked to remember something terrible and to give thanks that it would never happen again. Her mother had told her that they were remembering 'The Great War to End all Wars' and that Pam should be thankful that in her lifetime there would never again be anything like it.

In Whitely's department store near Paddington, the doors closed at 10.45 a.m. and shoppers and assistants together assembled beneath the vaulted roof at ten minutes to the hour. The Reverend Mr

Murphy, vicar of St Matthew's, Bayswater, invited them to sing 'Oh God Our Help in Ages Past', his Irish boom rising to the balconies four floors above before the hymn came to an end just before eleven o'clock as shoppers prepared themselves for silence.

In Selfridges a solitary bugler walked out on to the central balcony of the store overlooking Oxford Street and sounded his instrument to signal the approaching silence. At Harrods in Knightsbridge the fire alarms were rung. In the City at Lloyd's insurance brokers the huge 106-pound Lutine Bell rang out as it always did when the need arose to mark an event of national importance. A murder trial at the Old Bailey was interrupted.

In Baltimore, Maryland, the train on which the Prince of Wales was travelling was halted and in England the entire railway network of passenger trains, goods trains and shunting engines juddered and clanked to a standstill. Trading on the stock market ceased. Out in the Channel, ships stayed their course.

Just before eleven o'clock there was a tremendous burst of synchronised noise across the country. In the cities of London, Birmingham and Bradford, maroons were fired into the sky, and burst with a great clatter. Cities that even in the small hours of the night were never silent, were about to experience something unprecedented.

Town clocks struck with mechanical predictability and in village churches up and down the land peals of bells, so often used for cele-bration, with their repeated tumbling refrains summoned people to stand still and to remember.

In the coastal towns of Britain the signal for those in distress at sea which customarily caused families of sailors to flinch and pause with fear, rang out. At Piccadilly Circus, the place where London-ers felt the pulse of their city, the traffic was still thudding when the first maroon sounded. By the time the second maroon was heard the heartbeat was arrested, the man late for work no longer ran for the bus, families huddled at the edge of the pavement, poised to dash across the street, a window cleaner steadied his ladder, the violet-seller fell silent. Over them all, the elegant stone wings of Eros were as ever frozen in motion. For a moment or two as the traffic came to a halt, a faint under-hum could be heard; then all conversation ceased. The only sound was the splash of the fountain.

Far beneath the London streets all underground trains had ceased to run. Above ground London was normally so frantic that the police were often in despair. Motorcycles carried with them a particular danger, according to the mid-November issue of the *Saturday Review*, and seemed to drive 'at full speed at pedestrians', while the police were seen to 'scold instead of soothing the pedestrians who appeal for help'. But just before 11.00 a.m. motorcycles and cars waited obediently at junctions. Engines stilled as War Office lorries, taxis and motorbuses came to a halt. Horses exhaled deeply as they were pulled up by the side of the road.

Bicycles braked, road menders laid down their spades, telephone exchange operators unplugged their connection boards, factory workers switched off the machinery, dock workers stopped their unloading, schoolchildren stopped their lessons, miners downed their tools, shoppers stopped their purchasing, lovers stopped murmuring, and even villagers talking to one another over the garden fence held their tongues.

In London the King and Queen had sent their wreath to Whitehall in advance of their own arrival, and just before Big Ben's minute hand moved to the top of the clock, Lloyd George, white moustachioed, his long hair touching the collar of his dark tail coat, was seen walking towards the now rather dilapidated wood and plaster Cenotaph that had continued to be a focus for mourners since the summer. He was carrying orchids and white roses, woven into a circlet of laurel leaves. An announcement that the monument would be demolished early in the year had prompted a huge protest against the Ministry of Works for being 'utterly without soul or sentiment or understanding'.

But while Whitehall and Lutyens's monument provided the grand backdrop for royalty and statesmen and other leaders of the nation, this was really a silence designed for the common man. Men bared their heads, holding their hats before them in clasped hands. Only the act of breathing, the final affirmation of life, remained as the sign of human activity. In that fraction of a second before the silence began a reporter for *The Times* noticed a 'certain hesitancy' in the step, in anticipation of the moment, and within those small gestures an unmistakable determination not to miss it.

The first stroke of Big Ben announcing the hour of eleven gave notice of what was required as the nation fell still. 'Here and there an old soldier could be detected slipping unconsciously into the posture of attention,' wrote an observer. 'The hush deepened.'

At precisely 11.00 a.m. all movement stopped.

In that silence many prayed that the meaning of death would somehow be revealed. But some questioned whether such understanding would give them relief from unhappiness. No one who had lost someone in the war (and it was estimated that three million people had lost someone close) was immune from grief. Many tried not to give in to it, believing that acknowledgement of the intensity of their feelings would lead them to the verge of collapse. Some found that after the initial shock a state of denial was in itself a comfort.

Others were like Andrew Bonar Law, the Conservative Chancellor and Leader of the House during the wartime Coalition Government. Bonar Law had lost two of his sons, killed in action, and his friend Lord Blake described how Bonar Law was managing his loss. 'Night seemed to have descended upon him. For the moment he was incapable of work and could only sit despondently gazing into vacancy. All those dark clouds which were never far below the horizon of his thought came rolling up obliterating light and happiness.' Silence was unlikely to bring much comfort to Bonar Law. For within silence lies not only stillness but also agitation: the agitation of memory. For the agitated mind silence can become a place of threat and even of terror. At a time when the pain rather than the comfort of memory predominates, 'the great wings of silence continue to beat'. Absolute silence remains elusive.

That morning *The Times* reporter described how

> Even in the high Alps the solemn stillness which sometimes comes with the night is broken by the groan of the creeping glacier or smothered thunder of a distant avalanche. In the depths of a wood at twilight a leaf rustles or a twig snaps.

In London's Westminster the sudden sharp sound of a woman's sob was made all the more painful by its unexpectedness, its isolation and its quivering echo, coming and going, strengthening and fading between the tall grey buildings of Whitehall. Life, breath, sound would go on, but never again without being mistrusted or feared. Certainty and dependability had gone. This was, in Quaker terms, a 'living silence': those who took part were actively engaged in thought.

There were some in the crowd around the Cenotaph, who had come with their families to take part in the solemn moment, for whom the outside world no longer held any meaning. The damaging roar of the trenches had made many unable to hear even the slightest sound. For them silence was a permanent state.

But during lulls in the firing in France one unenfeebled sound had persisted through all, usually at its clearest with the first light of day. The unexpected and welcome sound of birdsong was often noticed by Duff Cooper, who had written from the trenches to his girlfriend Diana Manners in 1918 to tell her how 'still bravely' the larks continued to sing. 'Everywhere else in France they are shot by the Français sportifs,' he wrote. 'But here since neither the English nor the Germans can ever hit anything they are perfectly safe, with the result that the front line has become a regular bird refuge, and . . . one has anyhow always to be awake at dawn which as you know is their favourite hour for kicking up a row.' Maybe some of those who stood now, their heads bowed, their heads bared, were summoning from memory the beauty of the birdsong, perhaps the only thing of beauty they had encountered during four years.

The quality of this silence was strained, brimming over with pain. Tears streamed from the eyes of men and women.

As the two minutes ended there was a reluctance and uneasiness in resuming movement. This ending was not like the moment at the end of an examination in school, when chairs scrape back with audible relief, or of a church service, when the organ bursts into life and the congregation collects its belongings and re-engages with the daily business of living.

The moment that immediately followed the silence seemed to extend itself fractionally – before, as if in slow motion, hats were replaced, throats were cleared and the traffic once again began to move. This curious suspension of sound and movement had shown, as *The Times* commented, 'a glimpse into the soul of the nation'.

★

The day after the Silence, the motionless tableau of a shattered country was unfrozen, at least on the surface. Many, including the Prime Minister Lloyd George, hoped that the Great Silence would prove to have been a moment of national catharsis, the result similar to a massive, instantaneously effective blood transfusion. But the following morning, only a day after the country had engaged in its collective act of remembrance, *The Times* carried an unsigned advertisement in the personal columns.

> Lady of Gentle birth (clergyman's widow) insane through overwork, poverty, air raids, loss of husband, brothers killed in War, has two children. Inquiries welcomed. Nomination to suitable home or financial aid wanted to give her reasonable chance of recovery. Will anyone help?

Silence had not proved to be a cure for her.

For others less traumatised, the *Tatler* of that week carried a notice for Clincher Motor Tyres showing a woman draped in furs and a man in evening dress sitting in a beautiful car. 'When the old moon smiles these nights you can't help smiling back', ran the caption, going on to encourage the reader contemplating moonlit expeditions: 'Moonlight no longer betokens the possible visit of "Gothas" and "Zepps".'

That evening Lady Diana Cooper was still unable to stand without support as she appeared at the Albert Hall wearing eighteenth-century Russian costume for another Victory Ball. She was not enjoying the ball at all, immobile in her by now hated bath chair and confiding her misery to a very drunk but increasingly sympathetic Lord Beaverbrook in his private box, while her husband of five months had excused himself from the party and vanished. She was sure he was seeking out that annoying Diana Capel, the woman whose husband was rumoured to be having an affair with the clothes designer Coco Chanel, leaving his wife free to spend time with *her* husband. Duff had arrived at the ball wearing a false beard. His wife was annoyed to notice that earlier he had removed it during the course of the dancing and was looking more handsome than ever.

Outside, the snow began to fall across the country from Edinburgh to Dartmoor, but inside the Albert Hall the partygoers celebrating the first anniversary of the Armistice appeared as gay and light-hearted as ever. Paper streamers decorated the walls, and balloons floated high up into the huge ceiling vault. All thoughts of another formal pageant or procession were abandoned because, as the *Sketch* pointed out, 'Quite frankly people wanted to dance.' Reserve was thrown aside. The outfits were mesmerising. Gentlemen in satin knickerbockers, ladies in pom-pom frocks and thigh-skimming dresses whirled around the huge dance floor. A Mrs Ashley was spotted by reporters for the society pages holding a giant powder box fashioned as an umbrella, her skirt an elegant powder puff. Mademoiselle Edmée Dormeuil came as a bunch of large hothouse grapes, 'a full vine on her charming head'.

The time for national mourning was, Lloyd George continued to hope, now at an end and yet he sensed his optimism to be manufactured. At dinner with Duff Cooper a year earlier he had voiced those fears. He spoke to Duff of the long memories of the British. He spoke of those still alive who remembered the great famine of seventy years earlier, and 'that one should never rouse those memories because it was a dreadful thing to fight against ghosts'.

In 1919 there were ghosts in every town and village of the country – the ghosts of those who had fought for their country and who had been denied the burial and homecoming that their relations knew was their due. The Silence had aroused old feelings just as receding memories had begun to settle. Some wished for a more permanent silence. Others chose to carry on dancing.

10

Release

Early Winter 1919

The skies were filling with spectacular and record-breaking machines. Alcock and Brown's recent crossing of the Atlantic by air in June was still on everyone's mind when on 12 November a Vickers Vimy aeroplane departed from Hounslow airfield in Middlesex on a journey bound for the other side of the world. The Australian Captain Ross Smith, a pilot with an impressive flying record from the war, and his brother Keith Macpherson Smith planned to make the journey with twenty-one refuelling stops, including landings at Lyons, Rome, Cairo, Damascus, Basra, Bander Abbas, Karachi, Delhi, Rangoon, Bangkok, Singapore, and Bima, a distance of 11,340 miles. The journey felt like a means of escape to the other side of the world, to a continent where memories were not so clamorous. The Australian government offered a £10,000 prize for the successful completion of the journey.

On the same day Handley Page transport announced the production of an aeroplane large enough to carry fifteen people from London to Paris in two hours ten minutes and in considerable comfort. Passengers would be seated in velvet-cushioned armchairs, their feet resting on fitted carpets, their reading matter illuminated by electric light. The world seemed to be shrinking.

A month later a mesmerised audience watched as Sir Ernest Shackleton presented the extraordinary and heroic pictures of his attempt to cross the Antarctic and reach the South Pole. His 350-ton pine, oak and greenheart ship, *Endurance*, had left Plymouth on 8 August 1914 with a crew of twenty-seven men. England had been at war with Germany for four days. As the war continued, thousands of miles away the men of the *Endurance* struggled through the ice stacks, along needle-thin channels, using the ship as a battering ram as the ice floes, sounding like 'heavy distant surf', rose up into gargantuan towers all around the ship. Icebergs measuring thirty-two miles long and a hundred and fifty feet high resembled avenues of hostile sky-scrapers in which no human could ever take up residence.

Eventually ice had defeated the expedition. But to the lasting benefit of movie-going audiences, Australian cameraman Frank Hurley had made his way as fast as possible towards the listing, leaking, creaking, paralysed hulk of the ship. He dived into the freezing water of the hold, managing to rescue his films and photographic plates, smashing many but happily not all of them in his urgency to get back to safety.

The resulting film, entitled simply *South*, made the wintry London weather seem benign in contrast to the snow-bound beauty of the scenes shimmering on the screen, the ship's intricate rigging frosted with icicles. The seventy accompanying sledge dogs, half mad with hunger, existed on seal meat, emperor penguins and bleeding steaks gashed from the barnacle-encrusted flanks of furious bull sea-elephants. The men of the expeditionary force chewed hard on their pipes as they stared into the camera lens. One man provided the company with the 'vital mental tonic' of a banjo, while arms were encased to the elbow in vast fur gauntlets. By the time of their even-tual return in 1917, the crew had been out of touch with civilisation for nineteen months, protected from little except the knowledge of the grim progress of the war.

Audiences were amazed by man's resilience as they watched the terrifying black and white pictures of Shackleton's ship. First its rudder smashed, then the mast crumpled and finally the *Endurance* was lifted high up into the air by the force of the erupting ice below it, before sinking for ever into the freezing water.

Cinema and the taste for daring escapades provided one kind of release of emotion. Music and dance offered another. During the war the front covers of the *Tatler* magazine had mostly been devoted to black and white photographs of upper-class ladies, either newly widowed or in nurse's uniform. But on 26 November 1919 the cover carried a full-coloured drawing of a smiling soldier in full uniform throwing his sweetheart into the air. As his dancing partner, she is wearing an elegantly and daringly short, floaty skirt and is tossing back a glass of champagne as the bulbous stomached butler hovers nearby ready to refill her glass. At home gramophones were often contained inside a cocktail cabinet, and as the steel needle was lowered on to the thick wax record, the whole disc gently rose and fell seductively. The nation was in a mood to dance.

An ever-expanding troupe of five or six hundred freelance musicians would gather between noon and two each day in Archer Street just off London's Shaftesbury Avenue to meet entertainment agents and hope for a booking at a debutante's ball or for an engagement in one of the big hotels. New songs were being composed at the rate of five hundred a week and the players had to work hard to hold on to their individual repertoire of current melodies.

Grand dances in private house were being revived with gusto. A ball at Londonderry House in Park Lane had been held on 18 November for two and a half thousand guests, including doctors and nurses who had worked in the temporary hospital wards of the huge town house. The powerful hostess, Edith Londonderry, flanked by the Prime Minister and the leader of the Conservative party, stood at her usual place at the top of the celebrated double staircase – so wide that four guests could climb its stairs abreast. Edith wore a voluptuous black dress and her remarkable décolletage showed off to perfection the splendour of the family jewels. Her magnificent appearance more than made up for the shortage of flowers, a reflection of the wartime absence of gardeners.

Lady Cunard, the American wife of the shipowner Sir Bache Cunard and lover of Sir Thomas Beecham, had assumed the patronage of the Ballets Russes after the death of its pre-war promoter, the Marchioness of Ripon. On 4 December Emerald Cunard threw a fund-raising ball because, as she explained, 'the State refuses to support opera in any shape or form in this country'. She decorated Covent Garden in crimson, violet, yellow and green. Lady Beaverbrook came dressed as a blue butterfly, but not one that the *Illustrated London News* correspondent felt a naturalist might easily identify. Ivor Novello, the 26-year-old Welsh entertainer, was characteristically bejewelled from head to toe and Lady Diana Cooper, at last liberated from her bath chair, although discreetly holding on to a walking stick, came as Queen Anne in a rose-coloured gown garlanded with silver ribbon.

Those young, in love, aristocratic and keen to dance gathered at the famous underground Grafton Galleries in Piccadilly, site of the controversial pre-war Post-Impressionist exhibition, which in the evening doubled as a fashionable dancing club. The Prince of Wales was a regular. Proprieties were observed. White tie and tails were worn, and carnations were tucked into buttonholes. Nude pictures on the walls were covered with tissue paper, and no alcohol was served. The confectioner Gunter's would supply iced coffee and a brilliant pink drink called 'Turk's Blood', the innocence of the refreshments confirmed by the presence of teatime cakes and sandwiches. A favourite song, 'I'm Just Wild about Harry', was often requested, as was the pre-war waltz 'Destiny', the last song to be heard five years earlier by young uniformed men before their departure for the front. The nostalgic sound of the waltz filled the gallery as the couples competed for the length of time they could continue twirling each other round. The evening at the Grafton ended with the playing of the National Anthem. But the night was not over for those who left for Rector's, a club in a cellar in Tottenham Court Road where decanters of whisky were on offer in the gents' cloakroom, and powerfully sweet-smelling white face powder was piled into bowls in the ladies'. Here the band was less restrained than at the Grafton dressing up in firemen's helmets and circling the room while blasting out sexy tunes on their trumpets.

Dance was a recreation that all classes enjoyed. Dance halls up and down the country were attracting huge Saturday-night crowds as the saxophone blared out its foot-tapping, syncopated beat. The most spectacular of all dancing venues was to be found in London's old Brook Green skating rink which had been turned into the largest dance hall in Europe. Nearly six thousand tickets had been sold for the opening night of the Hammersmith Palais, the low cost of entry putting the dance floor within reach of pockets unable to afford West End prices. Movers and shakers, twisters and twirlers from Ealing, Richmond, Hampstead and Bayswater came gliding into the enormous salon beneath a copy of a 2,000-year-old Chinese sign that announced you were entering 'The Grotto of Peerless Height'.

Inside, the hall was decorated entirely in Chinese style with hand-painted glass and lacquer panels copied from old Chinese pictures and hung all around the dance floor. Tall, black-lacquered columns, decorated with Chinese lettering signifying good luck, supported the pagoda-like structure that formed the ceiling. In the centre of the highly polished dance floor of Canadian maple was a miniature mountain, with water cascading from it on all sides although the sound of water was entirely eclipsed by the music. The two bands took up their positions at each end of the floor under two mini-ature temple-like structures. As soon as the band at one end stopped, the other would take up the tune.

No one was able to resist the lure of the floor. The *Daily Mail* described the varied mix of participants: 'Women dressed as men, men as women; youths in bathing drawers and kimonos, matrons moving about lumpily and breathing hard. Bald obese perspiring men. Everybody terribly serious; not a single laugh or the palest ghost of a smile.' The floor was never empty. If you had arrived alone, a steward would find you a 'sixpenny partner' and off you twirled, the newly met couple happy with the arrangement, one a little richer, the other no longer clinging to the walls in solitary disappointment.

All around the edge of the floor were little tables, designed for tea and talk, if you were able to hear your partner speak. Their primary purpose was to provide a place to flop in an exhausted heap after the exertions demanded by the music. There was no licence for alcohol, but none was needed as the intoxication provided by the dancing was considered stimulation enough.

The Times' personal column was filled with advertisements for dancing lessons. At the Empress Rooms in Kensington you could learn the Hawaiian glide, the tango, and, for the very energetic, there was the paso doble. The editor of the *Dancing Times*, Philip Richard-son, became a figurehead for the dancing teachers' profession, organising an unofficial summit meeting for teachers to discuss their determination that dance steps remain 'correct'. They were anxious to unite against some of the outlandish exhibitionism seen on the dance floors and 'to stamp out freak steps, particularly dips and steps in which the feet are raised high off the ground'. Tips were offered for practising the new moves at home to the accompaniment of the gramophone, in order to get the swing and sway to accord exactly with the rules of the Imperial Society of Teachers of Dancing.

Suggestions included polishing the floor with Johnson's powdered wax that promised to give 'A Perfect Dancing Surface'.

The *Fulham Chronicle* announced that there would be eighty dancing instructors on hand at the new Palais, and, perhaps most surprising of all, that evening dress was to be 'optional'. During 'learner nights' one part of the huge floor would be roped off, as boys took one side and girls the other, the coloured heels of their dancing shoes matching the predominant colour of their dress, as they all waited their turn behind the corral. Girls took the art of dancing even more seriously than the boys, and in these post-war months the quantity of physically agile girls of dancing age outnumbered the men. Crutches and war wounds did not equip one for energetic movement.

The pre-war animal-like movements of the turkey trot, the bunny hug and the grizzle bear had given way to a whole new repertoire of dances from America. The sound of ragtime, the dance music that had engulfed the United States and become a nation's passion, had been led in part by the master of the art, Scott Joplin. But ragtime, along with previously popular dance routines, was on the wane. The twinkle, the jog trot, the vampire, the Missouri walk and the shimmy were all knocked sideways by the new craze for jazz. Audiences were invited to 'rock and roll', the phrase used in black slang to describe the act of love. The word jazz, or *jass* as it was originally spelled, dug further into African-American shorthand. Jass was only a short etymological beat away from *jissum*, and the sensual earthy music, with its insistent thump, mirrored the hip-thrusting energy of mankind's most basic creative activity. The Victor recording label of New York explained to somewhat puzzled new audiences in their catalogue notes how 'Out of the mass of sounds there emerge tunes, and as the music proceeds you get order out of chaos and a very satisfactory order at that: one that not merely invites you, but almost forces you to dance.'

In England 'jazzing' had begun properly with the arrival in London in spring of the Original Dixieland Jazz Band. Although the group's 28-year-old pianist, Henry Ragas, had died of a combination of Spanish flu and alcoholism two days before the band set sail from New York, the depleted ODJB had reached England on schedule.

Founded in New Orleans in 1916, the all-white band that played from memory and whose voices resembled the deepest of black soul singers had opened on 7 April 1919 at the London Hippodrome. The reaction was reminiscent of a life-saving manoeuvre on a choking body. London responded. The cornettist and leader of the band, Nick La Rocca, had an uncontrollable tic in his shoulder that had made him ineligible for the draft, but on stage his erratic arm movements had the unexpected bonus of making him disturbingly attractive. According to the *Tatler* La Rocca moved about the stage 'like a filleted eel about to enter the stewing pot'.

As a singer La Rocca was artistically hooked on compulsive and constant improvisation and the audience went wild for the new phenomenon. Whenever he walked on to the stage, every person in the theatre jumped to his or her feet, clapping, thumping, stamping, whooping and cheering. On the band's opening night at the Hippodrome, George Robey had been billed as the star. Robey was a performer who knew his worth, and was confident of his popularity with the crowds, often dressing for his act in women's costume and teasing the theatregoers with his double entendres, as he mock-beseeched them to 'Kindly temper your hilarity with a modicum of reserve'. The jubilant reception of the Old Dixieland Jazz Band left Robey feeling thoroughly upstaged. Seething with rage he swore he would never appear with them on the same bill again.

But the genie was unleashed and the visiting American musicians had immediately been snapped up for a two-week engagement over Easter at the London Palladium, followed by two months at Martan's Club in Bond Street (which promptly changed its name to the Dixie Club), then Rector's in Tottenham Court Road, while managing to pack in several shows up in Glasgow. Standing room only was available wherever they went. The King of England wanted to see for himself what all the fuss was about. A group of lorgnette-wielding members of the nobility were invited to join George V at a special royal performance where the group was scrutinised through the wand-held lenses as if, La Rocca said, 'there were bugs on us'. Two stamps of La Rocca's foot and a couple of shoulder jerks, and they were delivering a resounding 'Tiger Rag' to an audience more accustomed to assembling for a chamber music recital. Terror in the eyes of the audience gave way to cautious approval as, to general astonishment, the dour King himself led the way in enthusiastic applause.

The Hammersmith Palais had been quick thinking enough to book the band for their opening night in November. The response within the hall was ecstatic. The showiness of the performances with their excessive loudness, wildness and mock duelling with violin bows was irresistible. 'Mournin' Blues', 'Bluin' the Blues', 'Satanic Blues', 'Fidgety Feet', 'Clarinet Marmalade' and 'At the Jazz Band Ball' were among the favourite dance tunes. But it was 'Livery Stable Blues' and 'Tiger Rag', the song with 252 beats a minute and the 'Hold that Tiger' chorus in which the trombone imitates the roar of the beast, that proved the most popular. A variety of props and stunts added to the spectacular quality of the performance. Any combination of wood blocks, cowbells, gongs, saucepans masquerading as drums, Chinese gourds, tubular bells, tin cans, frying pans, motor horns and teddy bears swinging from cymbals could appear. British musicians would crowd around the bandstand trying to work out how so few players managed to make so much sound. Not many stood a chance of playing at the Palais in the near future: the ODJB had been engaged to play until June the following year.

Reactions to the dance craze were mixed, especially among the upper classes. Society's favourite magazine the *Tatler* was infected by the energy.

> They say the night clubs are opening up in rows and dressmakers say they're dizzy with the orders for dance frocks that keep on porin' in. And they just can't have enough niggers to play jazz music and I hear they are thinkin' of hirin' out squads of loonies to make the mad jazz noises till there are more ships available to bring the best New York jazz musicians over.

The press was bemused. The *Star* thought that La Rocca and his friends were doing their best 'to murder music', whilst the local newspaper, the *West London Observer*, considered the band's music to be 'the weirdest sound possible'.

Some like the Duke of Portland yearned for the more elegant mellifluence that he associated with dances before the war, as he decried the 'flat-footed negro antics to the discordant uproar – I will not call it music – of a braying brass band'. The *Daily Mail* was disturbed by the 'jungle' elements of the dances and of the primitive rituals of 'negro orgies'.

One Canon Drummond, interviewed for *The Times*, told the paper that in his view this modern form of dance reflected a lowering of morals and a sickness in the pulse of the country. The movement 'seemed to him to be a most degrading condition for any part of society to get into, to encourage a dance so low, and of such low origin – the dance of low niggers in America – with every conceivable crude instrument not to make music but to make noise'. And the liturgical community were not the only body to worry about a sickness. The physical effects of such strenuous exertions were causing concern to members of the medical establishment. They worried that all this jumping about could cause permanent damage to the arrangement of the internal organs as well as placing additional strain on the already traumatised nerves of many of the population.

Isolated pockets of the old values could still be found in the arts. *Lord Richard in the Pantry* was showing to packed audiences at the Criterion. The plot required his Lordship to assume the guise of butler Bloggins in his own house which post-war financial cutbacks had obliged him to let. When the 'butler', accustomed to servants doing everything for him, failed to get a shine on the dining-room silver because he was using boot-blacking polish, the audience fell off their seats in helpless laughter. But an appreciation of the remnants of the old ways was rapidly diminishing.

The new dance clothes did little to reassure stick-in-the-muds. Evening dress had become as short as daywear, the swinging beads and fringes attached to the hem giving the movement of the frock an extra sexy swing, while legs were encased in sheer silk stockings which shimmered at the same time as suggesting nudity. Legs were the chief attraction and men discussed the shape of every inch of the ankles and calves on show.

Bandeau brassieres flattened the bosom to prevent the uncomfortable agitation of the breasts while dancing. The French couturier Coco Chanel designed clothes that combined androgyny with femininity, simplicity with charm. Bright lipstick was applied to the mouth with a flamboyantly inviting flourish in front of anyone who cared to watch. The very impropriety of applying make-up in public, particularly lipstick, meant that it became the chicest thing to do.

The Duke of Portland was extremely worried by these developments. The Duke was a man who liked everything and everyone to have its proper place. He employed a man whose sole task it was to clean the housemaids' bicycles at Welbeck Abbey, the ducal seat in Nottinghamshire. The new order of things disturbed him. Smoking in public and ostentatious cosmetics both took a hammering. 'It is neither becoming or attractive for an otherwise pretty and charming young woman to appear with a half-smoked cigarette hanging from her vividly painted lips and with henna-coloured nails at the end of yellow nicotine-stained fingers'. He was bemused by this new world. 'In my youth I was taught that pearls fell from ladies' lips but that has all been altered of late.' Paint on the face or lips should be confined to use by 'ladies of the stage and demi-monde' while red-painted nails reminded him of 'the gory fingers of a Scottish ghillie after he had gralloched a dead stag or the unwashed hands of a butcher fresh from the slaughterhouse'.

Further changes in dressing habits included long necklaces, usually of large fake pearls, and elaborate corsages that disguised the fact that some of these young ladies were clothed in little more than a nightdress. *Punch* published a cartoon on 7 January 1920 showing one woman dreaming that she had got up from her bed, having been properly clothed for a night's sleep, and found herself at a party where the dancers were dressed in less than her. Labels were hung on the back of dining chairs carrying a printed warning that 'nothing farinaceous' was to be served. Slenderness was the look essential for fashion. Meanwhile the London underground observed proprieties by refusing to carry a poster for a film showing an actress in a backless gown.

The young Bohemians of London, who referred to their parents as 'Old Stick' as if they were fossils devoid of the energising blood of life, boasted a passion for the alternative. Everyday household items were put to entertainingly unconventional use. Butter was spread with razor blades, dishcloths became hairnets and tea was served in brandy glasses. The application of a drop of beaded wax applied to each eyelash, a fashion imported from Russia, helped the eye to glitter with youthful allure, though only if you managed to keep the weighted lid open. Middle-aged men were spotted in the street wearing schoolboy shorts.

Mrs Kate Meyrick, the ex-wife of a doctor, was making a good income from the craze for dancing. For the last few years she had lived in 'dull and dreary respectability' in Brighton, nursing many cases of shell shock, one of whom tried to throw the maid out of the window. At the end of the war, while in London looking after one of her eight children who had caught the deadly Spanish flu, she had seen an advertisement in the paper looking for someone with 'fifty pounds for partnership to run tea dances'. Sensing a way out of her monotonous life and an escape from the dreary doctor, she set up her club, Dalton's, in a cramped airless basement at number 28 Leicester Square with her partner George Murray. Soon she discovered that 'men will pay anything to be amused'.

Word of the liberal atmosphere of Dalton's got about and soon Belgian and Russian refugees, peers, princes and even the King of Denmark were all jostling against each other on the small dance floor. At first sight the club was filled with 'decent men and sweet girls', but Kate became aware of 'faces stamped with the unmistakable signs of a vicious life'. Nearby the area of Chinatown was taking decadence to a new level. Prostitutes mingled with the Chinese who allowed them into their restaurants. A reporter for the *Illustrated London News* was shocked by the scene he encountered. Customers ate 'in full view of passers-by with chopsticks, poking for choice morsels' and, opening their mouths very wide, proceeded to 'stoke themselves in a very alarming manner'.

In early December 1919 *The Times* carried a short report concerning the arrest of Mr William Change, an elderly Chinaman of Limehouse Causeway, who was charged with being in possession of 9.5 lb of opium and 10.5 lb of morphine. Mr Change confessed that he smoked no less than a quarter of a pound of opium mixed with morphine daily, pleading against his punishment that he was a victim to the drug and would die if he abandoned the habit.

Drugs were only part of a growing promiscuity spreading across all classes of society. Sir William Arbuthnot Lane, the Army's chief surgeon during the war, addressing the General Medical Council on the prevention of venereal disease, argued that 'It is an indisputable fact that irregular intercourse has greatly increased and that the average moral code of young women has altered very materially for the worse.' He continued in a voice of gloom, 'That moral degeneration especially among women will not disappear for a very long time in spite of all attempts to educate and improve the tone of the community.'

Marie Stopes's outspoken but sensible advice was almost entirely directed at heterosexual couples. But others allowed a sense of post-war liberation to overcome any lingering inhibitions. Men and women lived openly together. Not wishing to be committed by law and regarding such a union in Robert Graves's words as 'a social habit rather than a sacrament', these couples were referred to as being in a 'companionate marriage'. Women who slept with other women went to the opera dressed in male tuxedos and no one minded, much. In dance halls in the most emancipated parts of London, Chelsea and St John's Wood among them, lesbians took their licence from Berlin nightclubs and swung on to the dance floor with each other in an undisguised embrace. Homosexual men had to be a little more careful. Unlike the women, they were required to observe a law forbidding their union and Scotland Yard was reputed to hold a list of prominent suspects all of them listed in *Who's Who*. And yet the desire to be 'living one's life', as they reminded each other in the popular phrase, gave many homosexuals the courage to 'break cover'.

With the increasing awareness and encouragement of freedom given by contraceptive devices, the number of prostitutes in the country was said to be nudging 75,000. They too exhibited a new brazen confidence. In Salford two 'henna-haired girls from Cardiff' lived in a 'hovel' next to Robert Roberts's corner shop. Dressed in a combination of frills and nautical serge, they worked the docklands by night and bought their breakfast from the shop in the morning. Mrs Roberts was happy to serve them, but older men denounced them as 'trollops' and 'a bloody disgrace to the neighbourhood'.

A different class of 'moneyed and lonely women' were encouraged by psychiatrists to speak, for a fat fee, of their 'feelings'. The sceptical condemned the indulgence of talking about oneself in 'prattling detail' as a 'dredging up from the oozy depths of the mind childish memories of thwarted inclinations which would account for later aberrancies'. But the release of 'feelings' from the locked corners of the mind was a source of help that thousands longed for.

On the first day of December the country's figurehead, and embodiment of reserve and propriety, was waiting on the platform at Victoria Station. Queen Mary was wearing a new purple and gold toque with a favourite diamond arrow pinned to the front. She was a little nervous. She was aware that the new hat bordered on the fashionable. She watched her husband as he stood a little in front of her on the station platform, while the rain drummed down on the roof above, waiting for the train bringing their eldest son home from his four-month absence abroad on official duty in America and Canada.

The rain had been drenching London since dawn and hundreds of umbrellas like shiny black mushrooms had been unfurled against the weather. *The Times* said 'there never was, not even in London and in December, a more utterly hopeless heartbreaking day, the air full of yellow fog, a day in which a man would not stay two minutes out of doors to meet his best friend.'

Standing near the King was a damp collection of men dressed in tailcoats and top hats. These were the most senior members of the Cabinet and included the Prime Minister, Lloyd George, and Bonar Law, second in command in the Coalition Government, the Chancellor Arthur Balfour, the Foreign Secretary Lord Curzon and the Minister for War Winston Churchill.

The train pulled slowly into the station, the feathers of the Prince of Wales pinned to the front of the engine. As soon as the slight figure of the heir to the throne had stepped from the royal train on to the slippery platform, he told the waiting photographers and reporters that his long trip abroad had been 'a delightful and most valuable experience which will influence the whole of my life'.

For once Mary was unable to restrain herself. The moment the Prince finished speaking she gripped him tightly, relieved to see that the swelling on his right hand had subsided, and that the bruising, a result of an excess of enthusiastic New World handshaking, had faded. 'Put it right here, Ed,' he later told his mother, had been the constant and undeniable request.

The *Pall Mall Gazette* noted with appreciation that Mary 'gave him a truly motherly caress' while the Prince kissed her on both cheeks and then, most surprisingly, repeated the gesture to his father. His grandmother, regarding the return of her favourite grandson as a perfect present on the day of her seventy-fifth birthday, gave the young man a huge hug that produced the Prince's characteristic blush of pleasure beneath his fair skin. The scene as witnessed by the *Tatler* was one of 'a most astonishingly united family' and it commented approvingly that the Prince was 'better looking than ever by the way he carries his clothes and things and hasn't left behind him any of that charm – Barrie's immortal power'.

During his time in America the Prince had been attracted by the East Coast fashions, and in particular by the appearance of 'the slicker' style. Amory Blaine, a fictional young dandy who had recently graduated from Princeton, was the hero of a first novel by an ambitious 22-year-old writer called Scott Fitzgerald. *This Side of Paradise* had just been accepted by Charles Scribner, the successful New York publisher, and was due to be published shortly. According to Scott Fitzgerald, the hair of a slicker was 'inevitably worn short, soaked in water or tonic. Parted in the middle and slicked back.'

Lunch at Buckingham Palace that day was 'very cheery', Queen Mary was pleased to record, and later that evening family harmony was sustained at a welcome home dinner for nearly sixty friends, which to the relief of the Prince of Wales made no concessions to prohibition such as he had encountered at some places in the United States. Indeed *The Times* noted that a year had elapsed since the unsealing of the cellar doors at Buckingham Palace, after the wartime gesture of abstinence made by the King, which had proved not at all popular with several guests who found themselves required to make the same sacrifice. 'George made a charming speech and David made a charming reply,' Mary wrote in her diary that evening.

During the first few days after his return, the King pressed his son for information about America, fascinated by the size of the buildings, the quantity of cars. He was moved by the Prince's account of the tragic sight of an exhausted President Wilson. Three months after signing the Peace Treaty in Paris Wilson had fallen to his bathroom floor suffering a catastrophic stroke that had left him paralysed down his left side and blind in his left eye. The President had greeted the Prince from an undignified position inside Lincoln's bed in the White House, wearing what the Prince described as 'the most disappointed face that I had ever looked upon'.

The King was also hugely interested in the effects of prohibition and infuriated by the Prince's habit of whistling a catchy tune called 'A Pretty Girl is Like a Melody' that he had heard at the Ziegfeld Follies on Broadway. George was even more aghast to learn that Edward had bought a ranch near Calgary, while attempting a half joke that his son's new interest in property might well lead on subsequent trips abroad to the acquisition of a sheep station in Australia and an ostrich farm in South Africa.

But it was not only his family who were longing to hear about the Prince's adventures. The four-month separation from his married girlfriend Freda Dudley Ward had been difficult for them both, but Edward was determined to make up for lost time.

T. E. Lawrence was preoccupied by a different sort of urgency. That spring Lawrence had begun writing a memoir of the war that was turning out to be longer than he had anticipated. But he was not a naturally fluent writer and the process was becoming a struggle. He began writing more intensively, travelling up and down from Oxford to London by train, dividing his writing time between his dark oak-panelled rooms at All Souls and an attic room in Barton Street in Westminster that had been lent to him at the beginning of the summer by the architect Sir Herbert Baker. In the most basic of accommodation, without heat or hot water, he wrote throughout the night and slept by day, never smoking or drinking, and existing on bars of chocolate. When delirious with hunger after working for more than twenty-four hours without sleep, he would make an occasional visit to a nearby café for egg and bacon or fish and chips.

Shortly after the Great Silence he had been changing trains at Reading station before catching the fast service to Oxford. The manuscript of the nearly completed book, eight of eleven planned chapters all written in Lawrence's neat hand plus many original photographs and notes made while still in Arabia, had all been packed into an official army attaché case, similar to the kind used by bank messengers for transporting gold between branches. Lawrence was hungry and found he had a few minutes between connections. The refreshment room offered a delicious range of cakes, and safely storing his bag on the dining table beside him, he deliberated for a few moments over which cake to choose, after the self-imposed denial of the Westminster attic room. Suddenly the train to Oxford was announced and Lawrence had to run to catch it. One hour later, frantic telephone calls from Oxford were answered by the apologetic stationmaster who was obliged to report that neither a bag nor any ring-bound ledger had been found although the station had been turned upside down in the search. Yes, Lawrence was told, they realised there was only one copy. Yes, they realised how important it was.

Lawrence was distraught. But his great friend and mentor, D. G. Hogarth, Keeper of the Ashmolean Museum, persuaded Lawrence that he had no choice but to start again. Lawrence, a perfectionist, was appalled at the thought of the effort involved and L. P. Hartley, a young writer friend at All Souls, believed that 'only a masterpiece could satisfy his pretensions'. Lawrence began to write at ferocious speed, averaging a sizeable four to five thousand words a day, telling Robert Graves that he had once completed thirty-four thousand words in twenty-four hours. Sometimes he neither ate nor slept, nor changed his clothes for several days, although he would occasionally take a sixpenny dip in the Westminster public baths and every so often he would check himself into the Savoy, give all his laundry to the housekeeper and spend a night of luxury before returning to the Westminster garret.

The chapter which gave him most pleasure in writing was that devoted to a description of an aeroplane flight to Egypt. His friend and landlord Herbert Baker realised that 'his weakened nerve-batteries, as with so many but less sensitive war-shocked men, required recharging with the alcohol of speed'. As a way of relaxing Lawrence would ride his motorbike through the tram tunnel under Kingsway and down the Duke of York's steps. Lawrence mischievously suggested that the Prince of Wales might 'make more of a dash' if he drove his car up and down the same route from Carlton House Terrace to the Mall. The speed brought Lawrence a sense of supreme release from the tensions of a year of politics, writing and largely unwelcome fame.

There was no such release for the Prince of Wales who was, he began to realise, embarking on a seemingly unshakeable lifetime of demands although he shared with Lawrence a sometime aversion to the stardom that life had bestowed on both men.

11

Expectation

Mid-Winter 1919

A rich, twice-married American divorcee who lived in one of the grandest houses in the land was not an obvious candidate to represent the post-war female electorate. At Nancy Astor's house, Cliveden in Berkshire, there was a resident French chef to cater for Nancy, her husband and the five children. Horses wearing special boots designed to prevent their hooves from damaging the turf pulled the machines that mowed the smooth and lovely lawns.

But on the same day that the Prince of Wales arrived home, his exuberantly youthful appearance beginning to restore many people's faith in the future of the monarchy, an elegantly dressed woman was giving hope for a new future to millions of her own sex. With the vote now awarded to most women, with some qualifying restrictions, Nancy Astor was taking her seat in the House of Commons as the first woman Member of Parliament.

The by-election for the Conservative seat at Plymouth had arisen by accident. A month earlier Nancy's father-in-law, Lord Astor, had suffered a fatal heart attack after dining alone on a hearty plate of mutton and a glass of good red wine. On inheriting his father's title, Waldorf Astor, the MP for Plymouth, was propelled from his seat in the Commons into the House of Lords. An opportunity presented itself, and after much speculation in the press as they awaited her decision Nancy, at the age of 40, declared her intention to stand for her husband's recently vacated seat.

At once she became a symbol of hope for women throughout the country. Curiously it was her very foreignness that released her from the class constraints under which the well-born and smartly spoken Pankhursts had suffered. Her no-nonsense, non-militant, 'merry mixing' ways attracted many men as well as women. 'We are not asking for superiority,' she had said of her own sex, 'for we have always had that; all we ask is equality.'

At a campaign rally on 19 November she had not for a moment been put off her stride by a cynical question hurled at her from the audience, wondering whether there was a shortage of work for an American woman in America. Nor had she been thrown by an editorial in the *Sketch* full of potentially unsettling sarcasm: 'Lady Astor, I am sure, must have some definite reason for all this expenditure of energy other than the desire to be the first person to sit in Parliament. She would not waste her time and her own money on such a silly little motive.'

The *Saturday Review* of 15 November, however, had been openly hostile to the proposed candidate, accusing her of treating her candidacy as a 'nursery romp'. 'If we must have women in Parliament,' the journal expostulated in shrill tones, 'let them at least be English-women who have the peculiar knowledge of English habits and life and wants that comes only to those who are to the manor born.' Challenging Nancy's marital status, the magazine continued to table-thump. 'We deny that she has any qualification for the duty of representing Plymouth, particularly its women. Perhaps there is no subject more interesting to the female voters than the law of divorce. We are surprised that no elector has elicited Lady Astor's view on the question.' The journal accused the constituency of Plymouth of being the most frivolous and corrupt constituency in the country and called for its disenfranchisement.

A year earlier in the Coupon election, Countess Markievicz, beautiful, Irish and friend of the poet W. B. Yeats, had been the first woman to win a place in Parliament. However, after refusing to take the oath of allegiance, she had not taken up her seat in the House and now became one of Nancy Astor's fiercest critics, calling her 'upper class and out of touch'. In some ways the Countess was right. Nancy was poorly qualified to stand as a Member of Parliament. She was largely uninformed about the dominant political issues of the day and her charitable work was driven by a strong Protestant and fiercely anti-Catholic commitment and an unbending moral certainty. In her firm but musical voice she had denounced France as 'just one big brothel'. Her position as a Christian Scientist had become well known during the war as she made clear her belief that God was responsible for the good in the world, and that mankind must take the blame for evil.

But Nancy was a spirited and forthright woman and her political campaign had revealed her energy and her willingness to take on the hecklers, to stand firm, to visit the poorest parts of the constituency, even while wearing her best pearls and white gloves, her hands on hips as she stood to address them. Oswald Mosley, the youthful Conservative MP for Harrow who had his own ambitions for high office, was one of Nancy's campaign organisers and he marvelled at her electioneering technique. 'She had, of course, unlimited effrontery,' he observed. 'She was less shy than any woman – or any man – one has ever known. She'd address the audience and then she'd go across to some old woman scowling in a neighbouring doorway, who simply hated her, take both her hands and kiss her on the cheek.'

The people of Plymouth also admired her for her outspoken manner. She was not afraid to confront the disparaging comments that she knew were being whispered behind her back. And they simply loved her jokes. 'And now, my dears,' she would cry from her electioneering carriage, her silk-hatted coachman guiding the red, white and blue-ribboned reins of his horses through the Plymouth crowd. 'I'm going back to one of my beautiful palaces to sit down in my tiara and do nothing and when I roll out in my car I will splash you all with mud and look the other way.' The self-denigrating wit was hard to resist.

The election was held on Friday 28 November 1919, a cold winter day with ice on the ground, but the warmth that the people of Plymouth felt towards this dynamic American was undeniable. The result was announced that evening. Nancy had won the seat with a majority of 5,000 votes. Her son Bill, aged 12, made a touching little speech to the constituents. 'I have seen you elect Daddy,' he said in an impressively steady voice, 'and now I have seen you elect Mother. I thank you very much for it.'

Women were ecstatic at the unprecedented notion that they would have their own champion in the House. One of her campaign slogans had been 'Vote for Lady Astor and your children will weigh more'.

But tears welled even in the eyes of the most uncompromising of men who stood in the crowd on that extraordinary day.

The following Saturday morning readers of *The Times* were informed of Lady Astor's triumph. In the same edition of the paper the news was announced that the four magnificent classical bronze horses had been taken out of wartime storage and restored to their old place above the entrance to St Mark's basilica in Venice. The world was beginning to settle.

There had been some speculation as to what sort of hat, if any, Lady Astor would wear on her first day in the new job. On 1 December the new Member for Plymouth entered the tightly packed Chamber, until that moment an exclusively male preserve for over six hundred years. Nancy was wearing a black tailor-made costume with a long jacket and white collar designed by herself, set off by a velvet toque and polished, neatly laced black brogues. A hearty cheer went up. Eyebrows only rose when members noticed the strange sight of two women reporters high up in the press gallery, an area more conservative than the floor of the Chamber itself. Typewriters, for goodness' sake, had only been granted admittance into the precincts a few months earlier! Winston Churchill, the Minister for War, glowered perceptibly, having compared the arrival of a woman in Parliament to the experience of being spied upon by a member of the opposite sex while sitting in the bath with nothing more to protect oneself than a sponge. Never much of an advocate of female suffrage and irritated by Nancy's irreverence, Churchill, a daily devotee of Pol Roger champagne and more besides, could not bring himself to support a woman who was a vociferous advocate of teetotalism. 'One reason I don't drink', she explained, 'is that I want to know when I am having a good time.'

However, watched with an encouraging smile by her husband from his place above the Chamber in the Distinguished Strangers' Gallery, the new member responded to the welcoming words of Speaker Lowther addressed to 'members desirous of taking their seats'. She walked towards the Speaker flanked by her obligatory two introducers both wearing frock coats, the current Prime Minister on her left and a former prime minister, Arthur Balfour, on her right. Despite their differences, one married but nicknamed among close colleagues the 'Welsh goat' for his duplicitous attraction to women, the other an ascetic, unmarried Scotsman, they were affected by a similar nervousness on this particular occasion. As they processed towards the table at the top of the Chamber, Nancy had to hold out both her arms to try and restrict the undignified speed of their approach. Reaching the table all three were required to bow three times, but in his excitement Lloyd George forgot, so the choreography was at first spoiled. In the words of the sketch writer of *The Times*, the two elderly men 'behaved with the ingenuous shyness of boys at their first dance'.

After taking the oath and reading her declaration, there was another difficult moment when the elderly and short-sighted Clerk of the House failed to find the correct page on which Nancy was to sign the New Membership documents, and while he shuffled and fluttered the papers, Nancy was unable, even at such a solemn moment, to restrain her naturally garrulous nature, and turned to chat with a few of her Cliveden weekend guests on the front bench. Eyebrows were once again raised. Next it looked as if the only space left for Lady Astor was on the front bench itself, but she managed to squeeze into a corner that was still vacant near the gangway. Shortly afterwards, during a convenient lull in proceedings, she discreetly left the Chamber.

The following week the *Lady* summed up Lady Astor's arrival in Parliament as less that of a constituency representative than of 'a symbol of the patriotic self-denial, endurance and courage that, shown in times of national peril, made women the true comrades of men', and it saluted her presence as a signal that 'the right to help govern the land they helped to save is one that few can now deny'. Lady Astor's undeniable femininity encouraged women of all classes to expect their own professional ambitions to develop without any need to deny the characteristics of their sex.

During the war thousands of women had learned something of the role of men and even in the smallest ways attitudes had begun to shift. In his family's corner shop in Salford near Manchester, Robert Roberts noticed a new self-confidence among women. Wives no longer referred to their husbands as 'my boss' or 'my master'. Having grown accustomed to earning their own wage they went out into the cities, exploring a world of opportunities previously unknown to them.

Many widows had of necessity continued to assume the role of head of the household, although the incentive of a year's dowry awarded by the Government to all those who chose to remarry was attractive enough for 38,664 women to have found new husbands by December 1919. Even so, with a shortage of men from whom to choose, there were some who preferred to find a new and manless way of life. One woman, who had found the greyness of the preceding years more than wearying, was determined to find light and sunshine and used the personal columns of *The Times* to enquire:

> Would a lady wintering in a sunny climate who delights in giving pleasure to others take as companion a war widow who has done four years strenuous VAD war work. Now aches for sun and warmth.

Added as an afterthought and by way of qualification for this plum position were the words: 'four bridge player and golfer'.

But with the passage of the wide-ranging Sex Disqualification Act in December 1919 professional opportunities were opened up to single women in countless areas of work from which women had previously been barred, including banking, accountancy, engineering, law and Parliament itself. The war itself had forced through these changes. Only the priesthood and the floor of the Stock Exchange remained officially male preserves, although the Civil Service continued to exclude women from high office and several London teaching hospitals refused training for women doctors. Marriage remained a barrier to most of these jobs, the assumption being that managing a home and bringing up children still took priority for a woman over a remunerated occupation. Many were driven to conceal their marital status.

Votes for women had been part of a less specific but far-reaching rebellion against the traditional role that women were expected to follow. In January 1918, the 22-year-old Robert Graves had married the 18-year-old sister of the painter William Nicholson in the light, airy space of Sir Christopher Wren's church, St James, Piccadilly. The marriage vows so enraged Nancy Nicholson that her husband was taken aback to hear the quiet savagery with which she managed to mutter them, while at the same time appearing so feminine in her blue checked silk wedding dress. He of course undertook to cherish her till death did them part in a tone of formality that he had learned on the parade ground. She seethed against the world, and against the chauvinistic society that told her that women had a duty to maintain the diminished population. She persuaded her husband to join the Constructive Birth Control Society. And then she became pregnant.

Honesty, release and the expectation of a new freedom were all embodied in the philosophy behind the new designs for women's clothes pioneered by one French couturier. In November 1919 pictures of Gabrielle Chanel's chemise dress had filled the pages of *Vogue*: 'A gown that swathes the figure in straight soft folds, falling at the sides in little cascades'. The editorial commended Chanel's reliance on an uncluttered natural beauty, with a dress that showed only a slender pair of shoulder straps holding it up. The subsequent single-page spread devoted to Madame Lucille's chiffons and to Poiret's plumes seemed to be included simply out of respect for the old masters and appeared fearfully outdated. Poiret considered the Chanel look to encourage 'cardboard women, with hollow silhouettes, regular shoulders and flat breasts'. Once the matchless pace setter of individuality in fashion, Poiret snorted that her clothes resembled 'Cages lacking birds. Hives lacking bees.'

One other French designer, Madeleine Vionnet, managed to survive the transition through the war years and become part of the revolution in fashion. Vionnet cleverly amalgamated a still lingering desire for femininity with the wish to dress without the restricting discomfort of corsetry. Her bias-cut clothes were exquisitely desirable. But it was the androgyny promoted by Chanel that dominated women's fashion in Europe in 1919.

Chanel had been abandoned in childhood by her widowed father, a travelling salesman for ladies' corsets, to the care of several French aunts who threatened to sell her to the gypsies when she misbehaved. Her existence, she felt, was coloured black. Her hair was as black as a horse's mane, her eyebrows the colour of chimney sweeps' eyebrows, her skin dark like lava and she felt her character to be as black 'as the core of a land that has never capitulated'.

Chanel had spent several years in an orphanage at Aubazine where she learned to sew although not with great dexterity, never discovering how to avoid pricking her fingers. Rebellion undercut her childhood, before it established itself in her love affairs and her design for clothes. She was 'naughty, bad-tempered, thieving, hypocritical and eavesdropping'. She was, she said, 'a true Lucifer'. She dreamed of becoming a cabaret singer and started to appear in nightclubs, performing the two songs she knew best, 'Ko Ko Ri Ko' and 'Qui a Vu Coco dans le Trocadéro', which were so popular that the audience would simply clamour for 'Coco'. Her nickname was established.

Just before the war, at the age of 29, she had become the owner of a couple of shops where she specialised in selling hats which she made herself. Arthur Capel, an English mine and coalship owner of immense good looks, wealth and charm, financed the shops. Chanel loved him single-mindedly and he adored her in return. Despite his tendency to be unfaithful, he was no more capable of ending their relationship, he said, than of agreeing to 'chop off a leg'. Accompanying the slim, blond and beautiful polo-playing Boy Capel (as everyone called him) to the races, Chanel was appalled by the ill-fitting 'loaves' she saw on female racegoers' heads. The neat, austere head-hugging hats she designed in response were immediately coveted for their simplicity.

During the war she discovered the versatility of jersey cloth as used by stable lads for shirts for training sessions, and began to make sweaters and waistless dresses for women from the same supple fabric. The ornate Edwardian costume that according to a scornful Chanel had 'stifled the body's architecture' started to disappear. Chanel was after 'moral honesty' in the way women presented themselves. She had gauged the time for voicing these feelings to perfection. Thousands of women across Europe were feeling the same way. 'Elegance is not the prerogative of those who have just escaped from adolescence', she said, 'but of those who have already taken possession of their future.'

The flamboyant colours of Paul Poiret's pre-war designs and the theatricality of Bakst's influential costumes for the Ballets Russes suddenly seemed tawdry and overdone. Chanel declared their bright colours 'impossible'. They made her feel physically ill. She pledged to dress women in black. White and black, she felt, have an 'absolute beauty'. Women dressed for a ball in monochrome or pale colours stood out as 'the only ones you see'. And black, the colour of mourning, had always been the colour adopted both by rich and poor when in grief. Chanel's use of black with its attendant contribution to the blurring of class barriers through clothes was undeniable. She chose to accentuate an elegant neck rather than covering up fat legs, she lowered the back of a dress, redirecting attention from a sagging bottom. A look of luxury was achievable through the severity of simplicity. Expensive poverty was the aim. She dared to suggest that clothes themselves had ceased to matter and that it was the individual who counted.

She cut her hair short 'because it annoyed me'. Everyone cut off their hair in imitation. She designed fur coats from rabbit rather than mink. Warmth became available to rich and poor alike and within the simplicity there was an elegance of style that had a mass appeal. Secretaries on both sides of the Channel hugged their high-necked coats around them. The British aristocracy came to Paris to be close to the source of inspiration. The non-French-speaking Duchess of Portland arrived to shop, braving all language problems with a label stitched into the lining of her coat stating 'Je suis la Duchesse de Portland. En cas d'accident m'apporter au Ritz Hotel'. As hem lengths rose and flowerpot hats moulded themselves to the side of the head, a voluntary simplification of clothing spread across a wide spectrum of society.

Disapproval that had stirrings in the Women's Institute's own house magazine, *Home and County*, was voiced in the publication of a letter about the old-fashioned use of feathers from rare foreign birds of paradise. The correspondent estimated that it took the death or wounding of ten of these young exotic birds to create a hat. Before the war a staggering death cull of 300,000 albatrosses had been recorded in one single raid, as well as the sale of the skins of 162,750 blue and chestnut Smyrnian kingfishers and 152,000 ospreys.

H. J. Massingham, the celebrated naturalist, who was tireless in writing about and campaigning for the preservation of the old rural way of life, as well as founder of 'the Plumage Bill Group', begged for the practice to be halted and for members of Women's Institutes all over the country to demand from the Board of Trade the introduction of a Plumage Bill.

An advertisement addressing 'The New Poor' suggested ways the Sloane Street store Del Cot might help with cheaper fabrics and economic use of materials. Clearly the widespread use of second-hand clothes had prompted the advertisement. A retrenching in flashiness and consumption was mirrored by economic necessity even among the very rich. A popular 'Exclusive Dress Salon' in Buckingham Palace Road offered 'little worn models bought from society ladies'. Customers were assured that the first-floor windows were not visible from the street so all fear of being spotted in such an establishment by a friend or, heaven forbid, the donor of the dress herself was eliminated.

Despite a growing disbelief in the spiritual tenets around which the Christmas story was built, the run-up to Christmas was becoming increasingly frantic. Many families were looking forward to their first Christmas together for five years; the delays involved in demobilisation had meant that a huge number of soldiers had not reached their homes in time for the preceding Christmas. At the beginning of the month, on 2 December, a huge gale reaching speeds of 70 miles per hour tore through London and the Home Counties. A personal column advertisement from a demobilised soldier offered his £200 savings for a lodge or cottage 'whereby he may earn his living by writing poetry', thus giving him the best Christmas present imaginable.

In Kent, young Mary Beale, who had been so frightened by the hedge-hoiking false arm of Tom Noakes, was still waiting for her father's return. Her parents Dorothy and Os had married in 1916 while Dorothy was still in mourning for her mother who had recently died of breast cancer. On her wedding day Dorothy had worn a grey silk dress and a black hat. They had honeymooned over one weekend in a boarding house on the south coast and then Os had returned immediately to the front. They were deeply in love, and Dorothy missed her new husband dreadfully. In the spring of 1918, Dorothy had persuaded her sister-in-law Joan to accompany her on a reckless journey across the Channel and down to the south of France to meet Os. He too had been missing her and made the journey from Italy where he was stationed. Joan had turned an alarming colour with the motion of the Channel waves but Dorothy had assured her family that they would come to no harm. Privately, Dorothy did not care what happened as long as she could be guaranteed that Os would be waiting for her at the other end.

But when the Great War was nearly over, Os had been given no choice in the decision to send him to Russia to join the White Army in their fight against the Bolsheviks. Dorothy had no idea when he would return. Desperately disappointed, she felt more impatience than sadness. Unlike others she at least knew he would be coming back, even if once again it would not be in time for Christmas.

A lingering sense of the incompleteness of family life was backed up by fear of a return of the flu epidemic. Ovaltine continued to run advertisements reminding the public that 'the bodily and mental efforts that maintained the will to win were not exercised without a serious depletion of national health. Lowered vitality, diminished reserves of strength, exhaustion of nerve, brain and body and debility are some of the prevalent symptoms of post-war reaction . . . Ovaltine is the supreme nourisher for worn cells.'

But for those in the mood to celebrate – and many were – the shops and magazines gradually began to fill up with suggestions for Christmas presents. Oxford Street was bustling again with still black-coated shoppers, and butchers' shop windows had become invisible behind the packed rows of rabbits and turkeys hanging suspended by their feet outside. The opportunity to spend money had been denied for several years to those who had any and people were making up for lost time. Indeed the *Lady* magazine reported on 11 December that 'Christmas shopping is in full swing and never were shops more attractive or their display of gifts more temptingly charming'.

Among the ideas highlighted by Dickens & Jones department store as ideal gifts for ladies were a crêpe de Chine boudoir cap which came in a choice of colours including sky, pink, ivory or mauve. Mourning dress and in particular the black crape manufactured by Courtaulds had so long dominated the shops, but by 1919 the demand had dwindled and Courtaulds' profits had not fallen so low since 1914. For the fashionable woman about to enter a new decade there could be nothing more desirable than a pot of Unwin & Albert's liquid kohl, 'an oriental preparation for darkening the eyebrows and eyelashes' which achieved the much sought after Egyptian look. Make-up might come in handy for the households that were going to indulge in amateur dramatics. Black wax could be used for 'character' roles to make teeth disappear while some chemists were selling burnt cork as 'ideal for negro and minstrel parts'. Arthur's fur store had plenty of stock of the new skunk and opossum coats.

Women readers of the *Sketch* were invited to visit Madame Barrie's corset shop at 72 Baker Street where a new model of stays called 'Joie de Vivre' was on sale which promised to give 'a new figure as well as hope to numberless women'. Madame Barrie cautioned her customers to remember that 'there is nothing so unbecoming as a figure which is flat where the stick-outs ought to be and stick-outs where the flat should be'. The Joie de Vivre was adaptable for wear on the golf links, the hockey field or in the ballroom, and came garlanded with 'wee silk roses and forget-me-nots'.

In the early December edition of *Vogue* a helpful Christmas present list was divided by category. A debutante would undoubtedly enjoy a blue Moroccan writing case, inspiring even the most exhausted partygoer to write her thank-you letters promptly. The hostess would be delighted to receive an afternoon tea set or a cake basket, and *Vogue* could guarantee a husband's gratitude for a cigarette case complete with matches, a bridge set or a new Austin Sunbeam, in which he might invite house guests to join him on a motor tour of his extensive country estate.

Meanwhile the Savoy Hotel, within easy reach of the jewellers of Bond Street, had offered a Christmas shopping service to its discerning and busy clientele, employing a Cambridge undergraduate to choose individually appropriate gifts. Her brief from one guest included a must-have pair of emerald earrings costing £700. Another departing guest left his toothbrush in his room but sent the shopping service department a telegram with instructions for the safe return of the brush.

The *Lady* magazine was always ready with suggestions for those readers who might have a little spare time on their hands while the servants were busy preparing the Christmas feast. For example a Christmas table might be transformed 'by a scarlet linen cloth with a strip of wide lace insertion let in down the centre, and underneath a piece of bright green satin showing through the lace'. Small sprigs of holly would complete the look. If this did not appeal, why not join in the *Lady*'s own mince pie competition? Sybil in the *Lady*'s editorial office would be glad to consider all entries. A prize of a guinea would be awarded to the one that in Sybil's opinion proved the most succulent.

Meanwhile *Vogue* had not forgotten the lady of the house who had suffered financially in the war and had been left with a reduced domestic staff. She would surely find a vacuum cleaner useful as well as an artificial fuchsia plant to brighten her mood in her new circumstances. For the literary friend *Vogue* recommended Virginia Woolf's interesting essay on Kew Gardens as well as a special edition in a gold cover of T. S. Eliot's new volume of poetry. Well-off consumers could reassure themselves that the less fortunate were not forgotten over the festive period when they read in the society pages that the Duchess of Albany (wearing black satin and a large black hat with touches of gold) had opened the Christmas sale for the Crippled Children's Homes, in association with the Children's Union of the Waifs and Strays Society. Sometimes life seemed little different from before the war. The rich remained rich and the poor and disabled had little hope of change.

However, for the readers of the *Lady* small but troubling differences in post-war behaviour had not gone unnoticed. The magazine regretted for instance the demise of the excellent traditional St George and the Dragon sketches that children would perform on village porches in exchange for a few pence before 'we were plunged into the Great War'. Nowadays, the children simply contented themselves with singing a carol or two at the door, and the *Lady* tutted that 'these young folk take little pride in their efforts and it is hard to deny that they are out to snatch coppers the quickest and easiest way.' The children may have been forgiven a little cynicism of their own if they had been aware that owing to the unavailability of the male version, Queen Mary's Hospital in the East End had this year received a visit from Mother Christmas.

A week before Christmas, on 18 December, there was a national tragedy. A pre-Christmas trip to Paris planned by the flying hero of the summer, Sir John Alcock, was a light skip in comparison with the marathon journey he had made earlier in the year. He had agreed to deliver a new amphibian plane in time for a demonstration at an aeronautical show in Paris, but there was thick fog in France that day and twenty-five miles from Rouen Alcock lost his bearings. The farmer in whose field the plane crash-landed was able to identify the dead pilot only from an engraving on his diamond-studded wrist-watch. The whole world was shocked. 'Alcock's death was a true sacrifice for humanity,' said his friend and former co-pilot Arthur Brown on hearing of Alcock's death.

Talk both in and out of the retail trade was of another tragic accident. In October 1918 Coco Chanel's lover Boy Capel had married a widowed English aristocrat, Lady Diana Wyndham, who became pregnant with his child. But the child was not to grow up knowing her father. Capel was killed in a motor accident four days before the 1919 Christmas and left an emptiness and sadness in Chanel from which, at the age of 37, she did not expect to recover. She knew she was now quite incapable of happiness on a personal level. Her work became all consuming.

Christmas was not turning out to be the flawless holiday of pre-war memory, but the ritual of a Sandringham Christmas, an occasion that had always been observed with tradition and opulence, remained quite unchanged. It starred as usual one of the upper servants disguised as the royal family's personal Father Christmas in a red coat, black patent leather boots and a flowing white beard, followed by dinner where sweet-smelling roses filled silver bowls, and scarlet crackers were scattered along the crystal-glittering table. The festival to celebrate the birth of the Saviour resembled, according to the Prince of Wales, 'Dickens in a Cartier setting'. But none of this luxury did anything to dispel the feelings of panic and despair that occupied the Prince of Wales at the thought of his imminent separation from his girlfriend.

Freda Dudley Ward, the slight, elegant daughter of a lace manufacturer, was married to a Liberal Member of Parliament. She was hardly suitable girlfriend material for the future King. Cynthia Asquith called her a 'pretty little fluff'. But in the spring of 1919 David had fallen deeply in love with her. Freda was funny, laughed at his jokes and teased him. She discouraged his tremendous smoking habit, but played tennis and golf, and danced beautifully. Her high childish voice hid her intelligence and she encouraged him to read although he was not always familiar with the authors she suggested he try. 'Who is this woman Bront?' he asked her, wholly oblivious of the literary output of the Haworth sisters. Her husband thought it quite a compliment that his wife was involved with the heir to the throne and for as long as Freda remained married to Mr Dudley Ward, the Prince could remain secure in the knowledge that she could not marry anyone else. The question of his commitment following a divorce would have changed all that.

However, a second overseas tour, this time to Australia, taking him ten thousand miles away from her for seven months, was scheduled for March. He wanted desperately to get out of it. On Christmas Day, still clearly under the influence of his visit to the New World, he wrote to his private secretary, Godfrey Thomas: 'A sort of hopelessly lost feeling has come over me and I think I'm going kind of mad!' In a tone of distraught finality, he continued: 'How I loathe my job now and all this "press puffed" empty "succès". I feel I'm through with it and long and long to die.' Thomas wrote back urging the Prince to take more care of himself, to smoke and drink less and to rest more. But secretly Thomas was worried about the fragile state of his boss's mind.

Meanwhile in London at the Savoy Hotel the Christmas menu included bear from Finland, snails from France, caviar from Russia and Scottish plovers' eggs at a guinea each – all designed to illustrate the eighteenth-century gourmet and politician Brillat-Savarin's dictum that 'Beasts feed, Man eats, but only the man of intelligence and perceptiveness really dines.' For those who lived lives remote from the extravagant surroundings of the Savoy Hotel, the simple gathering of relations reunited round a table set for tea, with jam tarts and a huge currant cake in the centre, was enough.

On New Year's Eve a huge crowd gathered at midnight at St Paul's to sing 'Auld Lang Syne' and there was hardly a uniform in sight, a great contrast from the same occasion the year before. But amid this atmosphere of determined jollity a discordant paragraph had appeared on Christmas Eve in the *Sketch*. Suggesting that it was time to call an end to the refusal to face unhappiness and to the denial of loss, an editorial seemed to beckon its readers towards some admission of grief:

> The happiest people at Christmas are those who open their hearts instead of resolutely shutting them; a tear or two for the memory of a friend who has passed, a dear face missing from the table and the fireside will do you no harm. You will be happier for your moment of sorrowful reflection.

In one of its final editions of the year, the *Sketch* continued in a tone of undisguised disillusionment:

> The year 1919 which began with such glowing anticipation has not been much fun after all. The genuine rejoicings of November 1918 degenerated into the machine-made festivities of the summer.

The *Saturday Review* wrote of its fear for the future at the end of this first full year of peace: 'crushing taxation, impossible cost of living and an unseemly scuffle for jobs will probably drive many of our best men under thirty to push off and seek a newer world.' And *Vogue* detected a new tendency towards restraint. Immediately after the war the first reaction had been to 'eat, drink and be merry'. However, in the final month of 1919 the magazine felt 'a different spirit has begun to prevail': the post-Christmas sensibility was one in which 'We are beginning to face the facts instead of trying to forget them.'

The country seemed to be in a new, more honest if chastened mood.

12

Yearning

Early Spring 1920

The overcrowded London streets were still full of figures in khaki and the Government had begun to worry that the sight of uniform might be an unhelpful reminder of things best forgotten. An official instruction was issued for the removal of all military buttons, badges and shoulder straps from service dress. London's clubs and hotels provided a sanctuary for men who were beginning to remember the war with nostalgia. Some missed the heightened sense of awareness brought by the single-mindedness of war. It was as if some previous intervening darkness had thinned to reveal an insight into what really mattered in life. Although they remained silent on the subject, returning soldiers found they missed the friendships they had made almost more than they had missed their own families. Siegfried Sassoon said that every survivor would be 'everlastingly differentiated from everyone except his fellow soldiers'. Elderly men let off steam from deep within the red leather armchairs of London's smoking rooms, still arguing over the question of war debts and reparations, and discussing what the Allies would eventually do with the captive Kaiser.

Elsewhere conversations were full of a resolve to put the past behind them. Kensitas cigarettes were running an advertisement in the papers showing an officer and his wife smoking and relaxing together. The officer is confirming his wife's evident mood. 'You've seen it through. You don't want to talk about it. You don't want to think about it.' Women like Barbara Cartland, now 19 years old and embarking on what she suspected might be a life-long search for romance, made it her habit never to ask any of her many soldier friends about the war. 'We were young, the sun was shining, there was music to dance to, what more could anyone want?' she explained.

Although the military trench coats known as 'The British Warm', designed for officers as protection from the freezing winters of northern India, remained hugely popular, new fashions for men began to emerge. Timepieces strapped on to wrists became all the rage. They had been worn during the war by those engaged in aerial combat; now civilians adopted the fashion. A government allowance had been allocated for all demobbed servicemen, including thirty shillings for a suit and a further thirty for a decent overcoat. The *Tailor and Cutter* magazine confirmed that 'A man cannot make love unless he is wearing a coat cut within half a mile of Piccadilly', and the cloth cutters and seamstresses noticed a change of physique in their clients. According to the magazine, discharged soldiers had developed 'quite a different attitude of figure' in their upper body and arms which the magazine attributed to 'the drill, physical exercise and open air life'.

The Savoy had started 1920 with a bang, or as the *Tatler* put it, 'the season's simply biffed in'. Travel agents made plans for a record summer of expeditions to Europe and sent out alluring prospectuses. Opportunists predicted that the cost of living in Germany would soon drop and wondered if one day it might be an attractive place to settle. While the bereaved continued to make expeditions to the battlefields, seeking evidence of death in the place where their loved ones had fallen, London was one of the most popular places to visit for fun, particularly for Americans. Lucy Duff Gordon, who was herself planning to leave New York for Paris, was not surprised by the sudden activity all around her.

> Everyone was restless; people wanted to be in any place except the one where they happened to be. Old men and women who had lived all their lives in small towns in the Middle West sold their houses and came to New York, city dwellers went to the country, or took sea voyages. Young people went to victory balls, danced all night, got hilariously drunk and went to bed in somebody else's house.

Bookings at the Savoy were coming in faster than they had for years. The hotel forecourt was full of bicycles chained to the railings by their Gold Flake-smoking lady riders, and old customers were returning to the cocktail bar with relief to find that despite the official introduction of prohibition across the Atlantic on 17 January, teetotal barman Harry Craddock was in splendid form, shaking with gusto his newly invented martini, the White Lady, in the newly established American Bar. Harry reckoned to mix a thousand drinks in five hours.

But as the new American legislation to criminalise alcohol took effect there was a direct reminder from God of the wisdom of the alcohol ban. On 15 January a colossal molasses storage tank on the Boston waterfront burst open with no warning. The tank contained two million gallons of the glutinous brown liquid that on fermentation produced ethanol, the purest form of alcohol. The safety bolts in the tank had never been properly tested and a gigantic toffee-coloured wave measuring fifteen feet high and one hundred and sixty feet wide and travelling at a speed of thirty-five miles per hour rolled though the city engulfing everything and everyone in its sugary path. The steel girders of the Boston Elevated Railway buckled under its own weight, buildings came crashing down. Eyes, ears, mouths and noses were filled with the sweet-smelling sludge, and twenty-one people were killed and a hundred and fifty injured.

No such sign from above had appeared in England, however, to endorse Nancy Astor's best efforts to educate the British in the iniquities of drink. Nancy had painful experience of the matter, having been married first time round to an alcoholic. Her only concession to the needs of her bibulous house-guests was to allow the Cliveden butler to offer them a small glass of Dubonnet.

But exquisite excess was the way of the Savoy. The food there was back to its exotic pre-war standards. One guest with a discerning palate ordered woodcock, *bécasse au fumé*, a dish in which small slithers were lifted from the breast of the bird and flambéed in brandy at the table. But the guest had no desire to eat the finished thing. He was not hungry. He simply liked to indulge himself in watching the preparation process. A taste for the hitherto little requested frogs' legs and snails had developed in those men who had spent much of the preceding four years in France. Strawberries were a delicacy that provided a problem for one financially stretched guest who, at twenty-five shillings a dozen, treated himself by ordering a single fruit. More outlandish dishes were not always recognised. A plump haggis found itself despatched by a foreign maid to join the shelves of soap in the hotel laundry in Clapham.

The hotel remained under the management of its pre-war figure of authority and optimism, London's grandest and favourite honorary butler, Sir George Reeves Smith. He had recently been honoured by the Hotels and Restaurants Association with a silver cigar box for his wartime services to the catering trade, and for the unflagging maintenance of a hotel of the very highest standards. For Reeves Smith the comfort of his guests had always been his paramount consideration. Even after the rare unfortunate experience at the hotel guests invariably came back to stay. Reeves Smith had never forgotten the gratitude of the impresario Charles Frohman after he became stuck in one of the new high-speed lifts, stationary and alone between floors for several hours before being rescued. Frohman's gratitude arose, he said, from being given the first holiday he had spent in years. Frohman had been a passenger on the *Lusitania* and Reeves Smith continued to miss him.

Reeves Smith never overlooked the smallest detail. Returning lady guests were made aware of the special affection in which the hotel held them by the sight of a posy of their favourite flowers next to their plate as they sat down to dinner. Male guests who had survived the war but were missing an arm were given special consideration as Reeves Smith had made a small but significant change to the hotel 'facilities'. He had arranged for a row of nail brushes to be fixed to the wall just above the basins in the Gentlemen's washrooms. The surviving hand could be placed beneath the brush and cleansed without a second hand being necessary to hold the brush. All the staff mourned one post-war casualty. Ernest, the hotel goldfish whose party tricks included the ability to leapfrog over a floating cork, eventually succumbed to the avalanche of cigar ash that was carelessly tapped into his tank.

There were arrivals in the Savoy house team as well as departures. In March 1919 Signor Arturo Giordaneo had been appointed second in command. Originally from the Hotel de Paris in Monte Carlo he had recently run the Berkeley Restaurant in Piccadilly. Everyone called him Arthur; everyone loved him.

Among Arthur's many American guests later that spring was the much talked about novelist F. Scott Fitzgerald and his exuberant new wife Zelda. This golden couple appeared to their friends to have 'just stepped out of the sun'. Fitzgerald's novel *This Side of Paradise* had been published in New York at the end of March, and a week later Scott and Zelda had been married. They were honeymooning in Europe. Having signed her graduation photograph with the challenge

> Why should all life be work, when we can all borrow,
> Let's think only of today and not worry about tomorrow

the 19-year-old Zelda was enchanted by London. As she watched the changing of the guard at Buckingham Palace she was particularly charmed by the sight of 'the town hall with redskins walking around it'.

Expressions of love both old and new filled the corridors and staterooms of the hotel. Lord Lambourne, mourning the death of his wife, appeared nightly in the Grill wearing a withered brown twig in his buttonhole. The twig had been part of Lady Lambourne's wedding bouquet fifty years earlier. Harry Houdini, the Handcuff King, the greatest magician on earth, was welcomed back to England after an absence of six years and came directly to check in at his old room at the hotel. He had devised a new show called *Goodbye Winter, Welcome Summer* to add to the 'Vanishing Elephant' stunt and the familiar straitjacket escape. Audiences loved the way the fur-clad girl disappeared before their eyes only to be replaced at the sound of a pistol shot by another garlanded with flowers.

Staff were still discussing how just before Christmas Mr Jackson Gordon, a wealthy entrepreneur in the middle of financing a revolutionary process that would reclaim waste paper, had found time in his busy day to have a manicure in the hotel's beauty parlour. Mr Gordon had looked long into the 'largest and deepest of blue eyes' of the 'unusually beautiful' manicurist and begged her to become his wife. The ceremony took place in Holy Trinity Church, Tulse Hill, with a honeymoon in Bournemouth, and, as reported in the *Daily Express*, the new Mrs Jackson was lavished with diamonds and pearls, and the manicure department at the Savoy was renamed 'Cupid's Parlour'.

Not all Savoy staff were satisfied by the financial bonuses that came their way. The tip-pooling or tronc system was subject to such unfair distribution that the waiters and kitchen hands had gone on strike almost a year earlier, with the cashiers doubling up to serve at table and the housekeepers bending over potato peelings in the kitchen. The youths who worked as messengers and rush-abouts, the Savoy Button Boys, saw what was happening and wondered if they would have the courage to join the protest. What they minded about more than their wages, however, were the disgusting leftovers that were given them in their lunchtime break. What they would have given to be let loose on the guests' pastry trolley!

New opportunities for employment were opening up at the Savoy and in hotels and offices up and down the country, with the innovation of time-off accompanying the job, while offices were attracting thousands of domestic servants who craved a profession that combined independence and competitive salaries. Disillusionment had been spreading at the prospect of a future life spent in service, particularly among the younger generation, and many had become infinitely more skilled since the outbreak of war as illiteracy rates diminished even among the poorest in the country. During the war a hunger for news and for maintaining links with the men who were away had encouraged the skills of reading and writing in a population avid for communication. Corner shops sold a bottle of ink, a pen, writing paper and a packet of envelopes for a total of threepence, thus providing the necessary 'equipment' for staying in touch. And in the trenches a similar process of self-education had taken place as letter-writing habits were established among the ranks of new conscripts.

In 1919 the passing of the Restoration of Pre-War Practices Act had been designed to return women to the jobs they had left while men were away at the war, thus freeing up the men's jobs that the women had occupied. Demobilisation was all but complete by February 1920, with only 125,000 soldiers, airmen and sailors still waiting for their release papers, out of a total of four million who had served in the armed forces. With women's reluctance to give up their new independence and men unwilling to return to domestic service, the Act was proving difficult to enforce. Four hundred thousand servants had spent four years of freedom from domestic employment: they included cooks, maids of all sorts, butlers, grooms, chauffeurs, gardeners and gamekeepers, all of whom had been singled out by Lord Kitchener's long finger. Servants had been drafted to work on farms, in factories and in transport. Many women had joined the Women's Land Army and the Red Cross, happy to escape the fate of T. S. Eliot's

> damp souls of housemaids
> Sprouting despondently at area gates.

Women's enjoyment of wearing the trousers had contributed to the new sense of freedom, although the older generation was wary of where the habit might lead. Barbara Cartland's gardener feared the worst. 'Oi reckons if women start a-looking like men, we'll soon have 'em thinkin' like men, and then they'll be a-bossing us like men.'

Victoria Sackville had bombarded her old friend Lord Kitchener repeatedly during the war with complaints about the depleted service she was receiving at Knole. 'Do you not realise, my dear Lord K, that we employ five carpenters, and four painters and two black-smiths, and two footmen and you are taking them all from us!' she had expostulated in 1914. She was having to make do with parlour maids and as she told the Chief of the Defence Staff, certain of his sympathy, she had '*never* thought I would see parlour maids at Knole!'

Lady Randolph Churchill had employed 'footmaids' to replace the absent footmen, giving them most desirable uniforms of 'blue livery jackets, striped waistcoats, stiff shirts, short blue skirts, black silk stockings and patent leather shoes with three-inch heels'. Dinner conversation chez Lady Randolph was often patchy and attention wandered, particularly after the lady guests had withdrawn and the men were left alone not only with the port and cigars but with these distractingly alluring improvised attendants.

At the end of the war most of the servant-dependent upper and middle classes felt they had made do for long enough and were keen to return to being served. They were unprepared for a change of attitude. On their return from the war, however, servants were either in a position to bargain or had realised that the prospect of domestic employment was no longer obligatory. They now had a choice.

One of the dwindling group of servants who clung to pre-war standards was Eric Horne. Veteran butler and former servant to the highest in the land, Eric was a strict observer of the clean-shaven rule observed by all the best butlers. A moustache would have been quite inappropriate – unhygienic for one thing, and a privilege reserved for officers. But the half-dozen columns regularly given over in *The Times* personal advertisements for servants did not surprise him. People were desperate for servants of all sorts, including cook-generals, between maids, valets, menservants, scullery maids and cooks, and above all for dependable and experienced butlers such as himself.

In the first issue of the *Lady* for 1920 a notice for a combined mother and daughter position appealed to any widows with an older child who could share the cooking and housekeeping. Owing to the establishment's lack of a chauffeur or butler, or indeed any male servant at all, the mother–daughter team were required to have the skill to drive a bad-tempered donkey and its cart to the local village twice a day, in order to deliver and collect the children from school.

There was however a strong reluctance to accept live-in jobs and the market was overcrowded with women wishing to be cha ladies. The growing antipathy to a life-long career in service had, in Virginia Woolf's view, begun well before the war. The change had been gradual, and not as definite as if 'one went out, as one might, into a garden and there saw that a rose had flowered, or that a hen had laid an egg'. The 1914–18 interlude helped to deepen and define this shifting process so that by the end of the war change was already deep rooted.

The old employers and upholders of pre-war behaviour joined Eric in detecting a new and unwelcome stubbornness in their new staff. Lady Londonderry wrote to the *Evening Standard* in December 1919 to express her disappointment in the attitude of ex-service girls whose wartime experiences seemed to have ruined them for domestic service. The formidable Lady Londonderry, founder of the wartime Women's Legion, a voluntary organization for women set up in 1915, had found that these girls had become so exalted by the flattery showered upon them for jobs well done in the war that they had become 'unsuited for the humdrum of housework, expecting housing, food and warmth at double the wages, and will not learn from the old experienced servants who are fast disappearing'. *Punch* had recently carried a cartoon headed 'Insubordinate Maid' picturing a young, inexperienced but sympathetic mistress saying 'Would you like to go out this afternoon, Mabel?', to which Mabel replies in an insolent tone, her nose tilted upwards in undeniable arrogance, 'I am already going out, Madam.' Without so much as a by your leave, huffed Eric.

The sort of person now attracted to domestic service did not meet the standards Eric had been accustomed to all his working life. One brief spell of employment immediately after the end of the war had come to an end when Eric himself could not tolerate the snuffling cook. 'If there is anything I detest', Eric explained, 'it is to sit down to a meal with a person who snuffles over their food.' To make things worse, the cook's uncle's niece had been an actress, a talent which the cook thought flowed through her own veins. She would 'rave out the Soldier's March' from some old opera in a most off-putting manner.

Not only had staff become disillusioned with the demands placed on their time by a life in service, but the calibre of the employer had plummeted too. Eric was fiercely disapproving of those who had made financial capital out of the war. He found that his favourite saying, 'You cannot make a silk purse out of a soused mackerel', described the new regime perfectly. He felt a revulsion towards 'the newly rich' who had 'filled their pockets while Tommy was fighting', declaring with foreboding that for generations 'they will not get the stains off their hands'. And he felt a wave of nostalgia at seeing 'the old usages and traditions of gentleman's service . . . die with the old places, where so many high jinks and junketings have been carried on in the old days'.

Employers also offered lamentably unimaginative incentives to potential staff, including the use of the plumbed-in family bathroom (a famously tight-fisted dowager required her maid to bathe in the water that the dowager had just vacated), the opportunity to leave off the maid's hated mob cap, and the addition of the prefix 'Miss', lending the employee a little respect rather than the more familiar unadorned Christian name.

Recruitment of servants often took place in the hallways of smart shops like Fortnum & Mason where the chef, delivering his weekly order, would make it known that there was a vacancy at his house, and women looking for work would come to enquire about opportunities. In the North of England there were hiring fairs where girls who were prepared to work in the house or on the land would be inspected by farmers, and subjected to the qualifying question 'Do you milk or bake?' The servant class had their own employment agencies, referred to by the job-seekers themselves as 'slavey markets'. Here too insolence and contempt were on the rise. Eric fell into conversation with one man and his wife who were leaving the world of domestic service. The man amused Eric by remarking that he thought 'some of the gentry ought to be boiled', although personally Eric preferred the option of baking them alive.

A few faithful servants had returned to their pre-war work, among them another butler, Henry Moate, who had reappeared in the life of the Sitwell family, swimming into their midst 'whale-like', according to Osbert, in December 1918. Sir George Sitwell was cheered at the return of the old butler who brought with him 'the assurance of the past'. Before the war Moate had been an invaluable servant to Sir George as well as the devoted caretaker of the three children, writing long letters to Osbert, the elder son, while he was away, miserable, at boarding school.

As well as Moate's devotion to the Sitwell family, there was another reason for his return. Moate missed his Scarborough friends and in particular the company of the splendid Mr Follis, the grandest hairdresser in town. The two men had shared an on-off relationship for several decades. Sometimes they were close enough friends to attend a fancy dress ball together dressed respectively as Leonardo da Vinci and Captain Cook. On other occasions they vowed never to speak to one another again, while mutual black eyes revealed the occurrence of a never quite explained tiff. Lady Sitwell had invited Moate for Christmas after his demobilisation and his reunion with Mr Follis was a celebratory affair. Late on Christmas Eve Lady Sitwell was lying in bed and talking to Osbert when they were alarmed to hear a noise outside her bedroom door. The door opened and an enormous, wildly swaying figure appeared in the doorframe. 'My Lady, have mercy on an erring lamb,' Moate implored her with perfect mock dignity and composure, before wobbling round to face the other way and rejoining Follis in the cellar.

Some former butlers had become close to the men they served in the hardship of the trenches. Herbert Buckmaster, no longer happy in the companionship of his wife Gladys Cooper, had founded Buck's Club at the beginning of June 1919. The idea behind the club was to provide a specific place where the close friendships made in the trenches could continue. The club was in Clifford Street, just off Savile Row, and served sandwiches and oysters during the day, and after the theatre sausages and drinks were available until 2.00 a.m.

One day a letter came from Buckmaster's wartime manservant, Mr Hunstone, who was feeling his way gently through the subtle shift in the nature of the relationship. Equals they were not, but barriers had been loosened and in a letter thanking him for a gift the manservant permitted himself the use of a formerly unusable word. 'I shall appreciate the cigarette case always for it will serve as a lasting link to the times both pleasant and otherwise we experienced in France. I often think of those times not with envy of course but for once I found *friends* whose memory I shall always cherish.'

But in the same letter the servant Hunstone also asked for the address of Buckmaster's groom. Barriers may have loosened but those of similar backgrounds still stuck together. A return to the old servant–master relationship meant abandoning a sense of equality born out of shared hardship. So the bond lingered on. Barbara Cartland became accustomed to getting into taxicabs with upper-class young men who were clearly on extremely friendly terms with the driver. They had fought side by side. As the partition in the taxi was slid back, so the class barrier between the men was dissolved, leaving Barbara feeling that she had been excluded from an elite society.

Echoes of war could assail one anywhere: there was no forgetting. Barbara's grandmother's butler had become a Major, decorated with the DSO, and a peer of her family's acquaintance deliberately sought out limbless veterans as members of his domestic staff – the more limbless and disabled, the better – insisting they displayed their medals over their valet's or footman's uniform.

Eric Horne had been a highly regarded butler for over fifty years but now found his circumstances wholly altered. Most recently he had been working for 'a noble family' who had been financially ruined during the last four years. Eric had enjoyed this job so much that for the whole last year he had worked without any wages. He found himself taking on duties that he would never have considered part of the position of senior butler before the war. He had to understand lavatory ballcocks, repair and glue furniture and have a working knowledge of carpentry and painting. He even had to take up the carpets in the house, beat the dust from them and lay them back in place. The job was a heavy and long one with sixteen hours on his feet – something of a challenge for Eric, who was well beyond his allocated three score years and ten. He wondered to himself, in the diary he had now been keeping for several decades, 'what would the Trades Unions think of this little lot?'

Because he liked the family he did the jobs willingly but in the end when the indoor staff was reduced from twenty-five to three and numbers on the estate fell by the same proportion, the position became impossible. Eric found himself unable to find work, despite a strong network of friends in service, and the placing of advertisements in the *Morning Post*. There was less call for a butler of his experience, age and, it must be said, occasional intransigency. He began to imagine he had become something of a combined threat and irritant to younger staff, even though in his early days of employment he had taken instruction without complaint. In one early job he had scrubbed the silver coins from a gentleman's trouser pocket in case they had become contaminated with germs. At least he wasn't as badly off as a friend of his who had ended up in the workhouse. This old man kept a coat leftover from a more affluent era in Eric's brother's shop in the Fulham Road. Whenever the old butler came out of the workhouse he would come straight to the shop and put on his smart coat and imagine himself back in the old days.

Eric had already noticed a shift in what could only be called the 'class' of employer who could afford his wages in the years leading up to the war. After the war he became increasingly pessimistic at the effect the economy was having on the grand houses of the gentry. 'The way things are going', he gloomily predicted, it will not be long 'before they are all turned into institutions or schools or perhaps hotels' and 'homes for the weak minded'.

Plans to close up Devonshire House in Piccadilly were already rumoured, even though the Duke was out of the country in his continuing role as Governor General of Canada. Eric estimated that it would take a millionaire to keep up with the demands of a country estate 'with their deer parks, acres of gardens, peach and grape houses and bricks and mortar'. As well as the running costs, he foresaw a dearth of servants ready to return to their jobs of sustaining these great houses. The day would come when the gentry would fall so low in economic health that they 'would have moved into suburban villas and begun to grow scarlet runners instead of peaches'.

Liberal-minded members of a class a rung or two below the aristocracy applauded the emancipation of the servant class, while persisting in making use of the old system. Leonard Woolf, a committed socialist who felt 'the class war and the conflict of class interests' to be 'the greatest of curses', still employed a cha lady at the lowest of low wages impervious to any suggestion of hypocrisy.

Eric's own circumstances had become even more distressing in the spring of 1919. His wife Emma, or Aunt Em as the family knew her, had been gradually losing her sight over the years, and when she became blind the whole family, including Eric and Emily's son, daughter-in-law and grandson, had moved to Coronation Villas in Sutton and Cheam. Eric had taken the job with the snuffling cook and visited his wife whenever possible. But one snowy cold evening after an outing to the pantomime, Eric's son and his wife and child were unable to find an indoor seat on the bus home and were forced to take outside seats in the freezing night air. They all caught Spanish flu and passed it on to the weakened Emily. Within a day she had died, her daughter-in-law barely clinging to life.

The expenses for Eric and his family that first winter of peace were horrifying. Only one butler in a hundred had a pension and many, especially the married ones who had an extra drain on their reduced resources, ended up in the poorhouse. A special nurse had been called in to care for Eric's family through the worst of the crisis, as on top of the flu the young grandson had caught measles. Then there were the extra cylinders of hydrogen brought in to hydrate the sickroom and finally the most costly and saddest expense of all, Emily's funeral. Eric had saved £100 in the Prudential that covered it and he thanked the Lord for his own foresight.

After Emily's death Eric had stayed in London, partly to be near his brother Frank, whose taxi-driving skills had served him well during the war. Eric's flat in Bessborough Place, Victoria, was not much to write home about, being a stuffy garret at the top of the building, and on the long climb to the top Eric could feel his heart thumping in an alarmingly irregular manner. He was still writing his memoirs, his own safeguard against state poverty. He had been keeping the diary throughout his fifty years of service and thought he would end the book with an advertisement for a vacancy for a butler valet. Eric himself would be the ideal employee. The wording was specific and accurate. 'First class, life experience, strong, healthy, active worker, excellent references.' He thought he would add that any position would be considered 'where honesty and integrity would be appreciated' – a rare combination of qualities these days, Eric thought.

Living in the city, Eric also noticed how the pace of life, so leisurely and civilised before the war, had changed. The motor car, suddenly affordable to countless thousands, seemed to be in large part responsible for the change of speed. A year earlier, on the day the Peace Conference had begun in Paris, W. O. Bentley or W.O. to his friends, known for his manufacture of rotary aero-engines in the war, had announced the opening of a factory at Cricklewood, north London, where he planned to produce the most elegant car on the roads. 'Gentry need not leave their houses to go out to dinner until within a few minutes before dinner should be on the table,' Eric observed with a critical note in his voice. 'They dart up in a stinking car that sends out noxious fumes; offensive to everyone but themselves.'

But Eric had a still deeper anxiety concerning the moral laxity and fragmentation of society that went beyond inconvenience and selfishness. 'English home life is all broken up,' he observed. 'At any given meal time or at any entertainment, the chances are that the gentleman will be found dining with a "lady" not his wife and the lady dining with some gentleman, not her husband; and the chauffeur is waiting outside for hours in the cold and the wet. And the chauffeur is, by the professional rules of his employment, to remain silent about what he has seen.' Or, Eric might have added, not seen. The conspiracy of not speaking the truth pervaded all parts of society.

Some of Eric's younger relations rolled their eyes behind his back, realising for the hundredth time that there was no hope of accustoming Uncle Eric, now well into his seventies, to the new ways of behaving. But the eye-roll was undoubtedly of the affectionate kind. Everyone who knew him agreed that Uncle Eric was one of a kind and that they didn't make butlers like that any more.

For a brief interlude, however, Eric had been given a job that took him back to memories of happier times. Rajah Sir Harry Singh, whom Eric had served before the war, returned to London. He had taken a house in Curzon Street for six months from June 1919 from where he celebrated the Victory Parade. The Rajah, 'one of the most likeable men there has ever been', brought his own Indian staff with him for his immediate needs but he also took on several English servants and ran the house in a style that Eric approvingly noted was 'princely without being extravagant'. Here was a household where 'flowers and fruit abounded'. Visitors were served delicious home-prepared Indian curry and while the Rajah was an abstemious man he made sure the 'choicest wines' were served to his guests.

Only once, with Eric's help, did proceedings become a little excessive. On the night of the Victory Parade itself, the prince had taken a box at the theatre and when the beauty of the lady in the adjoining box was noted and remarked upon by the prince's all-male guests, Eric slipped next door and 'by the exercise of a little influence' with the butler there, conveyed champagne and supper into the box, whereupon the lady herself agreed to be lifted over into the Rajah's own box. Members of the audience who noticed this small transaction applauded with polite but envious laughter and the jollity of the evening helped a little in forgetting the recurring pain of Emily's death. Despairing of a return to the good old days of life before the war, Eric took comfort in his association with an Indian prince whose intelligence 'far surpassed any Englishman I ever met'.

13

Dreaming

Mid-Spring 1920

Driving days were over for Tommy Atkins, the former under-chauffeur of the Marquis de Soveral, even before they had begun. Having never managed to learn the skill since the humiliating incident when he was caught having a go at the wheel of the Portuguese ambassador's Rolls-Royce, Tommy was further ashamed to have been invalided out of the London Irish Rifles on account of his feet. He had enjoyed a moment or two of authority when guarding prisoners of war in the North of England. One day, overseeing some German prisoners digging a trench in the English mud and relishing his new-found gift for languages acquired in 'Paree', he asserted this authority with a German phrase that sounded pretty good to him even though he could not confirm its accuracy. As he bellowed out 'Ein Mun mit spaden', simultaneously indicating to the men that they should pick up their digging tools, he noted with pleasure how his words had the instant effect of making them jump to his command.

Tommy was the second youngest of twelve children and although Albert, one of his four brothers, had been killed in the fighting, Tommy was proud to know that the name of Private Atkins, a former engine cleaner for the London and South Western Railway Company, would appear in a special memorial plaque at Waterloo Station. Tommy had never had much time for religion, especially after he had seen his first dead German body lying in the mud with the words on his belt buckle still visible, *Gott mit uns.* No God, reasoned Tommy, could be on both sides of this ghastly carnage. Any belief he might have had evaporated immediately.

But Tommy's faith in human love remained undimmed. He had always been a romantic, although the sight of a couple in an unashamed embrace, or the lingering comings and goings between the milkman and the lady of the house next door, troubled him. He did not approve of public demonstrations of affection. However, he had been ecstatically happy to come back south to his sweetheart Kitty whom he had married immediately after the war. He treasured a photograph taken at Elstree of the two of them, their heads leaning into each other, Tommy jauntily bending his knee, his new moustache emphasising his handsome features. Everyone said he was a dead cert to win first prize in any competition searching for Mr Debonair. Tommy and Kitty were happy, despite having very little money, but he did not think that a return to life in service was for him even though most of his brothers and sisters had once worked for the gentry. Although Tommy had left school at the age of thirteen and was a bit of a dreamer, there was enough of an air of authority about him in the smart uniform that went with his new job as a meter reader in the Hackney Electrical Company.

Tommy and Kitty rented a room in a boarding house in Stoke Newington in London's East End run by a large woman called Annie who was three years older than Tommy. Marital prospects for Annie were slim not only because of the coldness of her expression but also because of her thrice-widowed and immensely demanding mother who lived with her and banged her stick on the floor whenever she wanted her daughter's attention. Annie was a hard-working woman, a seamstress by day, turning out exquisite panels of smocking which she would deliver to the factory up the road to be made up into children's dresses. In the evening she would cross London to fulfil her barmaid duties at Lambeth's Elephant and Castle Theatre, with its distinctive figure of an elephant sitting on the top of the entrance. Charlie Chaplin had grown up in a street not far away.

But Annie was not a happy woman. From the age of three her mother had farmed her out to be brought up by an aunt. Annie secretly dreamed of the day she would have a little girl for whom she could make pretty clothes and send to dance lessons in a theatre and for whom she would always be waiting when she returned from school. She would be a mother who might not be able to show much warmth, but who would make sure that when the occasion

was right she would let her daughter know that she loved her unconditionally. But even while Annie dreamed of finding a decent man
as a husband and father of her children, she knew the probability
was remote. Meanwhile her lodgers, Tommy and Kitty, in the first
flush of marriage, kept themselves to themselves.

Although Tommy's ambitions to drive a Rolls-Royce had not been
realised, the post-war passion for driving was increasing every year.
Douglas Ann, a dashing moustachioed ex-soldier, a passionate naturalist and owner of a modest farm in Sussex, thought he could make
some money out of this new craze for motoring. Immediately after
the war Douglas had married a plain but ambitious woman called
Drusilla. For two guineas a week 'all found' the enterprising Mr and
Mrs Ann had offered to train half a dozen well-to-do girls in the
skills of becoming financially self-sufficient, just in case the limited
post-war supply of wage-earning husbands should be denied them.
The eager girls mastered the care of the cow, the three pigs and the
varied selection of beautiful chickens including White Wyandottes,
Red Dorkings and Light Sussex hens kept by the Anns. By the end
of their stay and after several months immersed to their knees in
muck and mire, the girls had become qualified to run their own
smallholdings.

Meanwhile the enterprising Douglas and Drusilla had noticed that
the main road between Brighton and Eastbourne was becoming
busier. When a disused bone mill came up for sale, sitting in twenty
acres of empty land and only a stone's throw from the busy main
road, they bought it. They had a hunch that the new hobby of taking
the car out for a run would create demand for a tea shop and the
energetic Anns were determined they would have the most popular
tea shop in the county.

They took out an advertisement in the *Lady*, offering training
(still at the bargain price of two guineas a head) in the baking and
management skills necessary for opening a small tea shop. The
response to the advertisement was tremendous and soon the Anns
had their pick of a fully qualified staff. Douglas named the new
establishment after Drusilla. He would not have dared choose any
other name, given the fierce temperament of the woman who was

his partner in business and life. Only on Douglas's regular escapes down to the river to fish, or when chatting with the handsome girls under his tutelage, did he ever really feel free of Drusilla's never-ending and exhausting demands.

Within a short time 'Drusilla's' was providing the local villagers with much needed employment working in the kitchens and the tea shop and caring for the beautiful grounds. The tea shop, swiftly acknowledged to be one of the best in the Home Counties, served its visitors delicious cakes, eaten, on fine days, in large wicker seats down by the lake while looking at the glorious views of the South Downs. Soon 'Drusilla's' became a popular meeting place for motorists from all over Sussex. Archie from Eastbourne and his cloche-hatted wife Ethel would drive over in the lovingly polished Bentley for a rendezvous with their friends Harry and Maude, his new sweetheart. Harry had motored over to meet them from the opposite direction at Hove in his shiny new Lagonda and they would join all the other couples delighting in a day out in the countryside while showing off their new cars.

The Anns' commercial hunch proved correct. Soon a poster advertising 'Drusilla's' boasted that the car park was 'The Motor Show of the South'. Occasionally a demobbed sailor would visit the tea shop, bringing with him a brilliantly feathered and chatty parrot or a tiny shivery monkey, picked up in some exotic place during his wartime service. The Anns were happy to house these animals as they gave such pleasure to the children of their visitors. Some of the locals were amused and charmed to see the place turning into a miniature zoo.

Doris Scovell had worked in kitchens since the age of 14. She had left school just a few years short of the Education Act of 1918 when the number of teenagers remaining at school beyond that age rose from 30,000 to 600,000. But Doris was growing up in a different environment. In a manner of speaking, she was almost married to the cooking profession, having fallen in love just before the war with Will Titley, the under-footman in the smart household where she worked in Piccadilly, one door away from the Rothschild house.

Doris was born eighteen months after the death of Queen Victoria, making her just twelve years old when the war began. She had spent much of her childhood with her grandmother in High Wycombe, some thirty-nine miles from London and, for a young child, an impressive full day's walk from her home in Kensington. Accompanied on her way by her father, Doris would let her mother know of her progress by sending three postcards during the journey that, with the excellent pre-war postal service, would be delivered to London at intervals within the same day.

Granny Scovell was a naturally gifted cook and during Doris's visits to High Wycombe she acquired something of her grandmother's skill. Later on, wartime shortages of food led to a whole series of expressions related to quantities, all familiar to Doris and her grandmother as they talked of 'a lick of marge', 'a screw of sugar' and 'a marsel of cheese'. Ingenious ways to serve eggs had become a competitive habit, including infinite variations of scrambling. The dish came with anchovy essence, with grated cheese, sometimes with peas or tomatoes, with minced ham, diced sheep kidney, chopped mushrooms and sometimes nestled in a circle of spinach.

Food had been a major preoccupation during the war years. The Government's advice was to 'use as little as you can', and butchers, usually open for only one day a week, were often implored for any bit of offal that was going. A pound of meat a week was the average allocation, with perhaps a rasher or two of fatty bacon. Every flower bed and window box had been given over to growing vegetables. Only in gentlemen's eating establishments was the impact of rationing absent. At White's Oyster Shop at the top of Chancery Lane the oysters when *in* season were plentiful but on bookseller David Garnett's visits he would have a good lunch even *out* of season, with a choice of either lobster or crab, accompanied by brown bread and butter and a delicious chilled hock. After a plate of fine cheddar and a glass or two of port, he would continue puffing on a substantial cigar as he weaved his way back to the bookshop. Other city dwellers, however, without access to a gentleman's club or a plentiful rural estate, suffered. But country people like Doris's grandmother were endlessly resourceful. Rabbit was a staple and cooked in every possible way, in casseroles, pies, as pâtés and roasts.

In the early years of the war the stylish Marchioness of Tweeddale, who wore enormous hats even inside the house, took Doris on as a tweenie maid, and soon she was dashing between the upstairs and downstairs floors of the large house. She would help the cook with the vegetable preparation, tear upstairs to help the parlour maid with the bedmaking and dusting, scrub the floors and corridors and carry messages from the cook to the Marchioness with all speed. The other staff, the cook, the two parlour maids and the house-maids, all used to joke among themselves that the Marchioness didn't even know where the kitchen was! At least the Marchioness did not ask her maids to hold her knickers for her as she stepped into them, as some grand ladies were said to do.

One afternoon in February 1918, a few months after the intro-duction of wartime rationing of meat, butter and margarine, the cook's mother suddenly fell ill and the cook was called away to her bedside. The Marchioness was having an important lunch party for six ladies the following day and a semi-hysterical parlour maid came to Doris in the servants' hall, clutching a closely wrapped brown paper parcel. 'You will have to cook this,' the maid shrieked at Doris, shoving the package at the young girl, 'because I haven't an idea of what to do with it, to save my life.'

Scarcity such as was known in her grandmother's kitchen was not generally met with in the basement of the Marchioness's house; there was, it seemed, almost always plenty to go round. But on this par-ticular day Doris was taken aback at the quality of the raw ingredients. Unwrapping the layers of newspaper, she found herself looking at a whiskery face in need of a haircut. The insolent-looking eyes stared out of the complete head of a calf, daring Doris to reject it. But there was no question about it. Remembering the lessons she had learned from her grandmother, Doris was determined the lunch should go ahead.

Putting on her hat and coat she took the number 22 bus up to *The Times* bookshop in Wigmore Street, behind Selfridges depart-ment store. One of the new cookery writers, Agnes Jekyll, had a constructive way of dealing with shortages. In her recipe 'For the Too Fat' she suggested a meat jelly that would reduce the disad-vantages of being overweight, a state which she considered 'unbecoming, fatiguing and [which] impairs efficiency'.

But there on a high shelf was a copy of the condensed edition of the famous book that Doris was looking for, by the cookery writer she had heard her grandmother mention. In the index to Mrs Beeton's *Book of Household Management* Doris found the recipe for Boiled Calf's Head. The price of the book was marked at half a crown, a week's wages. She took it back to Hill Street, and after carefully consulting the instructions, began to prepare the dish.

Into the pot went the head, water, a handful of breadcrumbs, a large bunch of parsley, a knob of butter, pepper and salt, a tablespoon of lemon juice and a pinch of cayenne pepper. After four minutes of hard boiling, Doris grabbed the foam-flecked ear and heaved it from the pan before dismantling the warm head, chopping out the tongue, spooning out the eyes, 'the worst part of it', and snipping off all the whiskers before finally removing all the fine bones, until the head looked, Doris thought, 'as if it had been run over'. After returning it to the pot for three further hours of cooking, Doris skilfully put the baggy thing together again, puffing out the cheeks with whole boiled onions and carrots and cooking the tongue separately as a side dish. Would that it had been so easy to restore a facially damaged soldier with a few vegetables and a little culinary care.

The lunch was judged to be a triumph, and made the more so by the exquisite taste of the calf's head. Doris was launched on a career as a cook and the Marchioness was hardly able to believe her good fortune. The new cook began to develop her own instinct for recipe excellence and six rabbits were sent down every week from the Marchioness's Scottish estate so that the household could enjoy 'Rabbit Doris', a dish soon famed throughout smart London dining rooms.

Doris's career was on the ascendant and before long she had left the Marchioness for a new job at 146 Piccadilly, where she wore a cotton dress and a huge white apron, the required uniform for her job as assistant cook to the grumpy but talented French chef. Doris, known for her irrepressible laugh that continued to ring out long after everyone else had stopped, developed a formidable air of authority for one so young. She was proud to tell her family that she was never asked to wear the cap, the lowly headgear reserved for menial staff. Doris was going up in the world. And best of all she spent all her working days and most of the others with the dashing footman, Will Titley.

For the remainder of the war there was no shortage of food at number 146. The large country estates owned by the family continued to provide all the fruit, vegetables, game and meat that they needed. After the war Doris had remained at 146 even though the French chef gave her and Will a difficult time, believing romance should be kept out of the workplace. But Doris held her own, feeling that 'everything was going well for women when Nancy Astor was elected' and that a French chef should not interfere. They had watched the fireworks together on Victory Day when a usually cheerful Doris had whispered to Will, 'I won't let myself cry. If I started crying I might never stop.' Her uncle, her mother's adored brother, had been killed by a sniper on his way to the trenches in September 1914. To cheer themselves up they went to the movies at Hyde Park Corner.

Movies were affordable to all and Charlie Chaplin remained universally adored, long after cardboard cutouts of his bowler-hatted figure had been hauled up to the front by soldiers. Half the population of 1919 went twice weekly to the cinema where the doorman might be dressed to match the main feature. A vampire, a gladiator or a cowboy might offer a warm handshake of greeting. Inside, the steady crunch of peanuts combined with the noise of sucked oranges added to the other sound effects provided by the pianist who sat beneath the screen. In the big theatres a full orchestra accompanied the screenings. The programme was satisfyingly varied, catering to all tastes, and included a newsreel, a slapstick comedy and a travel feature before the main film itself. In the less sophisticated theatres with only one projector there was a slight delay between reel changes but no one minded the wait.

Doris and Will, the courting couple, considered Chaplin a bit 'past it' in 1919 but had enjoyed *Broken Blossoms*, one of the most popular films that winter, directed by D. W. Griffith and starring the much-loved actress, Lillian Gish. The lyrically affecting story of the relationship between a beautiful young girl and a Chinaman living in poverty in London's Limehouse district was playing to packed theatres. The innovative close-ups of Lillian Gish, filmed through gauze, revealed 'a child with a tear-aged face'. A rare note of contemporary realism was injected into scenes in which policemen were seen reading newspapers with headlines telling of 'only 40,000 casualties' as they remarked to each other that the casualty figures were 'better than last week'.

Griffith introduced elaborate colour tints, and for further depth the screen itself was washed with coloured lights. The subtitles alerted the viewer to the condition of the Chinaman as he walked through Limehouse 'with perhaps a whiff of the lillied pipe still in his brain', an atmospheric druggy haze drifting over the scene. Usherettes in Chinese dress guided the moviegoers to their seats and caged birds were suspended from the cinema's proscenium arch. Lillian Gish became so popular that her name was adopted into the shorthand of cockney rhyming slang, and Billingsgate market resounded to cries of 'Would you like a nice bit of Lillian for your supper?'

Doris and Will were huge cinema fans and had heard that synchronised words were soon going to be tied in to the silent pictures. But their favourite days were the ones when they left London for the clean air of the countryside. One morning they took a train down to Brighton and spent an unforgettable day out at the seaside. Their picnic included a smart blue tin of transparent crispy slivers of fried potato, a new product sold by a grocer, Frank Smith, who masterminded the frying from his Cricklewood garage. There were other new conveniences. Food in tins included exotic fruit from California and fillets of violently pink salmon. In the kitchen of 146 Piccadilly there was 'real artificial cream' in a pot that proved very convenient when the fresh supply from Scotland failed to arrive.

In March 1920 at the *Daily Mail* Ideal Home Exhibition the size of the ideal kitchen on display had been reduced and a new servant-free machine that washed dishes with its own in-built plumbing was introduced. The most astonishing exhibit was the All-Electric House with an electric towelrail heater and a heated pot for shaving water in the bathroom, a hair dryer, curling tongs, a milk steriliser for the baby and a massaging vibrator for tired arms for mothers exhausted by carrying the child round all day as a result of the shortage of nursemaids. In the scullery there was a washing machine with a basket that allowed the clothes to spin around while draining, while in the parlour an electric cigar lighter and a sewing machine that spun at the touch of a switch all drew admiring crowds.

Above: On 1 December 1919 the American divorcee Nancy Astor was the first woman to take a seat in the British Parliament after her election as MP for Plymouth

Right: The hugely popular Prince of Wales (the future Edward VIII), unofficial ambassador for Britain, salvation of the institution of monarchy and compulsive smoker, returned from an overseas trip in December 1919

The demobilisation process for the returning troops was so badly handled that some soldiers felt the respect given them was little better than that shown to the position of women in society. They proved their point by dressing up in women's clothes

Policemen in Whitehall pushing back thousands of unemployed workers, demonstrating for better pay and conditions within earshot of the Prime Minister Lloyd George

Right: On 26 November 1919 the cover of *Tatler* magazine carried a full-colour drawing of a smiling soldier in uniform throwing his sweetheart into the air. The country, or at least part of it, was at last in the mood to start dancing

Below: Six thousand movers and shakers poured into the new Hammersmith Palais in London when it opened in October 1919, featuring the sensational Original Dixieland Jazz Band from America

Lillian Gish, the much-loved star of the 1919 movie *Broken Blossoms*, whose name – as in 'Have a nice bit of Lillian for your supper' – was adopted as cockney rhyming slang at Billingsgate fish market

Coco Chanel, the greatest couturier of all time, was delighting her customers in 1920 with designs for daringly short but elegant black cocktail dresses

The Savoy 'button boys', fed up with the disgusting food in the staff dining room, caused chaos in the hotel's messenger system by implementing strike action in aid of a better quality of lunchtime cake

Dame Nellie Melba on the red carpet on 15 June 1920, poised to sing 'Home Sweet Home' during the world's first radio broadcast of a musical performance advertised in advance. Her voice was heard on radios as far away as Stockholm, Madrid, Warsaw, Paris, Rome and Malta

Right: Increases in taxes and the cost of living forced the ninth Duke and Duchess of Devonshire to sell their huge London house and to have the financially ruinous Great Conservatory at Chatsworth blown up

Below: Paxton's Great Conservatory, built in 1841, fell into disrepair as a result of neglect during the war, but it took over 450 electric detonators, 250 pounds of gelignite and many tears before the destruction was completed in the summer of 1920

The beautiful Slade student Edna Clarke Hall in a self-portrait at the time of her marriage to Willie Clarke Hall

Lady Ottoline Morrell by Simon Bussy, 1920. 'I love being really rather gorgeous'

Lionel Gomme, known as 'Tiger', stonemason, football fanatic and 'my beautiful boy', photographed by his lover Lady Ottoline Morrell in June 1920 at Garsington, Oxfordshire

Winifred Holtby, one of the first female undergraduates at Oxford to be awarded a degree in a ceremony in October 1920

Vera Brittain, once a firm patriot, lost her brother, her fiancé and her greatest friends in the war and became a lifelong pacifist

The Unknown Warrior represented the fiancé, husband, father, brother, son and friend to several millions of the bereaved who, during the war, had been denied the comfort of a funeral for their loved ones. He was buried among kings in Westminster Abbey on 11 November 1920

The Daily Mail Cookbook of the year included a helpful sequence of diagrams for the cracking and separating process of eggs. Many women had not learned the technique, having never entered the kitchen before. With fewer servants more involvement from the mistress of the house was necessary. Little known practical tips for handling a new world were offered. A lit cigarette allowed to smoulder in the hand was an infallible way of clearing nasty lingering onion smells.

Mills & Boon had published a perfect guide for the novice housekeeper. *Life Without Servants*, subtitled *The Rediscovery of Domestic Happiness*, was by a writer ready to identify themselves only as 'A Survivor'. The tiny volume measuring four by three inches, designed to fit handily into any pocket, was aimed at those who could not find a good servant or who could not afford the inflated prices of domestic staff in 1920. Further titles in the Mills & Boon series of miniature books designed to offer practical help of other kinds to their post-war readership included *A Little Book for Those Who Mourn* compiled by Mildred Carnegy and *Nerves and the Nervous* by a doctor called Edwin L. Ash.

Eileen Rafter was determined to escape from the domestic drudgery that she saw all around her. Eileen lived in Liverpool and the ever busy Merseyside docks had inspired in her a wish to see the world. Eileen had no ambition to go into service or to be a housewife, and would only marry, she told her mother, if she managed to 'land an Admiral'. That way, she explained, she could travel abroad on beautiful ships and visit exciting places. Otherwise she would stay firmly single and be in charge of her own life.

Clothes were her passion. The ragged black shawls and greasy braided hair of the older women who lived in the houses in her street filled her with horror. Their manner of dress had remained unchanged for three reigns. But standards in Eileen's own home were different. One day she remembered looking up at her elegant mother who was dressed for the ballet, wearing a hat 'with a jaunty little veil thing hanging off it, which was just to keep the flies off, but I thought to myself "oh she looks so lovely"'. The creamy panama-coloured broderie anglaise hat that Eileen herself wore each week to church in Birkenhead was so fussy that the lacy folds had to be ironed every Sunday. Mrs Rafter was a wonderful dressmaker and would make up patterns from the Weldon pattern book, but adapted under her young daughter's direction so that from the age of ten Eileen was the self-appointed 'style-setter' of the Rafter family. 'This dress has two frills at the bottom, but I think it would look better if you leave one of them off,' Eileen would advise her mother and Mrs Rafter would oblige.

As soon as she left school Eileen had applied for a job in a shop. Answering an advertisement in the *Liverpool Echo* for a cashier in Lewis's department store, Eileen soon became anxious that she 'would get a big bottom' if she remained sitting down in the glass box for days on end taking the money, and reading poetry in between trans-actions ('a novel would have been too frequently interrupted'). Here she learned the secrets of the commissions system and soon, after smiling winningly at the manager through the tiny window between her own office and his, she found herself employed in the haber-dashery department selling the new silk stockings. She had worked out from behind her cashier's desk that the commissions there were far higher than in the gloves section or even in the newly popular cosmetic department.

Shortly afterwards Eileen was transferred to the London branch of Lewis's where she slept in service block accommodation with other girls. Her room had a sofa that turned into a bed if you pulled it apart. 'It was very new and very strange.' But Eileen's eye for the stylish had impressed the dress buyer, Mr Leak, so much that he took her with him to Paris to view the collections and put her to work making sketches of the designs she saw there. The plan was to bring the drawings back to London and make copies of the clothes for important customers.

One evening in Paris Eileen was taken to dinner for pressed duck and champagne in the grandest of all Parisian restaurants, La Tour d'Argent. There, feeling herself to be well on the way to a lifetime's career in fashion, she renewed her intention to avoid the double horrors of domestic service and marriage. Her mother was proud of her child. She could never have imagined such a life for herself.

14

Surviving

Late Spring 1920

Adam Thorpe, born in the wonderfully sunlit year of 1911, wished everyone would forget about the war. In the early months of 1920, on successive rainy Saturday afternoons, Adam had travelled with his family from village green to village green, standing around in the mud listening to the bugler playing the Last Post as the all too familiar sound 'cut across a silence like the silence in a church before the coffin arrives'. On each of those cloud-filled Saturdays Adam had watched as the white sheets covering the still shapeless object fluttered to the ground to reveal memorial stones dedicated first to his grandfather, then to his uncle and finally to his own father and the other men of the village who had fallen with them. He watched the grief of his grandmother, his aunt and his mother and, with some impatience, wondered whether life would always consist of looking backwards.

Lucy Neale was still unable to believe she would never again feel the rough khaki uniform of her father's jacket brushing against her cheek during an embrace. Only when ten-year-old Lucy went to bed at night and remembered to say her prayers did her adored father's absence seem believable. In tears she would say her prayers just as he had taught her, but she found it almost impossible to sleep without receiving his kiss on her forehead or hearing the words 'Goodnight, Lulu, God bless you.'

For some the return of a parent did not add to the comfort of life at home, especially if the lack of a job contributed to lack of money. In the overcrowded homes of the very poor tension had intensified since the Armistice. Henry Freedman slept upside down in the same bed as his two brothers, trying to find space for his head between two sets of toes that agitated his hair all night. Despite the mass of bodies, they were cold, and a dusty red brick warmed in the fireplace joined them under the sheets. The ever present smell of carbolic and sulphur that hung over the bed was never strong enough to deter the bed bugs and the walls were covered in tiny insect-sized bloodstains indicating the moment when the squashed creatures had finally met their end. A stinking pot-pourri of tea, manure, tobacco, sweat, soup, fried fish and poverty rose up to the bedroom floor. Jobless men clustered on benches outside in the street, bored and apathetic.

Women struggled to find enough money to feed their children, starving themselves so there was more to go round, paying the doctor with precious ounces of butter, dreading the knock on the door that would bring the debt collector. Cleanliness was a mark of pride, but in the soot-filled back alleys of the cities there was little chance that the heavy sheets that had taken so long to wash would be clean by the time they had dried in the filthy air of the back yards. Keeping the dirt out of the house was a daily challenge. Outside taps, the only source of domestic water, would freeze over in cold weather. The temptations offered by the moneylender led only to further debt, but sometimes desperation won. Outside in the streets smells continued to identify the different areas of London's commercial districts. Commercial Street itself was thick with smoke from the cigars that were rolled in the factories there; from the furniture-making warehouses in Curtain Road came the smell of linseed oil and turpentine.

Unemployment had become the axis on which fear of destitution and shame balanced precariously. For the majority of the poor the ending of the war had not improved life. It was a world full of insecurity. And the middle classes developed a new contempt for the poor. Those who had enough money to celebrate their survival found the spiritlessness of the malnourished and the cynical hard to tolerate.

But children have a way of ignoring or not noticing the hardship that adults endure. Street games in the East End remained constant before, during and after the war. Empty cocoa tins threaded with a piece of string to form a support provided makeshift stilts. Hopscotch grids were chalked on to the pavement. Skipping was accompanied by rhymes handed down from parent to child. The click of marbles and the thwack of conkers in season were heard up and down the back streets, accompanied by childish laughter.

Away at boarding school Tom Mitford lived a lucky life that knew nothing of hardship. The spring holidays, at home at Asthall Manor in Oxfordshire, were the happy confirmation of the end of a long winter. While food at Lockers Park in Hemel Hempstead was not quite up to Savoy standards, Tom was relieved that the quantity had not suffered much even during the war years. What is more, he was allowed all sorts of dishes that he was never given at home; his mother, known to him and his sisters as Muv, had a rule that 'what was good enough for Moses was good enough for us'. The Mitford children therefore craved all the foods that were forbidden to the ancient Israelites, including bacon, lobster, pigeon, rabbit, hare and mackerel.

The girls who remained at home considered it most unfair that Tom was allowed some of these delicacies while away at school. And he never tired of detailing for them all the delicious things he had to eat there. 'The other day we had fried bacon for breakfast,' he wrote in his weekly letter home, adding, 'sometimes we have brawn.' And in case his sisters did not quite absorb the full joy of such a dish he emphasised that it was 'Oh! So Good.' As the sisters sat around sighing with irritation, Tom had not finished. Often, he told them, he was given 'sardines and sometimes tongue and sometimes ham and sometimes HOT ham for lunch'. The latter dish was 'scrumshus'. Other people's parents also understood what a growing boy needed. On a day out with the mother of his friend Gore, Tom was allowed *two* large helpings of roast chicken as well as one and a half sausages.

His mother responded at once to the barely concealed hint. Tom's next single-page letter was dominated by exclamation marks of gratitude for the 'LOVELY' cake, which the Asthall cook had baked for him, although he adds at the end to his mother that 'Sometime no matter when, I wish you would make me a cake with your own hands.'

Despite the superior standard of food at school, Tom was looking forward to the holidays, and to days filled with pony riding, mucking about with his sisters and as much cake as he could eat. And there was something else to look forward to. Everyone had told him that his mother's expected baby was bound to be a boy. Although he got along well with his sisters, coming exactly halfway down the family in order of age, after Nancy and Pam and before Diana, Jessica and Unity, it would be good to have someone in the family who could play football properly and be an ally against Nancy in particular who was such a brag. Tom often got his own back on her by replying in Latin to the show-off letters that she wrote him at school in Greek, and none of the sisters could compete with Tom's repertoire of thirty card tricks. Only his father was a match.

With five sisters it would be extreme bad luck and quite against the odds if his mother was to have yet another girl. The longed for brother was expected to arrive at the end of March and on the 30th he went into the garden with Pam and together they gathered for their mother 'some pheasants eyes, some enenemys, some cowslips and a few primroses' which he sent up with his father to London where the new arrival was scheduled to appear.

When the telegram containing the eagerly anticipated news arrived at the end of the following day, 31 March 1920, a dreadful gloom fell upon the household. Another girl. The housemaid Annie, very close to tears, immediately expressed her sympathies, voicing the thoughts of them all. 'Oh WHAT a disappointment!' she sniffed, while confirming to Nancy that she had heard from Mabel, the London parlourmaid, who had suspected the dreadful truth 'after taking one look at his Lordship's face'. Nancy was rather thrilled by the drama, telling everyone who would listen to her that the church bell had tolled as if for a funeral, the cattle in the surrounding fields had begun to moan at the news while inside the house the prospect of a nursery filled 'with another furious occupant, shrieking like a cage of parrots' had been greeted with horror.

However, Tom knew how important it was to muster the sum of his not inconsiderable sense of tact when he sat down the following day to write to his mother, while not forgetting that she always stressed the importance of telling the truth. 'My Darling Muv,' he began, 'I am so glad you have got a little girl', continuing, 'but of course it is a great pity that it was not a little boy but still.' And hoping that would do it, he went on with a bit of home news that he thought might cheer her up. 'Pam collected ten shillings this morning for the starving children and she is now keeping a shop or stall for them and she is going to have a box for collections.'

Tom returned to school for the summer term on 4 April, just before Easter, promising not to make too much of a fuss about going back if his mother would guarantee to send him some chocolates and some of his favourite *langue de chat* biscuits.

Pam Parish was also a happy member of a large family. Sometimes they all went to visit one of their grandmother's seven brothers and sisters, the favourites being Charles and Frank Beadle, who had both made a lot of money developing warehouses at Erith on the Kent estuary.

Charles's wealth had bought him Wood Hall, a beautiful Georgian house in Essex, with a lovely farm filled with horses, sheep, pigs and cows. Uncle Charles was a generous man who paid for the founding of a school at Erith and for the laying of a gas pipe to the village. He loved nothing better than sending a big limousine for his relations and friends and bringing them all to celebrate Christmas at Wood Hall in style. Pam loved her Great-Uncle Charlie so much that she would do anything for him. One day she handed him her favourite embroidered handkerchief to fold, but mistaking her intention he thanked her and put it in his pocket. Pam said nothing. Uncle Charlie was the only person she could imagine forgiving for inadvertently stealing her favourite handkerchief. But one summer, after spending a few days at the farm recovering from having her tonsils out, Pam became surprisingly reluctant to return with her parents and brother and sisters on these once-treasured expeditions.

Her mother could not get to the bottom of why Pam was making such a fuss about Uncle Charlie's friend Mr Humbert who had also been staying. Mrs Parish did not know that this man had, on more than one occasion during her previous visit, taken Pam on his knee, and leaned his whole body firmly up against Pam in such a way that no one else could see quite how close he was to her. 'I don't know how you can be so unkind to that poor man who really likes little girls and has no little girls of his own,' her baffled mother would say when Pam asked to stay behind while the rest of the family went

to Uncle Charles's. But Pam had begun to develop a profound distrust of grown-up men.

Older children and teenagers had become accustomed to a far greater
degree of independence than their parents had known, and this
younger generation was unwilling to relinquish its new-found
freedom. Face creams like 'Icilma' and 'Silver Foam', and pots of
rouge, were hidden at the back of the bathroom cupboard. When
the father of a young factory worker discovered his daughter's Dorothy
bag full of forbidden cosmetics, he accused her of polluting the house
and threatened to throw her out if she didn't dispose of 'this muck';
she replied that she would either continue to use the muck or she
and the muck would leave home together.

For schoolchildren that summer, the news of a scientific development was confirmation enough that a new and better world was
emerging. The world-famous Australian opera singer Nellie Melba
was already a hugely popular figure before 1914, but her charity con-
certs during the war had endeared her for ever to the Australian and
British people and she had been rewarded with a damehood. On 15
June she arrived at the Marconi Wireless recording studio in Chelmsford, Essex. There she was to sing to the British public in the first
ever nationwide broadcast by wireless. Twelve years earlier radio had
played a famous part in the country's life when a distress call using
Morse code was transmitted to nearby ships from the two radio
operators on board the *Titanic*. As a result hundreds of lives had been
saved from the engulfing waves. During the war wireless had been
used by the Navy to track the movement of the German fleet. But
these communications had been soundless and although amateur
radio enthusiasts had managed to speak to each other over the airwaves, there had not yet been an official public broadcast.

The ground-breaking occasion that summer of 1920 was spon-
sored by the *Daily Mail*, the newspaper once again in the vanguard
of technological development. As the deep, slow-voiced announcer
came to the microphone, an audience positioned just an inch or two
from its wireless, and listening from a distance of up to a thousand
miles from Chelmsford, was informed that Dame Nellie was about
to sing. Atlantic liners with receiving equipment had been told of

the fourthcoming 'séance', as some reports had it, and amateur wireless operators across the Channel and beyond tuned their sets.

Wearing a modest hat and dark patterned suit, her handsome chest poised in readiness for the opening bars, Dame Nellie stood on a strip of red carpet with her small square handbag held securely in one hand while steadying the six-foot high microphone with the other. At the last minute an unforeseen adjustment became necessary. Technicians were conscious that Dame Nellie's temper was volatile and that her celebrity made her at times demanding. There was a famous story of how the great Caruso had once teased Nellie for her occasional pomposity by singing 'Che gelida manina, se la lasci riscaldar' ('what a tiny frozen hand, let me warm it') while simultaneously pressing a hot sausage into Nellie's palm.

On this important day, however, the technicians were not going to risk anything going wrong with the broadcast and were prepared to make risky demands of Dame Nellie even if she objected. They were worried about the carpet. They feared that a rhythmic tap of a matronly foot on the deep pile might interfere with the purity and quality of the transmission. But as the carpet was rolled neatly back Dame Nellie made no objections and the sound of her glorious voice, accompanied on the adjacent grand piano by her friend the composer Herman Bemberg, came through with perfect clarity. The programme of music included the tear-jerking 'Home Sweet Home' that Nellie had sung to returning soldiers in 1918, just after receiving her damehood from the King. This song was followed by 'Nymphes et Silvains', and finally Mimi's farewell from La Bohème preceded a resounding rendering of the National Anthem. Dame Nellie's voice was heard by a marvelling audience as far away as Stockholm, Madrid, Warsaw, Paris, Rome and Malta.

Nellie Melba stayed on in England for the new season of the Ballets Russes. Since her own operatic performances at Covent Garden the preceding May, and despite her disapproval of the audience's informal dress, the seats had remained packed with opera lovers. On 10 June the seats were once again filled with ballet aficionados as Diaghilev returned to London and to the great opera house with Igor Stravinsky's new ballet Pulcinella that had been premiered in

Paris three weeks earlier. Pablo Picasso had painted the sets for a story based on an eighteenth-century Italian play, and once again London audiences ensured the ballets were a sell-out.

This new season had been hugely anticipated for months. Classical ballet, under the guidance of Serge Diaghilev, was continuing the revolution in style and content that had begun in London three years before the war. Despite Emerald Cunard's money-raising muscle, the expense of staging a production at Covent Garden remained impossible to meet with limited post-war funds. Instead the Ballets Russes had returned to London the preceding summer, opening at the less costly Coliseum.

A colour poster with Picasso's costume design for a character in one of the ballets had been pasted up all over the West End and throughout the Underground. Picasso himself had enjoyed an extended visit to London in the summer of 1919, staying with his new wife Olga Khokhlova at the Savoy and flaunting a fresh flower from the nearby Covent Garden market in the lapel of his new London-tailored suit. Picasso and Matisse were two artists out of only a handful whose reputation had been made before the war and whose creative originality and renown was extending beyond the Armistice. Picasso's visit had been centred around his commission by Diaghilev for the backdrops of *The Three-Cornered Hat*, which had its premiere at the Coliseum on 22 July that year. It formed part of a summer season which included the triumphant – some critics even thought perfect – production of *La Boutique Fantasque*. The new post-war stars of Diaghilev's stage, Léonide Massine and Lydia Lopokova, were greeted with as much rapture as had been lavished on the company at its first appearance with Nijinsky and Karsavina nearly a decade earlier.

Picasso had been both amused and flattered when he read in the *Weekly Despatch* that his poster had been 'defiled by the wretched scribbles of street urchins' who had added a beard and moustache to the picture. He saw the graffiti as part of the exciting and lively street art that he had come across in London, finding himself as 'charmed by the naiveté of these efforts', which he thought 'most instructive', as he was by London buses and the scarlet uniform of the British soldier on guard outside Buckingham Palace. During

Picasso's London stay Sacheverell Sitwell had climbed the narrow ladder to the top floor to visit him in the studio at 48 Floral Street and watched the carpet-slippered painter at work on the enormous backdrops for *The Three-Cornered Hat* – backdrops distinctive for their flamboyant use of colour combined with a pared-down and effective simplicity of composition. Seeing the artist 'moving about at a great speed over its surface, walking with something of a skating motion', Sitwell was prompted, in an outburst of excitement, to compare the scene to that of watching Tiepolo at work.

Later that autumn another new ballet had attracted huge crowds. Audiences at the Empire, Leicester Square, had been thrilled by Jean Cocteau's creatively daring composition of 1917, *Parade*. Set, curtains and costumes had again been conceived by the young painter Picasso; music was by Erik Satie, choreography by Léonide Massine and programme notes by the poet Guillaume Apollinaire. The leading ballerina was the popular Tamara Karsavina who played an ultra-modern American dancing girl.

Critics called the ballet variously 'a revolution', 'a comet', 'an earthquake'. Massine, who was the company's leading male dancer as well as choreographer, explained that, in their attempt to translate popular art into a new form, the combined creative team used 'certain elements of contemporary show business – ragtime music, jazz, the cinema, billboard advertising, circus and music-hall techniques', as well as musical references to the aeroplane, the typewriter and the skyscraper.

The Times critic was challenged to find the words to describe what he had seen. 'Cubo-futurist? Physical vers-libre? Plastic jazz?' he suggested, concluding that 'It is a world of nonsense, where anything means everything or nothing, yet everything is exciting to the eye, ear and mind.' But the audiences were large and Diaghilev wrote to Picasso from his suite of rooms at the Savoy telling him that London life was 'tres animé – on ne manque de rien on est bien chauffé et nourri' and adding that 'Les théâtres marchent mieux que jamais et nous travaillons comme des nègres.'

Audiences included the wife of the former prime minister, Margot Asquith. Her memoirs, 'an immortal addition to the chronicles of the super-egoists' according to the *Illustrated London News*, had just been published and were the talk of society. The critic Clive Bell, the Sitwell brothers and the poet T. S. Eliot with his wife Vivien had all been with Margot Asquith to watch the new performance. Vanessa Bell sent a message to Picasso who was by then back in Paris to say it was 'the best thing I have ever seen on stage', containing 'everything and nothing'. *Parade* held particular resonance for T. S. Eliot, who was working on his new long poem, *The Waste Land*: the arid post-war landscape of moral and spiritual apathy and stagnation was his inspiration and obsession.

Some of the dancers who had arrived a few weeks earlier for rehearsals for the 1920 summer season were staying at the Savoy, the Russian dancers' favourite hotel close to Covent Garden. They were mildly amused, though mildly inconvenienced, by the Savoy button boys who had finally summoned the courage to go on strike. But unlike the disgruntled senior staff who remained angry about the anomalies in the tipping system and had gone on strike several months earlier, the younger employees had a different grievance. The boys, increasingly fed up with the poor quality of food served during their rest breaks, objected in particular to the gristly lumps of cold mutton that was frequently presented in the guise of an edible lunch. On 25 May sixteen small boys had walked out of the main hotel entrance and crossed the Strand, skipping their way towards the excellent tea rooms opposite. In only two mouth-watering hours they succeeded in spending their entire and carefully collected strike fund on tarts, buns, tea and cocoa.

During the stand-off a group of senior staff had been drafted to walk the long corridors and the reception rooms while intoning the room number of a guest to alert him that a visitor had arrived. The baritone delivery was not sufficiently audible to many of the older guests whose hearing was no longer so strong. The management, realising the value of the button boys' treble and alto voices, quickly agreed to give the boys the best food that the Savoy kitchen could provide in return for constant and willing service. Members of the Ballets Russes were among those who were pleased that things were back to normal.

But while a certain nostalgia was satisfied by the return of the glorious pre-war ballet seasons, and while youth and the press were exhilarated by scientific excitement in the airwaves, many still struggled with the challenge of the new era. News of the worrying fragmentation of Germany filled the papers. Extremist militant groups were emerging all over the country. The Deutsche Arbeiterpartei, the German Workers' Party, founded in Bavaria in January 1919, was demonstrating an increasing hostility to capitalism and Jews. The party was growing in number of supporters and a young ex-corporal, Adolf Hitler, who had recovered from a blinding wartime gas attack, had recently joined them – their fifty-fifth member. Other groups were demonstrating against Bolshevism. The economy teetered. A general strike paralysed the country.

At home a controversial film was attracting crowds and comment in the cinemas. French director Abel Gance's raging damnation of the futility of war, *J'accuse*, was shown to its first British audience on 24 May 1920 at London's Philharmonic Hall in Great Portland Street. Six months earlier the Philharmonic audience had seen Lowell Thomas's Lawrence of Arabia show, but since December Sir Ernest Shackleton's film *South* had been presented in person by the exhausted, frustrated and increasingly alcohol-dependent explorer.

Gance's film was something very different. Accompanied by a full choir and a forty-piece orchestra, it starred two men from a village in Provence who, despite being rivals in love, put aside their enmity and fought together in the war. As the lyrical beauty of the opening pastoral scenes gave way to the harsh barren openness of no man's land, audiences realised that this was not simply a war film, but a tale about love, self-sacrifice and the fragility of survival. Gance had filmed the final tragic war scenes in the north-eastern town of Saint-Mihiel on 12 September 1918 during the actual battle in which over seven thousand soldiers were killed or wounded.

A French general watching Gance during the filming asked him whom he was accusing. 'I am accusing War,' Gance replied. 'I am accusing Man. I am accusing universal stupidity.' The film magazine *Kine Weekly* said that '*J'accuse* forms one of the most terrible indictments against war which it is possible to imagine', explaining that 'the effect is not produced by insistent horrors and sheer frightfulness' but 'by the emphasis of simple natural humanity'.

J'accuse was shown in cinemas throughout the country. *The Times* thought that a 'miracle has been achieved. A film has caused an audience to think.' No one who saw it could put the film's message from their minds. No one missed the title's echoes of Emile Zola's defence of the soldier Alfred Dreyfus twenty years earlier against anti-Semitic victimisation by the French government. If individuals could reconcile their differences, why did such a solution evade the politicians? What in fact had been the point of war? The content of the film reminded audiences of American director D. W. Griffith's huge wartime success, *The Birth of a Nation*, in which the American Civil War was celebrated while war itself was resoundingly condemned.

At the very end of Gance's film, in a horrifying hallucinatory sequence, the dead soldiers rise up from the waste land as Jean Diaz turns to the terrified watching civilians and, confronting their guilt, cries 'J'accuse.' The dead men are asking those who remain whether they are worthy of such sacrifice. For this Dante-esque sequence which made a nonsense of all the panaceas offered by spiritualists and practising seancists to the bereaved, Gance had borrowed two thousand soldiers while they were on an eight-day respite from the front at Verdun. While filming Gance was acutely aware of the implications of what he was asking the men to do. After the war he explained those feelings. 'The drama, the source of the psychological impact, stems from the acting of those dead men on leave. In a few weeks or months eighty per cent of them would disappear. I knew it and so did they.'

The experience of making and watching the film had a shattering effect on all involved. Women watching the film were so distressed that many were carried from the cinema in a faint. To a population who were in part beginning to put a distance between themselves and the slaughter, this film only reawakened the truth of the experience. The film was in some ways the cinematic equivalent of Wilfred Owen's verse, some of which was published in the same year. Moments of silence and national monuments could provide a temporary reprieve but could never eradicate the pain of truth.

15

Resignation

Early Summer 1920

Neither the ninth Duke of Devonshire nor his wife, Duchess Evelyn, were extravagant by nature. When the Duchess once attached a stamp to a wrongly addressed envelope she sent a footman on the ten-minute walk to the Chatsworth kitchens to fetch a newly boiled kettle so that she could steam it off. But Victor Devonshire had been forced to consider selling his huge London house well before the war broke out. A reduction in household expenses was a problem that many were struggling with, but a reduction in houses them-selves was a predicament reserved only for the few. As early as 1913 Duchess Evelyn had been looking for a way to meet the sum owed as death duties on the estate of Victor's uncle, the eighth Duke. 'Could you find out what sort of prices people now give for big houses?' Duchess Evelyn had written in February of that year to Francis Manners Sutton, the Duke's private secretary. 'So many have changed hands lately that someone ought to know.'

During the war years nothing was done about the proposition to sell but the financial repercussions of the four-year conflict had forced the ninth Duke to agree that the sale of Devonshire House was now inevitable and urgent. Disposal of the mansion would help with the enormous expenses of running the vast Devonshire estates. The agricultural slump of the war years, and the increased taxes imposed on rich landowners even before the war, meant that the Duke was now stretched beyond his means. In the past some of the huge sums owed to the Treasury had already been met by the sale of precious assets. Twenty-five volumes printed by William Caxton and the John Philip Kemble collection of plays were sold in 1914 to Henry E. Huntingdon who paid the Duke $750,000.

Devonshire House sat at the heart of London's Piccadilly, opposite the entrance to Green Park and a minute's stroll from the Ritz. With its dull-looking façade and high unadorned wall designed to keep out the din of street sellers it was not an elegant building when viewed from outside. But once inside first-time visitors would catch their breath at its glamour and grandeur. The Duke knew he would miss the glorious oak carvings of the London house, as well as the huge drawing rooms filled with masterpieces by Van Dyck, Rubens and Rembrandt, the dazzling crystal balustraded staircase and the ballroom, scene for nearly two hundred years of so many spectacular dances. But it was the garden with its two tennis courts surrounded by lawns and statues, fountains and ancient trees that he would find particularly difficult to give up.

The sale of Devonshire House would, the Duke hoped, be the biggest and final event of many such cash-raising ventures. During the last two years of the war the Duke had authorised the auctioning of land worth nearly £20,000. He planned to net several hundred thousand pounds by selling off property in London's Chiswick as well as farmland in Derbyshire, especially around the town of Chesterfield, some more from the Bolton Abbey estates in Yorkshire, and further acreage from other counties stretching from Lincolnshire to Somerset and Sussex.

The Duke had been particularly reluctant to part with Peelings, a glorious Jacobean manor house at Pevensey near Eastbourne. The estate agents handling the handsome property and its forty-seven acres had soon received an expression of great interest from the wife of the Minister for War. Clementire Churchill was a tremendous sea-bathing enthusiast and she loved the idea of living near the south coast. What is more, ever conscious of her husband's extravagance and always out to save or make a penny, Clemmie had spotted a little piece of land further down the coast that seemed ripe for development. She thought it would make a 'delicious little garden villa with good tennis courts, sailing boats etc'. But Winston resisted. He had always set his heart on finding a house in Kent. Since Winston had been a very young child, his old nanny Mrs Everest had impressed on him that with its wonderful fruit orchards and thick rich green hop gardens, Kent was undoubtedly the most beautiful county in England. Peelings remained on the market.

In 1916 the Duke of Devonshire had been appointed Governor General of Canada and proved to be successful and popular in the role. But by 1920 he was weary of trying to handle all the problems at home from such a great distance. On 14 March he left Canada for the week-long journey back to England. He planned to stay there for a month and a half during which time he had much business to conduct, most of it sad. He had no time to visit the Devonshires' lovely castle, Lismore in Ireland's County Waterford, and the increasing volatility of the country made it unadvisable for him to travel there.

The only bright engagement in his diary was the approaching marriage of his daughter Dorothy, scheduled to take place towards the end of April, a few days after a final ball was to be held at Devonshire House. Dorothy's fiancé, Harold Macmillan, had just joined his family's publishing firm as a junior partner, having refused to return to Oxford, a place that risked the recurrence of unhappy memories, after the loss of so many of his fellow undergraduates killed in the war.

Now aged 26, Harold had served as a captain in the Grenadier Guards and had been badly wounded three times. For the last year he had been an effective and likeable ADC to the Duke in Canada. Harold had ambitions for an eventual political career in Britain and was looking for a free seat to contest. With his intelligence and ease with people from all backgrounds, he seemed to his future father-in-law to be full of promise. The Duke hoped that this marriage would lessen the pain of the loss of another son-in-law, Captain Angus Mackintosh, who within a year of his marriage to Dorothy's elder sister Maud, and while serving with the Horse Guards, had been shot at Mons and died a month before the Armistice of pneumonia brought on by the Spanish flu.

Two days after his arrival back in Britain Victor Devonshire wrote in his diary that he still felt 'very bewildered and strange'. The sale of the London house, perhaps to one of the new American hoteliers, filled him with dread. On top of these anxieties there were worries up at Chatsworth in Derbyshire. During the war most of the gardeners had been away fighting and the dilapidated condition of Joseph Paxton's magnificent Conservatory was causing concern.

On its completion in 1841, 277 feet long, 123 feet wide and 67 feet high, it had been the largest glasshouse in the world. This amazing building, compared by one visitor at the time to 'a sea of glass when the waves are settling and smoothing down after a storm', had covered a quarter of an acre. Seven miles of iron pipes fired by eight underground coal furnaces that consumed 350 tons of fuel a year provided the heating for an unmatchable array of exotic plants with delicate temperaments. Mrs S. C. Hall, one of thousands of visitors to Derbyshire's beautiful new crystal palace, described it in 1851 as filled with 'the rarest exotics from all parts of the globe – from "farthest Ind", from China, from the Himalayas, from Mexico'. There were bananas, and grapes 'hanging in ripe profusion beneath the shadow of immense paper-like leaves' and, equally delightful, 'the far-famed silk cottontree supplying a sheet of cream-coloured blossoms', the deliciously scented cinnamon and 'thousands of other rare and little known species of both flowers and fruits'.

But the restrictions on coal usage during the war had caused the warmth-loving plants to wither and with the post-war shortage of fuel there was little prospect of maintaining the voracious heating requirements. Roland Burke, the Duke's chief agent in charge of the Devonshire lands at Hardwick, Bolton and Chatsworth, had written to Government House in Ottawa in January 1920 to explain that 'serious deterioration' to the surrounding greenhouses had taken place. 'A large quantity of the glass is in a thoroughly dilapidated condition and is worth practically nothing at all, the fruit trees themselves have of course suffered considerably by the wet continually dripping in.'

The ninth Duke was resigned. The Paxton masterpiece would have to go. On 14 January he had been advised in a telegram from Burke that an offer of £550 had been made for the destruction and removal of the kitchen garden greenhouses. In addition £3,600 was mentioned as a sum for buying the magnificent Great Conservatory in which Queen Victoria had danced over seventy years earlier, when 14,000 lamps had been hung around the upper gallery for the royal ball. Prince Albert's irreplaceable private secretary, Colonel G. E. Anson, had made it clear to the then Duke and Duchess that Victoria, although already a bride of three years, was to be seated next to her husband throughout the visit, and the royal couple as well as the Chatsworth fountains had danced the night away 'at an unwonted pace'. The following day, wearing a purple poke bonnet, the Queen had been given a special tour of the garden buildings by Paxton himself. Victoria pronounced the Conservatory to be 'the most stupendous and extraordinary creation imaginable'.

In 1851 Prince Albert commissioned another Paxton masterpiece. That year the Crystal Palace in Hyde Park became the centrepiece for the Great Exhibition and the achievement brought Paxton the reward of a knighthood. But in 1920 there was a risk that Paxton's Chatsworth structure, a thing of immense but fragile beauty, would simply fall apart in the hands of anyone attempting to move it.

Many of the same families had worked the great Devonshire estates for centuries and the Duke hoped the new generation would resist the lure of well-paid work in the surrounding cities. The Duke believed that men who had been marked by courage in battle fell apart when confined to an office, while those who could still breathe the outside air were certain to survive better. Roland Burke, his chief agent, was struggling under administrative pressure and, although not an old man, his irregular heartbeat was giving his doctor cause for worry. Burke had been warned that he might have to 'be put on the shelf' for at least six months, and to take a complete rest. Reluctantly Burke agreed, given that 'it seems a pity to go west at forty-nine'.

The Duke was fortunate in the individual he had chosen to run his affairs in his absence abroad. Burke was a man of energy, efficiency and also of compassion. The huge number of staff retained on the estates brought with it problems of a personal nature and in the Duke's absence Burke felt it important to boost morale. In a letter to the Duke at the beginning of the year he had to break the news that 'Elliot the under-keeper at Beeley has taken his life'. Poor Elliot had been suffering from depression and shot himself only the day before the switching on of the lights of the huge Christmas tree at Chatsworth. Burke told the Duke that he had managed to persuade Mrs Elliot to allow the two children to attend the tree lighting as usual; Burke knew how much children loved the occasion. He also knew how important it was for their lives to go on as normal.

And there were other problems. The vicar at the mining village of Pleasley near Bolsover was distressed by the habit of male teachers at the village school of caning little girls across the hands and shoulders. This misuse of male strength he considered 'positively revolting'. He had written to ask Burke whether he would implore the Duke to use his influence and put a stop to the practice. What upset the Reverend Pyddoke was not just the punishment itself but also the knowledge that it was administered by men because women were unwilling to do it and men were considered 'more expert floggers' than women.

The estate officer at Hardwick also wrote to the Duke informing him that there were staffing problems at the Hall with so many tempted by the competitive wages offered by employers in Sheffield and Derby. The absent Duke received the news that the bricklayers had almost all left already. Burke was further concerned that the much needed revenue from the new admission charge of sixpence was being rapidly exhausted by staff presenting Burke with 'deserving cases'. The rector's daughter was ill with typhoid and Mrs Herrington, the wife of the 'odd man' at the Hall, was dying of diabetes and 'her final wish is to have a small holiday by the sea'. Penrose had agreed to help out. What with one thing and another, he told the Duke, 'We shall all be glad when your term of office in Canada is finished, as no doubt you yourself will be.'

On 31 March the Duke went up to Derbyshire, delighted at first to be there after such a long absence. 'Cannot describe how nice it is to be back here,' he wrote in his diary, although the following morning his mood shifted as he walked round the crumbling garden buildings with Burke. 'It was', he wrote that evening, 'a melancholy scene.' Only a couple of decades earlier forty-six gardeners had been photographed at Chatsworth in front of Paxton's magnificent Conservatory. The wooden struts were now rotten, the hundreds of panels of glass all smashed. The decision was taken to demolish it, but the Duke could not bear to witness the event himself, so the day for demolition was set for 25 May, several weeks after his return to Canada.

Fearing that he might find another set of problems over at Hard-wick, Victor drove the twenty miles to Bess's magnificent sixteenth-century window-rich mansion, enjoying the pleasingly mild and sunny April weather. He was relieved to find Bess's old home 'in wonderfully good order' although he could not imagine the family ever living there again. Back on the Chatsworth estate, he had a meeting with the vicar after church on Sunday to discuss plans for the village war memorial. This was followed by a whole afternoon with Burke. There was so much to do and he anticipated a 'fearful life of difficulties before we get things straight'.

Complicated negotiations for the sale of the London house had been equally problematic, but the six-month long discussions had finally been concluded in the autumn of 1919, when contracts for the takeover were exchanged. A completion date of 25 March was arranged, with six weeks' notice beyond that given for all the con-tents to be removed. The plan was for the house itself to be demolished and for the land beneath it and around it to be devel-oped. The new owners, the famous building firm Holland Hannen & Cubitt, immediately made a further deal with a Mr Sibthorpe, a London property developer, who had a daring scheme for the land that had cost them one million guineas. A complex of sumptuous offices and entertainment facilities was envisaged with a magnificent cinema at the heart of it. Mr Sibthorpe was undaunted by criticism of his intention to get rid of William Kent's building. 'Personally I think the place is an eyesore,' he retorted.

And so the glories of the house remained in place for one last ball on 14 April, the necessitous times making it seem appropriate for guests to pay for their entrance tickets in aid of charity. For one last night a huge marble vase filled with orchids was placed at the bottom of the staircase and Newman's, the British band of the moment, supplied the music. The invitation had requested that guests come dressed in costumes reflecting the period 1760–90. The *Daily Telegraph* recorded the scene as guests arrived dressed in 'powder and patches, tall and nodding plumes above elaborately dressed hair, bro-cades and figured silks and uniforms that had stepped out of family portraits', and the huge rooms filled with music and dancing for the final party.

Princess Alice, Countess of Athlone, balancing a full white wig, was in a costume of pale yellow taffeta bunched up over a petticoat veiled with old lace and festooned with garlands of pink roses on silver ribbon. Lady Cynthia Curzon wore peacock blue taffeta, while some of the French ladies had followed the dress code to the letter, even ensuring that their faces were *poudré*. But in the newspaper's three-column report not a single mention was made of the family from whom the house for a few more days would take its name.

Marriage was in the air. The movie star Mary Pickford had been married to her sometime screen partner Douglas Fairbanks at the end of March and their arrival in London on honeymoon had prompted a riot, as enthusiastic fans crushed her when reaching out to touch the bride's hair at a party given for them in the grounds of the Royal Chelsea Hospital. Her new husband, in the custom of doting newly weds, had to lift her high in the air and carry her to safety.

A week after guests had made their farewell to Devonshire House they were once again invited to dress up for a ducal celebration. The wedding of the Duke's daughter Dorothy to Harold Macmillan on 21 April took place in St Margaret's, Westminster, where many Members of Parliament had married including, twelve years earlier, Winston Churchill and Clementine Hozier. The church was filled with the powerful scent of lilies and orange trees, their branches bending with ripened fruit. Dorothy looked enchanting in cream velvet with garlands of orange blossom encircling her waist, while her eight small attendants wore gowns of periwinkle blue satin, with wreaths of grapes hung on silver bands in their hair.

The Duke was delighted that his mother, who had not been well, was able to attend, albeit in her bath chair. 'She greatly enjoyed herself,' he wrote in his diary that night. He himself had 'spent most of the time with the Queen who was really charming' and the day proved to be one of the happiest of what was turning out to be a predominantly gloomy visit. News of escalating violence in Ireland inspired by the republican movement only added to the Duke's concern. In early April twenty-two offices of the Inland Revenue as well as over a hundred and twenty police stations in Dublin and other cities all over Ireland were burned down, and the anger and determination of the Irish Republican Army showed no signs of abating.

With a sailing date of 2 May and his time in England running out, the Duke went against his own better judgement to 'have a last look at poor old DH'. Hoping that 'the pain will soon pass' he tried to convince himself that 'Although I really could hardly face it, I am glad I managed to have another glimpse at it.' Spotted by a persistent reporter from the *Daily Sketch*, the Duke gave nothing away, but the reporter detected something of the effect the sale of the house was having on its owner. 'Although the ducal expression is scarcely expressive', he told his readers, and 'emotions have never visibly chased each other across the face of any Cavendish', he was in no doubt that during those weeks 'the Duke thought a lot'. His preoccupation with such changes in his life was evident to all.

Only the week before 250 pounds of gelignite was due to be ignited by 450 electric detonators attached to Paxton's magnificent glasshouse in Derbyshire, *The Times* reflected on how properties were changing hands all over England. The newspaper summed up the philosophical and resigned manner in which some of the wealthiest landowners were adjusting to altered circumstances.

> For the most part the sacrifices are made in silence . . . the sons are perhaps lying in far-away graves; the daughters, secretly mourning someone dearer than a brother, have taken up some definite work away from home, seeking thus to still their aching hearts, and the old people, knowing there is no son or near relative left to keep up the old traditions, or so crippled by necessary taxation that they know the boy will never be able to carry on when they are gone, take the irrevocable step.

On the night before Paxton's masterpiece was destroyed, electricians were working up until midnight finishing off the complex wiring of explosives. The story of the imminent explosion had reached the press, and one reporter, anxious for a scoop, wrote up the story without even travelling to Derbyshire. The following morning the published account described how some 'billion' pieces of glass had been scattered about the country. In fact the detonation had utterly failed. The edifice seemed obstinately indestructible. The following day they tried again, but after seven or eight efforts Burke told the Duke that 'Although very high charges were used it had not the slightest effect on the building, the roof remaining quite stationary.'

Poor Burke wondered if perhaps he had made a dreadful mistake. 'I am feeling quite guilty', he wrote to his employer in Canada, 'in having persuaded you to take the building down as if it can stand the terrific charges exploded beneath it, I believe it would have stood up for many years.' To those few people still alive who remembered the day when the glass palace had first gone up, the planned destruction promised to be a near-apocalyptic event. Newspaper editors smelled a front-page story and what Burke termed 'a cinema man' from Sheffield planned to come out to Derbyshire and record the whole sad sequence from ignition to demolition. Burke promised the Duke that if the film was satisfactory he would send a copy out to Canada.

The final week of May had brought unusually warm weather up and down the country, with temperatures of 82 degrees Fahrenheit recorded in London. On Saturday 29 May the inhabitants of the pretty town of Louth in Lincolnshire were getting ready to have tea when a massive storm hit the Lincolnshire Wolds. There was no chance for the moisture to be absorbed into the dry ground and soon the accumulated tons of water rose up into a fourteen-foot wave engulfing the River Ludd. All six bridges straddling the river were instantly destroyed by the tremendous torrent and the townspeople were given no warning before being swept up in the terrifying wall of water. One mother watched as her three children clung to the bacon hook in the kitchen. Soon their young arms gave way and they drowned in front of her. Twenty-three deaths were recorded that day and a thousand people were left homeless as, according to one survivor, houses were 'swept away like sandcastles'.

Over in Derbyshire the weather had been equally bad and on top of the Louth catastrophe, Burke had little news in his weekly letter with which to cheer the Duke. Thousands of young grouse had been drowned in the recent storms and 'one of the estate painters – old Hulley who lives in Edensor village' – had fallen very badly from a cart and severely injured his spine. 'The doctor is hopeful he may recover sufficiently,' Burke reported, but acknowledged that at the age of 68 there was no great hope that he would.

Meanwhile Burke had heard on the grapevine from London that the new owners of Devonshire House were still flirting with the idea of keeping the house intact and turning it into a luxury hotel. And he did have one good thing to tell the Duke. Earlier in the summer Lionel Earle, His Majesty's Officer of Works at Westminster, had been in touch with the Duke about the possibility of acquiring the Devonshire House entrance gates and using them on the opposite side of Piccadilly at the entrance to Green Park. He had offered £1,500. The Duke however was determined to hold out for a little more. Shrewsbury School had also been interested in buying them as a war memorial, although it was made clear that they could not afford 'a fancy price'. Burke now confirmed that the King would be pleased to erect the gates in Green Park and that His Majesty's Officer of Works would give the Duke £2,000 for the gates and pillars.

Back in Derbyshire the demolition plans had continued to go badly. The Conservatory had been built so carefully and solidly that all attempts to blow it up had failed to make an impact and the 'film man' gave up and went back to Sheffield. However, before he left he had managed to record some of the early attempts at detonation and on Tuesday 22 June Burke wrote from the estate office that he was sending the Duke a film of the failure to destroy the Great House.

One of the saddest witnesses that day was Paxton's own great-grandson, Sir Charles Markham. After demobilisation from the Life Guards, Sir Charles had spent a brief but notable period in the diplomatic service in Russia and Cairo before returning home to manage the huge fortune inherited from his father's coal-mining business in Derbyshire. He had made enough money to relieve another Duke of one of the many properties he too was selling to limit post-war expenses. Charlie bought Longford Hall from the Earl of Leicester in the very summer that he was asked to bring various pieces of apparatus over to Chatsworth to help destroy his grandfather's creation.

'Another heavy charge' was placed later that same evening and finally the whole roof caved in. The 'film man' was persuaded to return to take some photographs that he cleverly incorporated into his film. Shortly after the detonation a visitor to Chatsworth, amazed by the sight of the coconut palm with 'its head peering almost to the lofty arched roof', had watched as the plants withered and the Conservatory 'became a house of death'. He had stood in the rain looking with deep sadness at

> a dismal expanse of debris stretching away from my feet to where tall trees swayed down as if to hide the spectacle . . . Great iron pillars snapped in several places littered the ground. Thick baulks of timber, split and shivered, sprawled about. Over the turf was spread a glittering carpet of broken glass.

The violence of the final explosion forced one shard of iron to be carried through the courtyard of the house itself, shattering a windowpane and embedding itself in the tooled leather spine of a volume of Martius' *Flora Braziliensis*.

Burke stood the following day with an old man who had known the Great House for most of his life. They agreed that the disappearance of something quite so lovely was a calamity. The Chatsworth Conservatory that had brought light and warmth to living things had suffered and had died, another casualty of the war.

16

Hope

High Summer 1920

With her tumbling 'mass of chestnut hair' which, when unpinned, reached down to her waist, Ottoline Morrell reminded Osbert Sitwell of 'a rather over-lifesize Infanta of Spain'. But admiring comments on the drama of her appearance were no comfort to Ottoline. For several years she had slept alone in her schoolgirl-narrow bed at home at Garsington Manor. She was feeling increasingly lonely.

Two years earlier her husband Philip, a former Liberal Member of Parliament, had confessed to her in an agonising scene of remorse that he was 'dying of grief'. To his wife's distress he told her that within the next few months both his secretary and Ottoline's own personal maid were to have babies. Philip was the father of them both. This news had not surprised her as much as it might. Guests had been in the middle of a wartime dinner when the husband of the much loved Garsington housemaid burst into the room with a gun and threatened to shoot Philip. Ottoline wrote an agonised letter to her husband. He did not open it. The subject was confined to conspiratorial silence. Philip's political career had to be protected and besides, as Ottoline reminded herself in her diary, 'It does not do to show one is unhappy. People don't like one.' They never discussed the incident with others or between themselves. But the humiliation and betrayal had banished all thought of conjugal intimacy.

Ottoline's love affair with the philosopher Bertrand Russell had ended in 1916 when Bertie had fallen in love with a beautiful 20-year-old actress, and Ottoline missed the 'most divine' physical intimacy that the relationship had on occasion brought her. For a while she had clung, not always with dignity, to her friendship with Siegfried Sassoon. He had left the sanctuary of William Rivers's hospital at Craiglockhart, and she fancied herself in love with him. His feelings for her, although affectionate, were not what Ottoline was seeking.

The day before the Armistice she had greeted Sassoon at the large front door, a bright peacock feather in her hand, her delicate musky scent inescapable. Bach's music had filled the grey-painted hall, swirling round its pinkish-red curtains and the house smelled deliciously of incense and baskets of spicy oranges, their colour disguised beneath a skein of cloves. An invisible but all-pervasive mist had floated in from outside, clouding for a moment the ground-floor rooms, where the oak panelling had itself been painted 'a dark peacock-blue green'.

But Ottoline had found Sassoon in a highly nervous condition, talking incessantly and jumping from one subject to another 'He cannot concentrate his mind, stammers, and then dashes on all about himself,' she later wrote in her diary. She found him to be 'spoiled and his head very swelled'. In what Virginia Woolf called 'her queer nasal moan' used when upset, she announced that she never wanted to see Sassoon again, finding him 'so coarse, so ordinary' and so changed from the young man she had first met two years before.

The cost of running Garsington and entertaining all her friends had accelerated. The contributions made by its two full-time lodgers, the painters Mark Gertler and Dorothy Brett, were not enough to cover their upkeep but Ottoline did not press them for more. She never refused self-invited guests even though sometimes she confided to her diary that their presence depressed or discomforted her – 'I imagine them having dirty underclothes,' she wrote, and as a result she felt 'contaminated and damp'.

And yet she pronounced herself 'sick of the eternal money question' which 'weighs us down for ever'. 'We are ruined,' Philip told her as she went one more time to her jewellery box. This time, the most precious of all the jewels her mother had given her, 'the French crown jewel necklace', went under the hammer at Christie's. Ottoline was unsentimental about the sale. Just as she was unconcerned about eating a bun that had fallen on the floor (however dusty, it was there to give sustenance) so necklaces were there to bring in cash. A quarter of a century earlier, her mother had paid £500 for it, and this time the pearl necklace that had once belonged to Marie Antoinette netted her £1,300, which helped pay off some of the farm's debts. For now, Ottoline reasoned, she would far rather relinquish a jewel and be certain of remaining at Garsington. The bright vibrancy of its garden seemed to her 'a miracle of beauty', especially 'the long nasturtium border and along by it a double row of zinnias and behind them the asters and behind that the sun-flowers and some apricot roses coming up between'.

Money worries diminished in importance, however, when Otto-line allowed herself to dwell on her physical appearance. She was aware that she had developed 'an obsession with my own ugliness' and Brett had given her cold comfort when she cheerily dismissed her friend's looks as 'not so bad'. The psoriasis that Ottoline had suf-fered from for much of her life was becoming 'horribly depressing' and there were times when she felt as if 'every little pore is a possible spot'. Augustus John had recently finished a portrait of her for which she had dressed in a flamboyant black hat and a black silk dress which although dramatic had the unfortunate effect of flattening her bosom and eliminating much of her femininity. While she thought the top half of her face looked 'fine and tragic and like me' she was disappointed by everything from the nose downwards: 'the mouth is too open', she thought, 'and indefinite as if I was washing my teeth and all the foam was on my mouth.' Ottoline watched Virginia enviously, looking 'exquisite with her lovely lip and nose', although disappointed that Virginia 'has no ordinary human feelings at all. If one draws near to her and kisses her one finds nothing, nothing, no response at all, no drawing near, only delicate aloofness pushing away.' Perhaps the psoriasis repelled Virginia; that month the skin disease had erupted all over Ottoline's powdered face.

She tried to alter her appearance. She cut off her long hair which when short became thicker and curlier. And she went one step further. She dyed it bright red. She experimented with wearing dif-ferent fabrics as a means of cheering herself up, rejecting anything in wool, preferring silk and feeling more confident in things 'slip-pery and light'.

Her diary was her confessional although she was doubtful that the pages would ever be filled with any deep sense of satisfaction. 'Inside me is always the tossing search,' she wrote, 'to search for the hole in life in which I should naturally fit.' At the back of the leather journal she kept a running list of the books she was reading: the poetry of Dante, Ezra Pound, some Proust, and a novel by a new writer, Rebecca West, a tale of an army officer's homecoming called *The Return of the Soldier.*

T. S. Eliot and his wife Vivien had stayed one weekend and Ottoline immediately felt an empathy with Vivien whom she found to be 'so spontaneous and affectionate' and who, like Ottoline, suffered from migraines and gastric upset. The T at the end of Vivien's surname as she signed it in the visitors' book at the end of the weekend resembled a J with its long, tapering and slightly fragile tail. Ottoline had no interest in any romantic association with Tom, but she was frustrated by her own fear of his intellect and was determined to overcome it. After a 'delightful evening', Ottoline made 'a valiant effort' and invited Eliot upstairs to her book-lined workroom on the first floor of the house. But after they had talked in front of the fireplace, she was not sure how well the conversation had gone. 'He makes me very shy,' she wrote in her diary. 'I feel his mind is so accurate and dissecting and fits in every idea like a Chinese puzzle and my mind is so vague and floating. And I feel he must think me such an ass.'

The crude boorishness of post-war society troubled her. As a supporter of the Sinn Fein movement she had been to a volatile meeting at the Albert Hall where the sight of an old man being dragged out by his neck and another biting a fellow protestor in the leg convinced her that 'truly we are near primitive brutes'. That spring, though, there was an evening of joy for Ottoline, who never failed to be elated by the theatrical, when she heard a recital by the singer Raquel Meller and was enchanted by her 'Spanish, beautiful, liquid melting face and very lovely voice'. For Ottoline she encompassed 'a most absolute expression of poignant romance and feeling'. She told her friends of the beauty of the voice of the woman who by chance bore almost the same name as her mother's adored gamekeeper. On the bus back home she had sat next to a veteran of the Crimean War, a conflict that evoked Ottoline's irrepressible sense of romance. The old soldier told her how once, wounded and lying in a hospital bed, he had received a visit from Florence Nightingale who had bent over and kissed him.

In preparation for the summer Ottoline had indulged herself by buying a lovely new Chinese velvet coat and by having 'two pieces of stuff', one of yellow cloth, the other of grey blue satin, made into dresses at the dressmakers, Victoire. She also ordered a Henry IV-shaped jacket and full skirt in reddish plum satin. She could not really afford it but like Iris, the heroine of Michael Arlen's *Green Hat*, her sense of life's completeness evaded her even in the acquisition of her favourite clothes. 'I love being really rather gorgeous,' she wrote, while admitting that 'it is absurd too and in my other side I am so unhappy at the selfishness of getting so much for myself.'

Clothes and opera singers and friendships with poets were not enough to banish loneliness or to alter the circumstances of the narrow white-sheeted bed. She longed for either silence or the deep intimacy of requited love. She never seemed to have enough time or even patience for her 14-year-old daughter. Julian had whooping cough that May and the noise irritated and unsettled her. Ottoline went alone for a weekend to Underley, a large comfortable house in Cumbria where the 'no-noise velvet pile carpets' brought her a brief interlude of cherished quiet.

In June 1920 Ottoline pasted a photograph on to the blank page opposite her entwined initials. She wrote two words: 'summer' and 'Garsington' beneath the picture. The photograph had been taken in the sealing-wax red panelled Red Room. In the picture Mark Gertler, the ever-present Garsington lodger, sits beside her, half invisible inside the huge fireplace, boyish, curly headed. Standing next to her is T. S. Eliot, whose signature in Ottoline's visitors' book had become almost as frequent as that of Lytton Strachey. Eliot, large nosed, in tweed jacket and pale trousers, a book tucked under his arm, is looking down at Ottoline in her floor-length satin dress, from beneath which protrude her high-heeled, tightly laced shoes. She beams up at him from her seat in a high armchair in evident admiration.

That summer Ottoline's lawns at Garsington, stretching out into the Oxfordshire countryside to the water meadows beyond, were patterned with the yellow dapple of buttercups and cowslips. They seemed more crowded than ever with dons and students from nearby Oxford and the owners of the smartest local country houses. The notoriety surrounding both the lovely grey manor house and the hostess (whose large nose reminded small boys of a witch) meant that invitations to visit were contrived on the flimsiest of introductions. One neighbour, Margot Asquith, wife of the former prime minister, who lived at The Wharf, Sutton Courtenay, treated Garsington as a place of entertainment for her own guests, arriving – so one undergraduate, David Cecil, observed – with a medley of companions who ranged from 'international tycoons and foreign ambassadors to out of work actors and schoolboys on holiday'. They would spread themselves out beneath the branches of the holm oak that Aldous Huxley thought 'resembled a great wooden octopus'. Walking among them was their hostess with her 'antique irregular stones like childish molars' (Cecil again), the triple strand of pearls as ever at her neck, as she 'maintained an air of patrician detachment and an enigmatic gleam in her strange eyes'.

When the outside guests had gone home, Ottoline would exchange her ankle-gathered trousers and Grecian crêpe de Chine blouses for a 'pink maillot and peplum-style tunic in rainbow colours'. Dressed in this way she would descend into what Carrington called 'that cesspool of slime', the pond in which the Garsington guests all swam although the cowman had drowned in it and a huge black boar had once tumbled into its stinking fetid water.

A new employee, a young stonemason called Lionel Gomme, had come to help with some terracing in the garden. Lionel lived in the village with a famously intimidating and jealous foster-mother. His chief passions in life were football and cars. But he was a countryman, a child of nature, able to recognise every species of butterfly and to give a name to the tiniest beetle. He was 26. Ottoline was twenty-one years older. On 5 June, a day or two after he had begun work, Ottoline left her slim white bed and moved across to the open window of her bedroom. Below her in the sunshine she watched as, half kneeling, he began to form a new terrace, his shirtsleeves rolled right up to his elbows, his hands dripping with the sticky wet plaster that he was gently smoothing with a small trowel on to the grey Oxfordshire stone.

A few days later Ottoline brought out her camera and took a picture of the young man, hatless and wearing dungarees, holding her own pug and with a broad open-mouthed smile directed straight at the photographer. She stuck two of the photographs into the body of her diary. That evening she wrote her first impressions of this 'very remarkable boy' with whom she had not yet exchanged a word. He had 'a very intelligent face – and extremely beautiful'. What is more he looked 'like a poeT' – Ottoline's long and satisfied stroke to the T travelling fully, as if exhaled, along the whole length of the word.

She was apprehensive, however, reminding herself that 'the superficial talk that men get from living with uneducated men is such a barrier'. Though certain of the young man's intelligence, she feared he was unused to conversing much with anyone outside his work. For a brief moment also, she was doubtful whether she had the ability to attract him. Four days later she just happened to arrange to be outside in the garden, painting a metal seat a blue-green colour, while conveniently nearby 'my beautiful boy' was making a base for a statue. She was baffled at how to break through their mutual shyness. She knew not only that she needed to gain his trust but that she wanted to 'inspire and help him'.

In her diary she wrote down a further ambition, but on second thoughts crossed it out, at first with two firm strokes and then for double security with a neat dense coil of inky barbed wire. Ottoline was 47 but the jottings might as well have been those of a 16 year old. She was astonished and giddy with the realisation that she had fallen totally and all-consumingly in love. Over the next few weeks she gradually found the courage to talk to this beautiful young man, in her voice that could be at once emphatic and sing-song and which Bertrand Russell had described as 'very beautiful, gentle, vibrant'.

She began to call the object of her fascination by the name he had been known by in his family for most of his life: Tiger. One day at the end of the month she took Tiger into Oxford to show him the colleges, and two days later he came to her room, and took her hand in gratitude. He told her, she remembered later that night, that 'he felt I was a friend'. Ottoline's girlish delight in this new friendship and Tiger's evident response to these flattering attentions by his extraordinary employer began to dissolve barriers. The only obstacle remaining to its further development, Ottoline felt, was that 'I am old and he is young'.

In early July England's bishops were meeting at Lambeth Palace for the conference held roughly every ten years to discuss and assess the religious and moral state of the country. As well as issuing an official rejection of Christian Science, spiritualism and theosophy, all of which had done their part to shore up the ruins of many fragmented English souls, the conference came down firmly in defence of the underlying purpose of marriage and of the physical union between two adults. Not only was 'an emphatic warning' issued against any unnatural means taken for the avoidance of conception, but the Christian population of the country was reminded of 'the paramount importance in married life of deliberate and thoughtful self-control'.

In the same month, hungry for sunshine after the disappointingly chilly June, Ottoline went to Italy with Henry Lamb and Walter Sickert, confiding to her diary her by now consuming thoughts of the football-loving stonemason and the 'unexpected thrills' she received just by talking to him. She had seen 'a good deal' of him in the weeks before her holiday, boasting to herself privately that 'He is athletic, and loves games and sports and all sorts of manly things and then besides he has The Poetic Love of Nature.'

But Tiger had clearly given the prospect of taking his relationship further some thought and on her return he put up a polite but firm resistance to Ottoline's seduction techniques. All through the summer months Ottoline wavered between excitement at the smallest sign of encouragement from him and flat despondency when he pulled back. In the middle of August she wrote in the diary that he 'fades away and eludes one more and more – as usual I frighten'. She tried to justify his behaviour. 'He is afraid I think of the undiscovered country inside himself.' The gulf in their different backgrounds seemed insuperable. 'His loyalty to his comrades . . . makes him from self-preservation shy off from me', and then in a pang of self-pity she cried, 'I give and give and never receive.'

As the long summer days began to shorten it seemed that there would be no question of Ottoline and Tiger overcoming the barriers that prevented what Tom Mitford and his five sisters referred to as 'doing bodies'.

In the southernmost part of the country another woman was at last beginning to emerge from the reverberating effects of the war. Edna Clarke Hall was known to Ottoline, not as a Garsington guest but as someone with whose utterly lovely face, albeit on canvas, Otto-line was familiar. Before the war, Ottoline had a short but loving affair with the exuberant artist Augustus John. For £40 he had sold her a portrait of a beautiful young woman, a contemporary and friend at the Slade of his sister Gwen. Edna had dearly wanted to buy the picture for herself. It showed, as she described it: 'The figure on a cliff with bright green grass full of wild flowers and the sea . . . blue but dark and the sky almost gloomy . . . the face is turned full to the sky but the eyes are all closed. I feel proud and glad to have inspired him to paint it.' The spirit of freedom in the painting was the spirit that Edna had yearned to capture for herself. But without money to buy the painting, it was left to Ottoline to become the owner. She named the picture with the upturned head and raised arms *Nirvana*.

Edna was feeling trapped by the man she had married. Like Ottoline, she longed for some physical expression of affection. William Clarke Hall was thirteen years older than Edna and their marriage had come about in circumstances that made the confused adolescent Edna wonder whether she loved him or not. William was the leading barrister for the National Society for the Prevention of Cruelty to Children, which Edna's father Benjamin Waugh, a former minister of the Church, had helped to found in 1884. A growing awareness of the extent of the neglect and abuse of children within the home had moved Mr Waugh to take steps for their protection.

Willie Clarke Hall was appointed to be barrister to the new organisation. But Willie's interest in young children did not stop at the legal fight he undertook on their behalf. The poet Ernest Dowson, a friend of Willie's, detected that Willie joined him in being 'a devout follower of the most excellent cult of La Fillette'. A love of girl-children by adult men had not been unusual in the late Victorian decades, a proclivity that did not involve lustful intentions but rather a devotion and fascination with preserving virginal innocence. Willie Clarke Hall was mesmerised by these young girls chiefly because they were not, in his word, 'polluted'.

Edna had never forgotten how Willie 'would draw her to his knee, lovingly tease and talk to her' and whisper words of poetry in her ear. He described her as 'the child for whom of all things in the world I care most'. When they first met he was 26 and she was only 13. Within a year Willie had understood her passionate love of painting, and he persuaded Edna's father to allow her to enrol at the Slade. Here, among the easels over which Professor Henry Tonks presided, Edna found happiness. A new, inspiring world opened up in which, despite her protected upbringing, she was surprisingly unperturbed by the challenge of making her own watercolour version of Rubens's *Rape of the Sabine Women*. Mrs Clarke Hall was taken aback to come across her daughter standing on her bed, barely clothed, miming the repelling of seduction. Having posed as the model for her own dramatic picture, Edna won the Slade's coveted Summer Figure Composition Prize.

Edna's great friend Gwen John had introduced her to the painters William Orpen and Ambrose McEvoy and to her own soon-smitten brother, Augustus. But although the eminent painter was, according to young Edna, 'a handful' he desisted from any attempt to seduce this lovely young woman and Edna's gratitude to Willie for helping to give her this new life was enormous. But gratitude was not enough. Willie wanted Edna for himself, and three years later, with the encouragement of her parents, she agreed to become engaged to Willie. In 1898, when she was 19 and he was 32, they were married.

In the legal contract that now bound them, the seductive power of Edna's youthful purity vanished. By sleeping with his wife, as a husband was required to do, Willie himself had destroyed the precious innocence he had loved. His 'immense delight' in 'the constant charm of childhood' would have to be found elsewhere. He lost interest not only in Edna as the child-woman he had pursued but also, and perhaps more importantly, in Edna as the artist, whose talent he had once encouraged.

Within the first few months of their marriage Edna began to feel as if she had been abandoned. 'I was left standing like a confused child by an unkindness I could not interpret.' She rapidly fell into a deep depression, feeling herself to be 'in space, sick with desire for a near intimate touch'. Her regard for her own work was by then so diminished that she would sweep her paintings from the floor into a corner with a broom. Gradually she started to paint in secret as if her creativity was a shameful thing she needed to conceal. She could not bear Willie's antagonism to her art.

But if Edna had something to hide, so did her husband. Friends and family knew about the coldness of Willie's behaviour and did not like it. Furthermore the family thought that his search for uncomplicated emotional and physical pleasure meant that he 'pursued his way a bit too much'. They thought he should have 'restrained' himself and hoped Edna was unaware of her husband's infidelities. But she knew all too well.

During the war Edna had developed an abhorrence of the 'organised hatred' that summed up the conflict for her. The distress affected her ability to paint, but under the influence of a new friendship words for a while became her chief creative currency. The writer Edward Thomas was billeted at the army training camp at Hare Hall in Essex near the Clarkes' new home, Great House at Upminster Common. Marriage had been a disappointment to them both and for eight brief but precious months Edna and Edward drew towards each other in an intimacy and companionship that had been missing from both their lives. They walked for hours through the fields and woods and along the lanes together, talking about the natural beauty of things that mattered to them both. And Edna fell in love with him.

Edward made Edna feel like a woman embarking on the beginnings of a love affair for the first time. Every small gesture filled her with excitement. And one evening she asked him to her studio, filled with 'heather and flowering reeds – candles, pens'. They stood together 'by the open garden door with the darkness beyond' as she read him the poem that she had finished writing only moments before. The ink was still wet on the page. 'He became curiously tender and drew me lightly to him as I stood there and felt me trembling.' He pronounced the poem 'quite beautiful', then pulled her closer and, she remembered later, 'leaned his face against my breast'. They stood in silence, 'the silence so eloquent there was no need of further speech'.

These moments, the sensibilities of two artists meeting in silence and alone, became the riches of Edna's life. And when one morning he arrived at her house and embraced her, she wrote some lines expressing her gratitude.

I did my best
The clothes they were neat pressed;
The hour was early
Even my pinafore was blue
And in the sun stood you;
Your kiss took me to heaven!

Edward left one day in August 1916 smelling of what his wife Helen called 'that queer sour smell of khaki'. Nine months later, on 9 April 1917, he was killed at Arras.

Almost a year after Thomas's death Edna was still protesting in her diary at the cruel way that dreams can make death seem an illusion: 'I forgot you had died and were hid in a grave. I do not believe you are hid in a grave, for you came to me then gave to me more than I can ever return unto you till I die.' His death triggered a long-repressed nervous breakdown. She tried at first 'her very best' to master the onset, spending one afternoon painting a frantic grief-induced series of forty drawings 'relating to life at sea and life at Great House, all intimate and vivid'. During those few heady hours Edna was 'urged on by a divine madness almost as if I had died'. When she showed the paintings to her old professor from the Slade, Henry Tonks, he pronounced them to be 'little gems all of them'.

But Willie had insisted that Edna and her younger son Denis go further into the countryside to escape the bombs that were now falling on London and that were threatening the surrounding counties. Isolated from her much loved sisters, and separated from her elder son Justin, who was away at boarding school, Edna felt waves of guilt and loneliness sweep over her. Edna knew Willie was 'just, wise and very kind'; she was aware too that the compassion he showed towards the troubled children under his care impressed all those who knew him. But he denied her the intimacy she longed for. By some queer misfortune the reverse of his double-sided nature was the side he showed to Edna. She was only one of thousands of women who envied those who had loved their dead husbands. For them even death could not take away the memory of their love, whereas the reality of a living but unloving husband was inescapably painful.

After the intense strain of concealing a sadness that sometimes possessed her 'for weeks with hardly a break', she descended into a state of mind 'akin to those who plunge shocking live razors and carving knives into their gizzards'. Only her own poetry prevented her from some ultimate act of madness. In these lines the whole range of emotions finds expression. Sometimes she wrote in anger, sometimes in despair, occasionally with nostalgia for the love her husband had shown her when she was a child, always with the immediacy and spontaneity that she had used in her paintings. Although she was not using paint to express herself, her love of colour and image spilled into her written words:

> The sense of colour is my wealth,
> With careless loveliness it lies
> Cast on the chair, or on the shelf,
> Above the hearth to lift my eyes;
>
> In earthen jug, in cloak of blue,
> In sober brown of cupboard door,
> In time-stained walls of pallid hue
> And sunlit grey of boarded floor.

At Tonks's urging she agreed to see Henry Head, a close friend and colleague of the Craiglockhart doctor, William Rivers, and the same portly, friendly psychiatrist who had once tried to help Virginia Woolf with her episodes of mental collapse. Head's compassionate recognition of her loneliness helped Edna recover. 'His profound interest in the psychological aspect of my painting and poetry in relation to experience, and his deep sympathy and understanding of the intricacies and the subtle things that matter in that experience were worth much to me,' she wrote in gratitude. At his suggestion she spoke to Willie and persuaded him that her mental well-being would benefit from a room or a place of her own in which to paint.

In the summer, with Willie's blessing, Edna and Denis went alone to their cottage on the Cornish coast. Denis was ten years old and between schools. His brother Justin was to join them later. For Denis, the journey itself was entirely thrilling and he later recorded the familiar adventure in detail. The trunks were weighed at Paddington and labels were then stuck in the top of the trunk stating the destination in large letters. At the same time the flame-licking firebox, a monstrous insatiable engine painted in gleaming green, with fittings in brass and steel, was being stoked prior to departure as Denis climbed into the brown and cream carriage with his mother. He hung out of the window for as much of the long journey as his mother would allow, wiping from his eyes the smuts that were carried down the length of the train from the engine. But things got even better when 'the real excitement started with the Exe estuary, the red cliffs and the red deserted beaches of Dawlish'. The journey was not yet over as the Clarke Hall carriage was disconnected from the body of the train and pulled by a small tank engine up the hill, through the country-side and over the 'rickety timber bridge' towards Helston.

There a pony and carriage was waiting to carry the family 'along narrow granite lanes between stone walls and hedges and verges covered with wild flowers'. At one moment at the top of a hill, the horses paused panting at the exertion, while Edna and Denis caught their own breath. For there, glimpsed for a tantalising moment between the fields, was the gleaming open sea, before it vanished again behind the curve of the hill. Eventually they were down on the shore, their cottage only a pebble's skim from the water's edge. And there was Willie's sailing boat, waiting to carry them out to sea.

Willie had taught his young sons to be confident sailors. As the summer warmth began to plump out the air, Denis would spend his days in the dinghy 'rowing out to sea trailing for mackerel, sometimes from dawn to dusk, rowing for hours, going miles out until the land appeared a haze'. His mother's trust in his safe return was absolute, even after he came back one evening to tell her that he had broken an oar and had pulled up a floorboard in order to row himself home. Being alone in the water did not scare him. In fact, he recorded that 'isolation at sea' fascinated him and he would spend all day, totally naked, the boat bobbing over the waves, his clothes stashed under the seat to keep them dry.

One day his solitariness was interrupted when he spotted an old man with a bald head and a whiskery face swimming along near him in the open sea. As Denis rowed cautiously nearer the ancient figure, it suddenly vanished. Whether it was a walrus, a seal, or some mysterious gentleman from the bottom of the ocean who had not been expecting human company, Denis never knew. Anchoring off Nare Point, he would let down his line, and fall asleep knowing that the boat would rock and wake him the moment he got a bite. Hauling up a resistant conger into the boat meant that he occasionally ended up flat on his back. But he loved bringing home the catch for his mother to cook for supper. One day at anchor he heard a loud drumming and saw the clear dark blue water turning a deep black. All around him silver flashes were moving on the surface of the water. Entranced, he realised 'I was in the middle of a shoal of surfacing mackerel.' The unpredictable magic of the sea never failed to disappoint.

During the final years of the war it had been Edna's habit to record the children's daily activities in her diary in the smallest detail. She had recorded the day Denis came into the kitchen with cabbage leaves covered in caterpillars; she had recorded her visit to the boys' school where she was appalled by the art teacher who told her that she could not get the children to draw Bo Peep 'properly'. She had recorded Denis telling her on the final Easter Day of the war, 'It will not be a happy Easter in Germany or Austria or Italy or France or England or in fact in the whole world – nobody is so happy as before the war – even children!' Edward Thomas had been killed a year earlier, on Easter Monday.

Now, as the memory of the war began slowly to recede, she recorded the detail of her children's lives on canvas. Justin had joined them for the school holidays, and throughout those summer months Edna drew their seaside life, dashing off her crayoned drawings almost as if she had an accelerating device on a camera. In dozens of watercolour and coloured pencil images she caught the speed and constant movement of a child's daily activity in scene after scene, as the boys fished, swam, lay in the sun at Gillian Creek or stood on the top of the cliffs, pummelled by the wind. She drew them as they peered over into rock pools, in red shirts looking out at the sea from the dinghy, in blue shirts staring at sunlight flickering over the shallow pools. She painted them with tenderness but without sentimentality. There were pictures of Denis in the dinghy, of both boys on *Lorna Doone*, the half-decked sloop, of Denis with his lobster pots and of Justin leaning over the gunwale. There were pictures of the boys together, in the cottage eating an apple or by the sea, filling the hours with all the absorption of small boys fascinated with the drift and swell around them and with the abandoned riches that lay scattered on the shore.

> Feather or shell or it may be
> The white bleached wood cast up from the sea,
> A smooth fine stone, blue glass or a flower,
> Gathered and loved in an idle hour.

The habits of that holiday were as simple and uncluttered as the drawings. Wearing a sleeveless dress, graceful and bare-legged among the nettles, Edna hung the washing out to dry, singing as she did so in her pretty voice, fetched water from the well before sitting round the kitchen table drinking tea out of unmatched cups, or having lunch at funny hours, free to do so without the critical scrutiny of Willie to inhibit her. And she began to get well.

17

Trust

Early Autumn 1920

The summer was over having once again brought triumph for France on the grass courts of Wimbledon. Last year's 20-year-old champion Suzanne Lenglen had won the women's singles trophy for the second year running in a skirt apparently several yards shorter than the preceding summer. Now the autumn with the inevitable echoes of a new school term brought new beginnings.

Mrs Roberts had managed the family grocery shop in Salford since the war, and had saved £100 cash in the bank. The shop itself she estimated to be worth another £450 and with this money she hoped to leave the impoverished streets of her neighbourhood and move to her dream house near a park and within walking distance of a library. She hoped to find a place with a small garden, and to have 'a few decent years' with her family. This thought gave her 'courage to go on'.

Ottoline was savouring her own victory. Despite the lengths she went to keep her feelings discreet and at least outwardly disguised, her friends noticed a new effervescence about her. Ottoline and Tiger had at last consummated their love. In her diary she wrote without fear or shame, 'I have loved to give – now I am allowed to receive. It is a miracle.'

D. H. Lawrence and Frieda Lawrence had once been frequent Garsington guests, and in the huge gloomy spare room with its sloping floor and its view over the courtyard at the front of the house darkened by the high yew hedge, ornaments were thrown in tempestuous arguments audible throughout the house. Husband and wife would reappear downstairs and, according to their discomforted hostess, 'sit about with their arms around each other's necks'. The novelist Katherine Mansfield had described Frieda to Ottoline as 'that immense German Christmas pudding'. But Ottoline no longer spoke to Lawrence. She had learned through friends of his impending betrayal of her in the character of Hermione Roddice in his new novel *Women in Love*, due to be published in New York in November.

Mark Gertler, delighted by the happy transformation in his previously dejected hostess, was friendly with that other Garsington regular, Dorothy Brett, who in turn remained friendly with Lawrence. Rumours that Ottoline was sleeping with the gardener had reached the novelist who had not forgotten the Baroness Bolsover (Ottoline's mother) and her deep but platonic affection for the Bolsover estate gamekeeper. Nor had he forgotten what the gamekeeper was called. Mellors might be an excellent name for a fictional character, he thought. But Ottoline was writing her own true version of events and asked 'whoever reads this in years to come' that they should not 'mock or laugh'.

One other relationship appeared to have reached a resolution that summer. After nearly two years of an existence powered by intense sexual passion, Violet Trefusis had been forced to relinquish her lover. Vita Sackville-West had returned to her husband Harold Nicolson and to her two small boys, Ben and Nigel. The French soldier's uniform, including the fake blood-stained bandage worn by Vita during the war, had been packed away in a trunk in the attic at her home in Kent. Vita and Violet had not once been recognised as they walked in disguise, arms entwined lover-like, through the streets of Piccadilly. Harold, who had retrieved his wife by following the two women in a biplane to a hotel room in Amiens, hoped the affair was well and truly finished. It had nearly destroyed his sanity.

The mental health of Sir Arthur Conan Doyle was, however, of growing concern to friends, critics and the public in general, who were convinced that he was still living firmly in his fictional world when he began work on a piece for the *Strand* magazine about the nature of fairies. On examining some photographs of two girls playing with winged sprites at a waterfall in Cottingly in Yorkshire, he considered them 'remarkable'. Others considered that the pictures were clever but demonstrable fakes and that Conan Doyle was slightly mad.

Diana Cooper was looking forward to the autumn. During the summer she had spent many weekends convalescing at her aunt Norah Lindsay's house at Sutton Courtenay in Berkshire. Here Diana could almost recapture the feeling of life before the war when her aunt would dress in tinsel and leopard skin. At last the constant pain in Diana's damaged leg was beginning to ease, and she and Duff had found a new house in Bloomsbury's Gower Street. Duff's warning that excessive use of morphine might damage her looks had been enough of a deterrent to keep her use of the drug within safe limits. And there was an alternative. Alcohol, the socially acceptable anaes-thetic, was equally effective in numbing pain, fear and lingering grief.

The Coopers were always short of money and Diana's face, unlike the poor plain dairymaid at Belvoir, as Diana had once observed, was indeed her fortune. A £12,000 offer from a movie producer for a small part in *The Glorious Adventure: A Restoration Melodrama* would hopefully lead to a lucrative career in the cinema. The war had also left Diana with a growing terror of illness. In July a hardness in her breast convinced her that she was dying of cancer. Despite her doctors' assurance that there was nothing to worry about, Diana's almost hysterical anxiety was only tempered when the King of Spain made an extravagant pass at her at a dance given by the Earl of Pembroke, thus confirming to Diana that her looks were firmly intact. All further thoughts of cancer left her head.

As trust in healing and in a more permanent future began to settle on the country, people were starting to lay plans. Gabrielle Chanel began to investigate whether she could create a distinctive bottled scent with a subtlety that would produce an entire evening's worth of evaporation. Chanel deplored the harsh intensity of existing per-fumes that began the night with an engulfing strength before vanishing within an hour of application.

Nick La Rocca, the curly-haired, shoulder-shrugging sensation of the Original Dixieland Jazz Band, was preparing to return to America. He felt he had had a lucky escape. In between playing engagements at the Hammersmith Palais de Danse he was rumoured to have found romance with innumerable English lovelies, but on the day of his departure, 8 July, he had been alarmed to see the furious face of Lord Harrington, the father of one of the loveliest ladies of all, chasing him down the Southampton boardwalk, a loaded shotgun in hand, shuddering with rage at every step he took.

Death, the war and the call to arms were all beginning to feel a little more distant. On 9 June the King had opened the Imperial War Museum at Crystal Palace, mainly staffed by ex-servicemen, where John Singer Sargent's huge and horrifyingly evocative painting *Gassed* had been hung in a prominent position near portraits by William Orpen of Earl Haig and Marshal Foch. A museum, not a current newspaper was the proper place for it now.

Harold Gillies was still looking to bring hope to the damaged. After completing thousands of facial operations over the last few years, he had left Sidcup in the summer. He was delighted by the Government's recent decision to give the full disability allowance for 'very severe facial disfigurement': the same sum given to those who had either lost two limbs or a limb and an eye, or suffered total paralysis. He was already feeling some nostalgia for the beautiful grounds at Sidcup where he would often relax by sketching his own watercolours. He had been happy in that place, practising his golf swings in the corridors between the aisles of beds. In order to recover from three years of intensively draining work, he was spending time with his wife Kathleen in a small cottage at Hothfield near Maidstone in the Weald of Kent. There he had been writing a medical textbook and in the afternoons he would fish, coming to know 'the wonder of the mayfly, nightingale and nightjar'.

Earlier in the year Gillies had been staying at a hotel in Yorkshire and happened to notice that the chambermaid had a disturbingly malformed nose. Leaving the page proofs of his book on the desk in his room open at the pages in which he described the ways in which he could improve noses, he went downstairs for dinner, leaving the room empty for the chambermaid to come and turn down his bed. A few weeks later he was not surprised to see her standing in front of him in his consulting rooms.

His awareness of the distress caused by deformity went well beyond the urgent cases on which his efforts had been concentrated for the last four years. Cleft palates, harelips, car accidents, birthmarks, and even botched attempts at plastic surgery made lives miserable, as he well recognised: 'the link between the psyche and the surgeon becomes more and more evident'. An amazing variety of cases came to his surgery for help. A woman, who had breasts that hung huge 'like vegetable marrows' right down to her waist, had never felt able to swim or even to dare to dance with a boy in case his arm encountered the pendulous growth. Gillies removed the equivalent in weight to four large sacks of flour and his infinitely lighter, more agile and happier patient was married within months. A factory worker whose glorious long hair had been caught in a machine was scalped so severely that 'a red Indian could not have done it more thoroughly'. She was provided with a new forehead after Gillies used his miraculous pedicle technique, unrolling the new flap of skin 'like a carpet being laid'. To the amazement of her colleagues she was back at work within weeks of leaving hospital.

He dealt with burns, with injuries from dog bites and injuries incurred during boxing matches. One woman who had been badly burned in a car accident allowed Gillies to persuade her husband to donate the skin from his bottom to make the necessary large graft possible. The husband took great pleasure in telling Gillies that whenever his mother-in-law kissed her daughter goodbye he felt as if he was 'getting his own back'.

But even Gillies, who had seen almost every variety of physical deformity, was challenged when a housemaid arrived in his consulting rooms and 'crossed the room with great lumbering strides and vaulted on to the couch like a rugby player'. Since entering service at the age of 15 this unfortunate woman had always been acutely embarrassed when undressing in front of the other maids, and became bewildered when she found herself head over heels in love with the laundry maid. Gillies's examination revealed that she was suffering from hypospadias: the ambivalent appearance of her genitals had meant that she was wrongly identified at birth as a girl. Under Gillies's surgical guidance she became the muscular husband of a farmer's daughter.

Interventions in nature's handiwork were on the advance and Gillies was fascinated by the news that Serge Voranov, a Russian-French surgeon, had on 12 June successfully infused a few youth-endowing slithers from a baboon's testicles into the tissue of a human scrotum. Meanwhile the 424 pages of the book with 844 often frightening and detailed illustrations that Gillies had been working on was complete and *Plastic Surgery of the Face* was published at a price tag of three guineas. Immediately it became the authoritative text and doctors expected no more comprehensive book on the subject to be written in their lifetime. The *British Medical Journal* had 'no hesitation in saying that this is one of the most notable contributions made to surgical literature today'.

On 27 October 1920 a celebratory dinner was held at the Savoy to mark the centenary of the renowned stationers W. H. Smith, who had maintained a shop in the Strand since 1820. During the sumptuous dinner a letter from Lord Northcliffe was read to the assembled company congratulating the firm on its role in pioneering the 'trading in books and newspapers at railway stations, a system now universal the world over'. Much cheering followed and then Lord Riddell, former proprietor of the *News of the World* and representative of the press barons at the Paris Peace Conference, read a special poem:

> There are gold smiths and silver smiths
> The choice one of the tribe
> There are blacksmiths and white smiths
> Whose arts I can't describe
> There are tin smiths and the smiths of iron shoes
> But the best smiths of all the smiths
> Are the ones that deal in news.

The eulogy brought smiles and tears to the eyes of the toughest tradesman present.

At Oxford, male undergraduates that autumn were steadying themselves for the day when their female counterparts would join them in the Sheldonian Theatre. Women students were to receive their degrees for the first time. Nearly two years after scenes of uncontrolled chaos during which a woman had hitched her skirts above her waist in celebration of the first day of peace, Oxford had grown calm. Winifred Holtby had been startled by the beauty of the city that summer. The exuberant undergraduate, 'superbly tall and vigor-ous as the young Diana with her long straight limbs and golden hair' as her friend Vera Brittain saw her, had missed the ancient stone buildings and the hidden courtyards. She had missed the delicious sense of mystery and privilege in pushing open the small wooden doors set within the large college gates, and stepping over the thresh-old into the perfect grassy quadrangles beyond. Winifred had interrupted her studies at Somerville in 1918 to spend a year in a signals unit crammed into a hut at Abbeville in France; she was delighting once again in the contrasting freedom and space that she had found on returning to Oxford in the autumn of 1919 to com-plete her history course. This last summer the buttercups had been so prolific she had never seen the like and the whole city seemed affected by the brightness of the season.

She had been sharply aware of the rhythm of the academic year, enjoying 'burlesques and school discipline and Dostoevsky and porridge' in the spring, when 'the air is frosty and the road is dry', and moving on to the matchless exhilaration that fills an Oxford undergraduate's summer days. Against a background of champagne and punts, love and poetry, anything that life, glorious life might offer seemed within her grasp. Winifred had heard some exceptional lectures during the Trinity term. The poets Hilaire Belloc and Laurence Binyon had come to the University to speak about the business of writing poetry and plays, but it was the talk on the craft of the short story given by John Masefield, the Poet Laureate, that Winifred had enjoyed most. In fact it was the best talk she had ever heard. The Schools hall where he spoke was 'crowded from end to end'. Admission was by tickets, so coveted that they quickly sold out, resulting in more cheating than 'in a card sharper's den'. The lucky seated undergraduates, including Winifred, were delighted by Masefield's 'charming personality' and his 'glorious' sense of humour.

Afterwards down on the banks of the River Cherwell Winifred and her friends had filled their arms with wild roses and watched the darting, hovering blue dragonflies and 'a flurry of bees and swal-lows'. England was free at last 'of the blight of war'. Just as the busy life of the High Street had resumed and the bicycles 'swarmed once again' through Carfax at the junction with Broad Street, so Winifred was pleased and calmed by the rhythm of the river where she watched 'some very admirable and astute little water rats bustle in and out among the flags'.

Robert Graves had moved to live at Boars Hill near Oxford, after taking up his place at St John's as an undergraduate. That summer, he had taken a short holiday with his wife Nancy. They had bicycled to Dorchester, passing the now empty army camps near Stonehenge that had been built to accommodate a million men. They had spent some time with Thomas Hardy who on 2 June had celebrated his eightieth birthday. They had discussed the dangers of the overworn phrase in poetry. Hardy urged Graves to omit 'the scent of thyme' from one of his recent poems. Graves begged to be allowed to keep it. They discussed how the local church had once been for Hardy the musical, literary and artistic hub of village life. He told Graves how the clergyman on whom he had modelled Mr St Clair in *Tess of the D'Urbervilles* had written to the War Office to object about the brass bands sent to disturb the discipline of the Dorchester barracks. The older poet confided to the younger something that had been troubling him. Out gardening one day, the full realisation of a new story had come into his head as he pruned a rose bush. Character, plot, sensibility, all were assembled in his mind. Hardy continued to chop down the wayward branches, unintentionally eliminating something more than he had intended. On returning to the house he found that the entire story had evaporated irretrievably. He told Graves of an essential rule for so many writers. He reminded the younger man of the evanescent imagination which needs to be tethered to paper and pinned there if it is not to escape.

After the euphoria of the summer when fine weather eases the pain in men and women's souls and the autumn term was imminent, Winifred wrote to a friend in some despair, 'England's in a horrid mess . . . we're all running after the moon.' The result of everyone fighting for 'rights' when it seemed to Winifred that although 'they don't know what they are, they intend to have 'em' was that the tally of lost working days in the nearly two years since the end of the war was now, according to government estimates, nudging over sixty million. On 18 October a group of unemployed servicemen from the North of the country came down to London, arriving in Whitehall just as a meeting between Lloyd George and the mayors of the London boroughs was being disbanded. Emotion could not be contained as the startled mayors saw angry men rushing towards them waving the Red Flag and lobbing bricks at the Georgian windows of Downing Street. The police arrived and charged, injuring forty men.

But Winifred deplored the way the Government was universally condemned for every problem both personal and financial, along with the accompanying sense that everyone deserved 'pensions, indemnities, two shillings a week rise in wages, cheap coal, electric massage, twopence a case divorce and railway transport'. She thought people behaved as if Lloyd George had found a gold mine in the back garden of his official residence. Men were not living up to the standards women imposed on them as heroes of war.

A few months earlier *Vogue* had thrown up its hands in disgust at the extremes to which 'old and decrepit' men would go in the pursuit of eternal youth. 'When they show signs of senility [they] are to have the glands of young and skittish monkeys grafted onto them and hey presto! They will immediately become hale and active.' What on earth was to follow, *Vogue* mused? 'Will they take to the trees? Will tails begin to sprout?' The magazine could only imagine what future generations might think of this lunacy, a folly comparable in absurdity to the notion of reviving the bowler hat, musical comedy, or even Cubist painting!

But the search for beauty and eternal youth was on the increase as seldom before. The *Sketch* joined in the derision concerning the claims that the grafting of the interstitial gland of the monkey could bring back lost youth. Will Cabinet ministers begin tangoing across Downing Street, the newspaper wondered? 'We weep', wrote Winifred, half laughing, 'because we can't make archangels out of men all in a hurry, forgetting it has taken a good many thousands of years to make a man out of a monkey.' The legacy of primates was further evident to Winifred when, having thought that 'now and then we see his wings sprouting, we weep to find that the only superfluous excrescence on his person is a remnant of his monkey's tail!'

By a grim irony, on 25 October, in the very same week that primates were causing Winifred to puzzle over man's aspirations and just as the *Illustrated London News* was reporting the rising fashion for monkey fur as a trimming on hats, Alexander, King of Greece, died from the effects of blood poisoning caused by a bite from by his own pet monkey.

The absurdity and unpredictability of life continued to trouble Virginia Woolf. In her diary that day she questioned, 'Why is life so tragic, so like a little strip of pavement over an abyss? I look down. I feel giddy. I wonder how I am ever to walk to the end.' Everywhere she looked she saw unhappiness and resistance to change. Although continuing to meet her Bloomsbury friends at gatherings of the quasi-nostalgic Memoir Club they had founded in the spring, she spent much of her time at Monk's House in the village of Rodmell in Sussex which she and Leonard had bought the previous summer. She was working on a new novel, *Jacob's Room*, and consciously shifting her writing away from the more traditional style of her previous two novels, *The Voyage Out* and *Night and Day*.

On 11 October the Prince of Wales returned home from another long promotional tour abroad, to face a parental dressing down for allowing his picture to be taken with his new aide Louis Mountbatten in a swimming pool. 'You might as well be photographed *naked*,' his father expostulated. Yet at Oxford there was a general feeling that the time had come to cast off prejudice and inhibition. The increasing recognition of the invaluable role women had played in the war was hard to ignore even in establishments and professions that had previously done their best to do so. Winifred went so far as to surmise that there were only three anti-feminists left in the world: the Foreign Secretary Lord Curzon, the lawyer Lord Birkenhead, and Mrs Humphry Ward, president of Britain's anti-suffrage movement. The Sex Disqualification Bill had become law the preceding December just after Lady Astor had taken her seat. Women solicitors had formed their own '1919 Club' in celebration of the new law that allowed them to practise for the first time and Oxford University had incorported the membership of women in the University into its statute.

On 20 October Winifred was pleased to boast that she and her great friend Vera Brittain had been welcomed into the Sheldonian, the beautiful golden-stoned theatre sitting proudly at the centre of Oxford's academic nucleus of buildings, to take part in the matriculation ceremony and to be 'initiated into the mysteries of degrees at last'. Shining in the sunshine, the scarlet hoods of the students were out-glamourised in their vibrancy by, Vera noticed, 'the wine red amphilopsis which hung with decorative dignity over walls and quad-rangles'.

Cambridge had not yet agreed to allow this huge gender barrier to be demolished, and on that sunny autumn day in Oxford only a few of the 4,181 male students were gathered for their own academic crowning and the few looked so abashed they might have been inter-lopers. As the Principals of the five women's colleges, who were all to be awarded MAs as part of the process of raising the status of women in the University, processed up the aisle of the theatre there was 'rousing applause'. Ghosts of women long dead, 'women who did not care whether they saw the end so long as they had contributed to the means', beamed down on their protégés. But this was a show, an act of theatre in which the players strutted and posed, the women adopting expressions of 'demure severity' while the men 'assumed an attitude of determined conviction that nothing special was happen-ing'. The atmosphere was 'tense with the consciousness of a dream fulfilled'. The Vice Chancellor became so agitated by the novelty of the proceedings that he mistook his mortarboard for his Bible, and matriculation took place with the help of a tap from his hat.

The women, among them a young published poet, Dorothy L. Sayers, who had left university in 1916 and now returned to claim her degree, stood in their specially designed caps and oversized gowns. Perhaps the sight was not particularly glamorous but it certainly incorporated, according to Winifred, 'the visible signs of a profound revolution'. Later that Friday the High Street was filled with the unprecedented sight of women on bicycles, wearing their flimsy female versions of mortarboards with their 'deplorable habit' of slip-ping down over one eye, and trying not to get their unfamiliar gowns caught in the spokes. Male undergraduates responded with courtesy. One newly gowned young woman grasped a young male hand, exclaiming in ecstasy that she had waited decades for this day, only to receive the polite response that she did not look her age.

Winifred's friend Vera Brittain, who had interrupted her time as an undergraduate at Somerville to become a Voluntary Aid

Detachment (VAD) nurse, had returned to the University, changing her degree course from English to history. There was another reason for her return. With the deaths of her brother, his greatest friend and her own fiancé she found herself deprived of 'the alternative lives that I might have lived'. She had been absent from Oxford for four years and in the seclusion of her grief found the atmosphere 'abnormally normal'. The students seemed determined to continue with the gay life that had preceded the war. At the age of only 26 she had become one of the huge number of suspiciously regarded spinsters who, verging on the outer age limit for marriage, were thought, without the fulfilment of children or sex, to be running the risk of going mad. The only thing, she told Winifred later, that held her to life was her own personal ambition to succeed.

One day in her first term after returning to Oxford, Vera had been attending a history tutorial with the Dean of Hertford College when a young woman burst into the room. Her physical appearance, bronzed by the summer sun in contrast to the small pale Vera, was astonishing. Dressed in a striped coat with an emerald green hat sitting on top of golden hair that seemed to illuminate the dull atmosphere of the study 'like a brilliant lamp irrepressibly shining in a dark corner', the figure glowed with 'the vivacity of health and unquenchable spirits'. This was Vera's first encounter with Winifred. She took an instant and contemptuous dislike to her, behaving with 'barely concealed hostility'. Soon they clashed fiercely and publicly at the debating society. Vera confused Winifred's ease with life with superficiality, and in her turn Winifred had been taken aback at Vera's sense of superiority towards anyone who had not experienced the agony of war at first hand.

Another Somerville undergraduate, Hilda Reid, was struck by the contrast in the two young women. Winifred was full of fun and 'very good company' while Vera was prone to melancholy, 'a very little creature with wet brown eyes' who found thunder and mice equally terrifying. And Winifred's all-embracing nature, her open-mindedness towards people, her passion for reading, for writing poetry, meeting men, buying clothes and involving herself in politics had the result of enraging Vera still further. Winifred's vitality, she found, had the effect 'of a blow upon my jaded nerves'.

But eventually Winifred's strength of personality warmed the silent, angry older woman. One day when Vera was ill, an uninvited visit from Winifred to her sickbed brought grapes and gentle sympathy. And Winifred brought more. There was an apology for the argument at the debating society and an exchange of reminiscences about the camp at Abbeville. Vera began to change her mind and lose her distrust of this vibrant and compassionate individual.

On the eleventh day of the eleventh month of 1919 the two women had accompanied each other to observe the two minutes' Great Silence at Christ Church Cathedral in Oxford and to remember those they had loved. The pain of the service was eased for both of them by their growing friendship. By the spring of 1920 the two had became inseparable.

This unlikely friendship gave Vera a lifeline, a reason for living. From June 1918 when her brother Edward was killed in Italy until that April of 1920 she had not known anyone 'to whom I could speak spontaneously or utter one sentence completely expressive of what I really thought or felt'. Winifred had changed that. But even Winifred was ignorant of how profound an effect the war had made on Vera. After a day spent walking in the fields around Box Hill and laughing together at the poets Edmund Blunden, Robert Graves and Roy Campbell, who kept a shop and wore red leather slippers and lived on goat's milk and cheese, Vera would return to her room and to her solitary nightmare. She dreamt that her face was changing and that in the morning she would wake to find that she had been transformed into a witch or that she had grown a full beard overnight. Rushing to the mirror she would see her own hairless face staring back at her in relief and horror combined. Terrified of uncovering a suppressed awareness of the 'thinness of the barrier between normality and insanity' she did not even dare tell her friend about the nightmares she suffered. The truth remained a shared secret between her sleeping and her waking self. She drifted 'to the borderland of craziness' but was too frightened to admit it.

A daytime fear haunted her as well. Her new lodgings in Keble Road that Trinity term of 1920 were overrun with mice. Images of the sights and sounds and smells and fears and cries of pain that had filled the trenches and which she knew so well from Roland and

Edward reverberated around her room. 'Armies of large fat mice' transformed a sanctuary into a prison. And what is more the room was filled with five separate mirrors. Dreading a sudden appearance of five identical hags as if on a Macbethian heath, she would cover her eyes to avoid seeing her own reflection. Fearful that the mice would re-emerge in the middle of the night, and desperate to prevent a recurrence of the dreaded visionary hairy growth, she would barely sleep a wink all night.

Vera was unaware that only a few miles away Robert Graves was imagining Beowulf 'wrapped in a blanket among his platoon of drunken thanes in the Gothland billet'. Nor was she aware that in the middle of one of the English literature lectures Graves would 'have a sudden very clear experience of men on the march up the Béthune–La Bassée road' and that the smell of the French knacker's yard nearby would rise up from the desks of the lecture theatre and swamp him. Gradually the fear began to recede as her mind concentrated on her own writing and her new life-enhancing friendship. Hope and trust were proving to be the cures for grief.

18

Acceptance

11 November 1920

No one who had lived through the war and lost someone they loved had been able to ignore the moments of false hope which were still capable of flaring up. The sound of a postman tipping the letterbox flap, the bark of a dog at the click of a garden latch, a knock at the door, the ring of a telephone – the cruel mind-game of false hope flourished in a context where there was no proper evidence of death.

The Lutyens monument, with its coffin-like presence, provided a receptacle in which, in the imagination of those still grieving, a body could be laid. For nearly eighteen months the temporary wooden Cenotaph had been acquiring increasing poignancy and significance not only for all who saw it but for all those denied a body and a coffin in which to place it.

To be in the silent presence of the Cenotaph, the mind paradoxically was free to express anything it chose. Here at last was a tangible object on which to focus personal grief. Lacking any inner substance of its own, it seemed to be the silence of grief made visible, the absence of the missing men made real. For a Christian, the very emptiness of the Cenotaph held a symbolism like that of Christ's tomb after the Resurrection. Comfort came in many guises and for some the Cenotaph carried with it a suggestion that the dead were perhaps not finally dead, but had risen again to a better life. The *Morning Post* noticed that 'Near the Memorial there were moments of silence when the dead seemed very near.'

Despite being a construction of wood and plaster, the monument in its colour and size resembled something permanent, substantial. Its presence interrupted the flow of six lanes of traffic, but suggestions that it be moved to Parliament Square were dismissed. Lutyens had designed the thirty-five foot high Cenotaph to dominate the great sweep of road that is Whitehall and his wish was respected.

Every day since the unveiling, the base of the monument had been concealed by the bouquets, garlands and wreaths heaped upon it. Further armfuls of flowers were continually laid at its foot – flowers brought from country meadows, from allotments, from back gardens and great estates. Here at last was a place where the mourning could begin and the horror recede. Here was a place where four years of pent-up sorrow could at last express itself, and where the bereaved could gather to remember. Passengers on the top deck of passing London buses removed their hats in salute.

But still the sound of tears was rarely heard. The Cenotaph remained a place for quiet reflection, where the manifestation of noisy emotion was, by silent agreement, discouraged. The author J. M. Barrie was one of hundreds of thousands of mourners who found Lutyens's monument a place of comfort. His adopted son, George Llewellyn Davies, had been killed in 1915, the body never found. Barrie had met Lutyens on the boat to France when searching for George's grave. He wrote to the architect that 'The Cenotaph grows in beauty as one strolls alone o'nights to look at it which becomes my habit.' Finding in the building an echo of Milton's definition of poetry, 'thoughts that voluntarily move harmonious numbers', Barrie applauded his friend for creating such a harmonious number. 'I feel proud of it and you,' he wrote.

In Whitehall Sir Alfred Mond, head of the Board of Works, had become increasingly irritated by the ever mounting and rotten-smelling hillock of flowers that smothered the foot of the Cenotaph. The summer temperatures of 1919 had on occasion beaten the records set in 1911 and the flowers soon wilted. 'A mass of decaying flowers needs almost daily attention,' he grumbled; he was thinking of suggesting that perhaps it would be more hygienic and tidier if flowers were permitted on only two days a year, the anniversary of the Peace Treaty in June and perhaps at Easter.

But the temporary monument, a construction that had started out as a stage prop for the Victory Parade, had assumed a significance that the people were not ready to surrender. The building of monuments became infectious. Memorials founded by money raised in individual towns and villages were being built all over the country – in high streets, at road junctions, on village greens. Each one was different. The proposal to erect an identical headstone for the millions of bodies that awaited burial abroad in the colossal cemeteries that Kipling called 'the silent cities' was causing debate in the letters columns of *The Times*. Some felt that this 'was a camouflaged effort to do things on the cheap'; others argued that visual uniformity and the sense of fellowship with colleagues, officer and soldier alike, would dignify the look of the stone.

For more than a year, ever since Sir Alfred Mond had given him the agreement to proceed, Lutyens had been working on refinements and alterations to his temporary structure. He was worried that London's rain and smog would destroy the fragile fabric of the fluttering silk flags that hung down the sides of the Cenotaph and that 'anything less calculated to inspire reverence or emotion than a petrified and raddled imitation of free and living bunting' was hard to imagine. As he found in T. S. Eliot's poetry, Lutyens felt it was the half said and the half complete that proved to be the most eloquent expression of the gaping hole made by death.

Mond had tried to convince Lutyens that stone ensigns would do the job better. Knowing that the artistic demands for creating new faces at the Tin Noses Shop had diminished, Lutyens had initially invited his old colleague Francis Derwent Wood to make the new flags as well as to sculpt the stone wreath that would be placed halfway up the stone sides. But in May 1920 Lutyens's wish to retain his original design was accepted: the silk flags remained, the sculptor reassuring Wood that he would find a place for the redundant work in one of his many other war memorial commissions.

On the eve of the second anniversary of the Armistice, when the new monument had been completed and before the sheets had been thrown over it in preparation for the unveiling, the casual passer-by strolling down Whitehall noticed little if any change. Lutyens explained that the subtle differences in the curves were almost imperceptible 'yet sufficient to give it a sculpturesque quality and a life that cannot pertain to rectangular blocks of stone'. Lutyens refused to be paid for this particular piece of work.

★

But there was something that continued to feel incomplete about the celebrations for the observance of the second anniversary of the Armistice. The coffin-like Cenotaph was of course empty. There were no plans to fill it and yet its very emptiness emphasised a void.

During the war an army padre called David Railton, guiding an itinerant wartime parish through the middle of the body-thick mud of France, had been deeply moved, one still, unusually silent evening, by the sight of a small fenced garden which contained in one corner a grave marked by a simple wooden cross. Someone had taken a black pencil and written on the crosspiece the words 'An Unknown British Soldier'. Could not one of these unidentified men, Railton wondered, serve as a symbol of comfort and courage to the whole armies of people who had no body to bury? The lack of a funeral had denied hundreds of thousands the chance to accept the finality of death. Perhaps one single body could be brought out of the mud of France, never to be identified but to fill the gap left by a father, brother, husband, son, fiancé, lover, uncle, grandfather, friend – a loved one who could be made to symbolise and fill that void. His invisible face could be invested with thousands of familiar faces, all much missed and much loved. The suggestion seemed to offer a retreat from the terrifying emptiness of the tomb, with its attendant silence, and instead an emphasis on the continuing vitality of the common man.

Railton hesitated to air his suggestion, worried that such a mawkish idea would be rejected. He said nothing about it, spending the summer of 1920 by the sea in Margate where his peacetime parish lay. But his wife persisted, encouraging her husband not to drop his simple and daring scheme. Finally, as autumn approached, Railton wrote a letter to the Dean of Westminster, the Right Reverend Herbert Ryle. At once the Dean understood the brilliance of the suggestion and wrote himself to the King and the Prime Minister asking for their agreement to proceed with the plan.

The King recoiled, not this time at the impracticality of the scheme, but rather, as Railton had feared, at its distasteful sentimentality. Indeed, the King questioned whether the very act of seeing a coffin pulled through the streets of London in a further scene of national mourning would not reawaken, with a ghastly reality, the pain that was beginning to dull. Was the whole idea not 'poised precariously on the tightrope of taste'? Would it not all become a morbid sideshow? Would the solemnity of the unveiling of the Cenotaph not be diluted? And there was more. Would a decomposing body give off a distasteful smell in the Abbey?

The King was not alone in his initial response. Siegfried Sassoon was among those who considered the idea sentimental. But the Prime Minister shared the Dean's enthusiasm, and by early October had succeeded in persuading the King to give his consent.

In the village of Saint Pol-sur-Ternoise, twenty miles west of Arras, a small tin hut had been adapted to form a makeshift chapel. Four days before the second anniversary of the Armistice four bodies, deteriorated so badly that they were beyond identification, and from whom the vivid smell of death had long since dissipated, lay inside the chapel wrapped in sacking and covered in the Union flag. From these four bodies one would be chosen to represent all those who had died during the Great War. A few hours earlier they had been gently retrieved from beneath the mud of four different battlefields. The Aisne, Arras, the Somme and Ypres had all given up a soldier from hastily made graves commemorated simply as 'Unknown British Soldier': none carried any identifying mark beyond being clothed in the uniform of a British soldier; all of them precious in life only to a handful, but one of them in death about to provide the emotional focus for millions.

At midnight on Sunday 7 November 1920 Brigadier General L. J. Wyatt, the General Officer commanding the British troops in France and Flanders, entered the dimly lit chapel at Saint-Pol and put out his hand towards one of the flag-draped bodies and touched it. The choice was made. The body was sealed in a coffin made by the British Undertakers Association from the wood of an ancient English oak tree from Hampton Court. It had been sent over to Saint-Pol accompanied by two undertakers, Mr Nodes and Mr Sourbutts, and by an ancient battle trophy. The King, who over the last two months had moved from a position of distasteful scepticism to impassioned advocacy of the imminent ceremony, had selected one of his own ceremonial swords to accompany the coffin on its journey home.

Enough earth to fill six barrels had been dug up from Flanders and travelled with the soldier's cortège as it made its way through northern France. At Boulogne the coffin was placed on the destroyer HMS *Verdun* to make the crossing to Dover. Halfway across the Channel, six more destroyers were waiting and as the *Verdun* came nearer, they lowered the Union flag in the manner usually reserved for the approach of the Monarch.

On the English side all shops in Dover had been closed for the day and as the reverberations from a nineteen-gun salute faded, a band on shore began to play 'Land of Hope and Glory'. The huge crowds gathered at the quayside stared fixedly at the coffin as if wishing to imprint this scene on their minds for ever.

The coffin, secured by two thick black straps wrapped round it like string round a parcel, was placed in the same luggage van, number 132, that had brought home from Belgium the body of Nurse Edith Cavell in May of the preceding year. The inside of the luggage van had been fitted out by the railwaymen of the South Eastern and Chatham Railway Company a few days before. It was draped with purple cloth and hung with a frieze of sweet-smelling bay leaves, rosemary and chrysanthemums; outside, its white-painted roof ensured that everyone watching, from bridges and railway cuttings, even in the November darkness, could identify the carriage in the light of the moon and know that it contained this most special of cargoes.

As the train pulled into Victoria Station at 8.32 p.m. the steam clouds from the engine billowed up into the station's high ceiling. The police had to work hard to restrain the huge numbers of people who had come for a glimpse of the white-roofed carriage. There was no ceremonial that night, simply a mass of ashen faces, many in tears, straining to see the carriage in which, guarded by officers of the Grenadier Guards, the dead soldier lay.

Early on the morning of Thursday 11 November the streets around Westminster Abbey were not silent. Voices were hushed but people were talking with some excitement of the events they were to witness. Many wore black armbands. All wore hats. Some were in uniform. The majority were dressed in mourning. The misty November sunshine bathed the grey buildings with a pale light that softened their sharp edges. Large sycamore leaves, some still whole despite their dry fragility, others showing traces of their earlier golden colour beneath the late autumn dappling, rustled in the gutters. There was a tenderness to the barely discernible breeze. If the unknown soldier had himself imagined his own homecoming he could not have wished for a lovelier day. And, 'if he was a Londoner', *The Times* said, 'he could not have wished to see his city more beautiful'.

Just as they had waited all night nearly eighteen months before for the march of peace, now they came early to wait for a return too precious to miss. Tired eyes occasionally dropped downwards towards hands protecting drooping bunches of carnations shrunken in the cold, trying to will them to cling to life for just an hour or two longer so they could place the flowers at the monument in front of them. The sun too was struggling to appear from behind a white mist. And as it broke through, the King arrived wearing the uniform of a Field Marshal. The slow beat of the drum came ever nearer. George V shielded his eyes from the shafting light, as he looked in the direction of the road along which the gun carriage would travel. Thousands more eyes, tired with the waiting but a little brighter now that the moment had arrived, followed his. The King and his subjects had at last gathered together for a funeral.

After leaving Platform 8 of Victoria Station, where the unknown soldier had spent his final night on earth, guarded in the darkness by the silent officers of the Guards, the black gun carriage emerged from the western arch of the station into what *The Times* called 'the kindly sunshine of a mellow day'. Six black horses pulled the carriage with its precious burden as they made their slow rhythmic progress over two and a half miles.

Accompanied by four admirals, four field marshals and two generals, as well as officers and other ranks from the Royal Navy, the Marines and the Air Force, the procession travelled slowly from Grosvenor Gardens, through Grosvenor Place to Hyde Park Corner, and down the long slope of Constitution Hill to the Mall. From there it passed through Admiralty Arch until it eventually came rolling down the empty stretch of Whitehall. The crowds in places were between ten and twenty deep. Behind the carriage the heads of the armed forces and four hundred former servicemen marched four abreast. As the procession passed by, the pattern of colour changed.

Dark naval blue gave way to the yellow and khaki of the army and finally to the slate-coloured uniform of the air force. The flecked black and grey of civilian clothes brought up the rear of a slow-moving river of men bound together by what *The Times* described as 'the mysterious and indefinable bonds of comradeship'.

Among the watching masses, hats, removed as the silent crowds 'uncovered' at the approach, were not returned to heads even twenty minutes after the procession had disappeared. It was as if the extended emotion and the indelible memory of the coffin had brought a near-total paralysis.

By now there was no music, apart from the funeral drums, and although sand had been spread over the tarmac to muffle all noise, the hard echo of the horses' hooves struck the cold November pavements. When daylight emerged that day some heard the sound of a lone thrush. A few weeks earlier the bird had stopped singing for the winter months, but had suddenly returned in the late-appearing dawn for a final song. Choosing 'to fling his soul upon the growing gloom', as Thomas Hardy had written twenty years earlier as one century gave way to another, a darkling thrush brought 'some blessed hope' to crowds bereft of such an unaccustomed feeling.

On the lid of the coffin was the brass plate confirming that this was the body of 'A British Warrior who fell in the Great War 1914–1918 for King and Country'. Covering the coffin was the faded flag, ragged and stained, that David Railton, when serving as a padre, had used as an altar cloth – a piece of the life so many had come to remember and to forget. This was a flag that had travelled from the Western Front to the heart of London, a flag that had been used for services on makeshift altars before the battles at Ypres, High Wood, Passchendaele, Cambrai and the Somme. This was a flag that had been used to cover shattered bodies, to shield them from the indignity of death. This was a flag covered in death mud, and in blood. The colours of the flag were almost the only colours to relieve the black-drenched scene.

As the carriage came nearer, its joints creaking slightly with the weight of the load, sobs ineffectively suppressed were prompted again and again by the sight of the poignant familiarity of the soldier's webbing belt and modest, dented steel helmet on top of the coffin.

Perhaps at that moment more than any other, the dead soldier was invested with the millions of identities that the bereaved willed upon him. Here at last was lying that father, brother, husband, lover, son or friend that had been taken from them. The scene was magnificent in its plain depiction of death.

In an instant the entire crowd was bareheaded. The sword strapped to the top of the coffin was the very one that had belonged to the King. The clock on Big Ben announced that it was ten minutes to eleven. General Haig handed George a wreath of bay leaves and red roses and, stretching up a little to reach the coffin, the King gently placed it on top. On the card attached the King had chosen to include the eternally hopeful words of St Paul's Epistle to the Corinthians: 'In proud memory of those Warriors who died unknown in the Great War. Unknown, and yet well known; as dying, and behold they live.' Nearby the Abbey choir, standing in the brisk November air, sang 'O God our Help in Ages Past' and then joined the Archbishop of Canterbury in the Lord's Prayer.

For a moment those assembled in Whitehall stood motionless and silent. Then at the thundering sound of the first of Big Ben's eleven chimes, the King pressed a button that released the flags shrouding the Cenotaph. Nearly ten years earlier, even before his Coronation, George V had stood in the Mall beside his first cousin, the German Kaiser, and pressed a button that had revealed the huge marble statue of the grandmother they shared. She had been the figurehead of an Empire and a Europe at peace. He now made the same gesture and unveiled a monument commemorating a period of war – a period in which the monarchs of Europe had seen Victoria's peaceful rule ruptured.

'The Glorious Dead', read the inscription on both sides of the monument. A day earlier General Haig had written in *The Times*: 'All generations of British men and women shall look at it forever with pride, for it stands for the Nation's glory.' Yet could there be glory in the four years that the tomb commemorated? The *Illustrated London News* did not think so. This had been, it said, 'the strife that has filled the world with agony, destroyed millions of men, broken millions of lives, ruined great cities and hamlets'. And there was more: the war had left 'a belt of earth ravaged, crowded the world with maimed men, blind, mad, sick men flinging empires into anarchy'.

The new monument, elegant in its severity, stood unadorned except for two Union flags. The upended shape was reflected hinge-like in the horizontal coffin lying beside it.

Big Ben completed its eleven strokes and England for the second time edged its way towards that unfamiliar state of absolute silence. During those two minutes the previously inexpressible was, for some, at last articulated. For others the silence and the containing of emotion was almost intolerable.

The observance of silence was not confined to England. All the other countries except Germany that had fought in the war respected the Great Silence. In Australia, Belgium, Canada, France, India, Italy, New Zealand, Portugal and South Africa silence fell as the anniversary of the Armistice was remembered. Only America was too busy to stop.

As the acute, pain-triumphant notes of the Last Post sounded and the silence was broken, thousands of heads were raised, throats were cleared and crumpled handkerchiefs dampened the fists that held them. The crowd watched as first the King laid his second wreath of the morning at the foot of the Cenotaph, followed by the Prime Minister. And then the tableau, a still life only moments earlier, began to move. After such stillness the King appeared to be in a hurry. The horses pulling the gun carriage slowly made their way towards Parliament Square, the hollow clock of their hooves echoing through a still silent Whitehall.

When the procession reached Westminster Abbey the coffin was lifted from the gun carriage and carried in through the doors towards the west end of the nave, where one hundred recipients of the Victoria Cross formed a guard of honour. The grave was positioned so that for ever after no one, not even a king or queen approaching the altar at their own coronation, would be able to avoid side-stepping the grave of the man who had given his life for his country.

No one from a foreign government had been invited to the final ceremony. But this was not only an exclusively British occasion. This was also a time for women – for queens representing their countries and for one thousand especially chosen mothers and widows of men who had given their lives for their country just as the unknown soldier had given his.

The service was short. The Twenty-third Psalm and a reading by the Dean from the Book of Revelation followed Beethoven's beautiful Equale for Trombones. Then the steel helmet, the webbing belt, the King's sword and the flag were lifted from the coffin, and, unadorned, the heavy oak container was lowered into the permanent silence deep beneath the floor of the Abbey. The choir sang 'Lead Kindly Light' and the King was handed a small silver shell from which he scooped little handfuls of now dry earth: what once represented fear was now contained within a handful of dust. He scattered the earth on to the wooden lid, earth taken once again from the fields of France. The last hymn, 'God of our Fathers', was written for Queen Victoria's Jubilee by Rudyard Kipling, a man whose son might well have been occupying the coffin in front of them. The final lines broke down all remaining restraint as the words 'Lest we Forget, lest we forget' sounded their agonising caution over all those present. Simplicity held the emotion at the appropriate level. All rhetoric would have seemed false.

The watching women had managed until then to maintain their composure. All except one. Queen Mary was unable to maintain her self-control and her distress was plain for everyone to see. The Last Post sounded and the guard of honour passed by the grave. The slab of Tournai marble that was to cover the grave, was inscribed simply 'An Unknown Warrior', and the battlefield mud that was to be packed around the coffin (so that in Brigadier General Wyatt's words 'the body should rest in the soil on which so many of our troops gave up their lives') were waiting to be put in position. Somehow it seemed important that the visitors to the grave should be allowed one last glimpse of the flag-covered coffin. The waiting queue already stretched back to the Cenotaph.

After the service was over, back in Whitehall the people continued to move towards the Cenotaph with their tributes. Around the base of the new monument (already wholly invisible) were the flowers – elaborate formal wreaths made up of exotic species shining perfect against evergreen leaves; red roses, the symbol of love; violets bought from roadside hawkers. A tiny child approached the monument holding his mother's hand tightly. As he bent to lay a posy among the mass of flowers already there, he shouted out in such a loud voice that, despite the huge sob that engulfed his words, the listening crowd thought they must have mistaken his age. 'Oh Mummy,' he cried, 'what a lovely garden Daddy has got.'

Winifred Holtby had not been to the unveiling of the Cenotaph that day. Nor had she followed the later procession that moved slowly past the monument. The whole event seemed to her both stagey and hypocritical, something of a sop to those who could not summon the strength or vision of their own to carry on. She could not bear 'the nobler sentiments about the Unknown Hero and the rest of it when Ireland and Belgium were still staggering under men's murderous ways'. The whole show seemed like 'an appeal to sentiment to carry England away from the realisation of a practical evil'.

But survival and youth combined to give the lucky ones the chance to hope and to look forward. This had been the war to end all wars, and in the beauty of those last autumn days when 'the sun shines and the air is clear and frosty on the hills' Winifred noticed something else that floated, visible if untouchable, in those valleys beneath the Oxfordshire hills where 'every tree is aflame with vivid leaves and berries'. Amid the quietness of the valleys 'the grey mist lies soft as an unborn dream'.

Dreaming and hoping were the tenets of the present. Why, she wondered, must men spoil what is lovely in the world? In that moment, a glorious day in which alone in the silence of her own company it seemed that 'every colour was clearer, every air was fresher than on ordinary days – as though the world was having a birthday', she challenged anyone to contradict her when she cried, 'How can one help loving it?'

Dramatis Personae

Nancy Astor (1879–1964) Britain's first woman Member of Parliament, she took her seat in the House of Commons in December 1919. Remained MP for Plymouth until 1945. Rumours of Nazi party sympathies dispelled much of her earlier popularity. But her notoriety within the 'Cliveden Set' remained undimmed especially during the 'Profumo affair' of 1963.

Violet Astor (1889–1965) Widow of Charles Petty-Fitzmaurice (killed in the war in 1914) and wife of John Jacob Astor. When in the 1960s her grandsons reached the age of 21 Violet retrieved the cufflinks that had belonged to her first husband (their grandfather) from a bricked-up recess in her private sitting room at Hever Castle and gave them to the boys as birthday gifts.

Tommy Atkins (1892–1974) One time under-chauffeur, soldier, gas meter reader and would-be Vaudeville star. His first wife Kitty died in childbirth and soon afterwards he married his landlady Annie. They had a son Ronald and a daughter Eileen who acknowledges that she owes much of her theatrical gift to her father.

Mary (Stearns, née) Beale (1917–) Mary grew up to marry Stanley Stearns, a local farmer, and they had four children, James, Michael, Richard and Linda She now lives within a mile of Bettenham, near Sissinghurst in Kent, where she is the life, soul and inspiration of the community.

Vera Brittain (1893–1970) Writer, feminist and pacifist. *Testament of Youth*, Vera's account of her war years and those immediately afterwards, was published in 1933 and continues to be a bestseller. In 1925 Vera married George Catlin, a political scientist and philosopher. Their son John (1927–87) was an artist, and daughter Shirley Williams (born 1930) is the distinguished Liberal Democrat peer.

Coco Chanel (1883–1971) Most influential couture designer of the century and creator in 1925 of the iconic scent Chanel Number 5. Despite having many lovers she never married.

Denis Clarke Hall (1910–2006) Younger son of the artist Edna Clarke Hall. Distinguished architect, who never lost his childhood love for the sea.

Edna Clarke Hall (1879–1979) Painter, poet and beauty. Mother of Justin and Denis and wife of Willie, barrister and co-founder of the National Society for the Prevention of Cruelty to Children.

Lady Diana Cooper (née Manners) (1892–1986) Society's beautiful eccentric. Daughter of the Duke of Rutland, wife of Duff Cooper, diplomat. Became something of a film star in the 1920s and later the glittering Ambassadress at the British Embassy in Paris following the liberation of that city in 1944.

Duff Cooper (1890–1954) Politician, diplomat and author. Served as Member of Parliament in the 1920s; became British Ambassador to France in 1944.

Victor Christian William Cavendish, 9th Duke of Devonshire (1868–1938) British politician. Between 1916 and 1921, served as the Governor General of Canada. Owner of several of Britain's greatest houses including Chatsworth, Hardwick and Belton as well as Devonshire House which was demolished in 1924.

Lucy Duff Gordon (1863–1935) Prominent Edwardian fashion designer. Sister of the writer Elinor Glyn. She opened branches of her prestigious London couture house in Paris, New York City and Chicago. Fashions changed and she died in poverty.

Thomas Stearns Eliot (1888–1965) Poet, playwright and literary critic. Received the Nobel Prize for Literature in 1948. Among his most famous writings are the poems *The Love Song of J. Alfred Prufrock*, *The Waste Land*, *The Hollow Men*, *Ash Wednesday* and *Four Quartets*.

HM King George V (1865–1936) Crowned King in 1911. Son of Edward VII, husband of Queen Mary, father of Edward VIII and George VI, first cousin of Kaiser Wilhelm II of Germany and Tsar Nicholas II of Russia, and grandson of Queen Victoria.

Harold Gillies (1882–1960) New Zealand born, London based, widely considered as the father of plastic surgery and pre-eminent restorative surgeon at Queen Mary's Hospital, Sidcup. Became mentor to his cousin Archie McIndoe, founder of the Second World War's 'Guinea Pig Club'.

Lionel Gomme (1894–1922) Football-mad stonemason nicknamed Tiger and object of a grand passion of Lady Ottoline Morrell. Died suddenly of a brain haemorrhage in Ottoline's arms, aged 28.

Winifred Holtby (1898–1935) Pacifist and undergraduate at Somerville College, Oxford; friend of Vera Brittain. Among the first group of women students to be awarded a degree. Later became a journalist and novelist.

Eric Horne (*c.*1850–1935) Former butler to royalty and the upper reaches of the aristocracy. Compulsive diarist and author of *What the Butler Winked at* and *More Winks* – both bestsellers.

Jeremy Hutchinson (1915–) The five year old with an amazing memory became a highly distinguished lawyer and life peer. Married first the actress Peggy Ashcroft and then June, daughter of Boy Capel, the one-time lover of Coco Chanel.

T. E. Lawrence (1888–1935) British soldier who became known for his role during the Arab Revolt of 1916–18. His book *Seven Pillars of Wisdom* and the story of his camel-bound life in the desert, as portrayed by Peter O'Toole in David Lean's 1962 film, have made him world famous as Lawrence of Arabia.

David Lloyd George (1863–1945) War-time Prime Minister and Leader of the Liberal Party.

Sir Edwin Lutyens (1869–1944) Leading twentieth-century British architect, who designed many memorials to the First World War including the Cenotaph in London's Whitehall.

HM Queen Mary (1867–1953) Wife of HM King George V and mother of six children including the future Edward VIII and George VI. Her youngest child, Prince John, died in January 1919.

Tom Mitford (1909–1945) Schoolboy with an irresistibly winning manner. Only son of the second Lord and Lady Redesdale, Tom joined the army before the Second World War, served in the African and Italian campaigns and was fatally shot in Burma nine weeks before the war in Europe ended.

Lady Ottoline Morrell (1873–1938) English aristocrat, patron of the arts and society hostess. Wife of former MP Philip Morrell, Lady Ottoline had many affairs including two years of passion with a young stonemason, Lionel Gomme (q.v.).

Pam Parish (1916–) Pam was three years old when she observed the first Great Silence in 1919 on her knees at home in her village of Sidcup in Kent. Married during the Second World War to the distinguished psychiatrist Denis Leigh and mother of five children, she lives in Kent and continues to drive herself around the county she has known all her life.

Nick La Rocca (1889–1961) Jazz cornetist and trumpeter and leader of the Original Dixieland Jazz Band. According to La Rocca he was 'The Creator of Jazz', and he moved about the stage like a 'filleted eel about to enter the stewing pot'.

Siegfried Sassoon (1886–1967) English poet and author who wrote satirical anti-war verse during the First World War. Friend of the Bloomsbury group and cared for at the famous psychiatric hospital, Craiglockhart in Edinburgh, with contemporary and friend, the poet Wilfred Owen.

Doris Scovell (1903–2008) Tweenie maid who ran between the upstairs and downstairs floors of smart Edwardian homes. Became a first-class cook and married Will Titley, the footman she had met in her earliest days in service. She died aged 105, her infectious laughter intact to the end.

Lowell Thomas (1892–1981) American writer, broadcaster and traveller best known as the man who made Lawrence of Arabia famous by bringing his story through film and lecture to the American and British public.

The Prince of Wales (1894–1972) Eldest son of HM George V and Queen Mary. Saw service in the First World War. Thereafter unofficial ambassador for Britain, spending months at a time touring the United States and the British Empire. Became King of the United Kingdom and the British dominions and Emperor of India from 20 January 1936 until his abdication on 11 December 1936. Married Mrs Wallis Simpson on 3 June 1937.

Bibliography

Archives

The Chatsworth Archive
Private Papers and Diaries of Edna Clarke Hall
Fulham and Hammersmith District Archive
The Meteorological Office Archive
The Mitford Archive
The Royal Archive at Windsor
The Savoy Hotel Archive

Newpapers and magazines

Daily Mail
Daily Sketch
Daily Telegraph
Fulham Chronicle
Guardian
Illustrated London News
Lady
London Evening News
New York Times
News of the World
Punch
Sketch
The Spectator
Tatler
The Times
Vogue
West London Observer

Books and articles

Ackroyd, Peter, *T. S. Eliot*, Hamish Hamilton, 1984

Adams, Jad, 'Private and Public Childhood: "Your Child Forever"', *English Literature in Transition 1880–1920*, Vol. 49, no. 4, 2006

Airlie, Mabel, Countess of, *Thatched with Gold*, Hutchinson, 1962

Alexander, Caroline, 'Faces of War', *Smithsonian*, February 2007, pp. 72–80

Alcock, John, and Whitten Brown, Arthur, *Our Transatlantic Flight, Badminton Magazine*, 1919, and *Royal Airforce and Civil Aviation Record*, 1920

Alsop, Susan Mary, *Lady Sackville*, Weidenfeld & Nicolson, 1978

Arlen, Michael, *The Green Hat*, W. Collins Sons & Co., 1924

Arthur, Max, *Last Post: The Final Word from our First World War Soldiers*, Weidenfeld & Nicolson, 2005

Ash, Edwin, M.D., *Nerves and the Nervous*, Mills & Boon, 1911

Asquith, Cynthia, *The Diaries of Lady Cynthia Asquith 1915–1918*, Century, 1968

Bailey, Catherine, *Black Diamonds: The Rise and Fall of an English Dynasty*, Viking, 2007

Bailey, Hilary, *Vera Brittain*, Penguin, 1987

Barham, Peter, *Forgotten Lunatics of the Great War*, Yale, 2004

Barker, Pat, *Regeneration*, Viking, 1991

—— *The Eye in the Door*, Viking, 1993

—— *The Ghost Road*, Viking, 1995

—— *Life Class*, Hamish Hamilton, 2007

Barrett, Michèle, *Casualty Figures: How Five Men Survived the First World War*, Verso, 2007

Battiscombe, Georgina, *Queen Alexandra*, Constable, 1969

Beaton, Cecil, *The Glass of Fashion*, Weidenfeld & Nicolson, 1954

Beechey, James, and Shone, Richard, 'Picasso in London 1919: The Premiere of *The Three-Cornered Hat*', *Burlington Magazine*, October 2006

Beeton, Mrs, *Household Management*, 1861

Benson, John, *The Working Class in Britain 1850–1939*, I. B. Tauris, 2003

Best, Nicholas, *The Greatest Day in History: How the Great War Really Ended*, Weidenfeld & Nicolson, 2008

Blythe, Ronald, *The Age of Illusion: England in the Twenties and Thirties 1919–1940*, Hamish Hamilton, 1963

Bourchier, Christine, 'Rituals of Mourning: Bereavement, Grief and Mourning in the First World War', Department of History, University of Calgary, 2001

Brittain, Vera, *Testament of Youth*, Gollancz, 1933

—— *Testament of Friendship*, Macmillan, 1940

—— and Four Friends, *Letters from a Lost Generation: First World War Letters*, Little Brown, 1998

Brown, Jane, *Lutyens and the Edwardians: An English Architect and His Clients*, Viking, 1996

Brownlow, Kevin, *The Parade's Gone By*, Secker & Warburg, 1968

Brunn, H. O., *The Story of the Original Dixieland Jazz Band*, Jazz Book Club and Sidgwick & Jackson, 1963

Buchan, John, *These For Remembrance: Memoirs of Six Friends Killed in the Great War*, privately printed, 1919

Buckle, Richard, *Diaghilev*, Weidenfeld & Nicolson, 1979

Buckmaster, Herbert, *Buck's Book*, Grayson & Grayson, 1933

Carrington, Charles, *Soldiers from the Wars Returning*, Hutchinson, 1965

Cartland, Barbara, *We Danced All Night*, Hutchinson, 1971

Churchill, Winston and Clementine, ed. Mary Soames, *Speaking for Themselves*, Doubleday, 1998 (their personal correspondence)

Clarke Hall, Denis, 'Some Reflections on Sailing in a Very Different Age 1918–1938', unpublished

Clout, Hugh, *After the Ruins: Restoring the Countryside of Northern France after the Great War*, University of Exeter Press, 1996

Collins, Michael, *The Likes of Us: A Biography of the White Working Class*, Granta, 2004

Cooksley, Peter, *The Home Front: Civilian Life in World War One*, Tempus Publishing, 2006

Cooper, Diana, *The Rainbow Comes and Goes*, Rupert Hart-Davis, 1958

Cooper, Duff, *Old Men Forget*, Rupert Hart-Davis 1955

—— ed. John Julius Norwich, *The Duff Cooper Diaries*, Weidenfeld & Nicolson, 2005

Davenport-Hines, Richard, *Ettie: The Intimate Life and Dauntless Spirit of Lady Desborough*, Weidenfeld & Nicolson, 2008

De Courcy, Anne, *Circe: The Life of Edith Marchioness of Londonderry*, Sinclair Stevenson, 1992

—— *The Viceroy's Daughters: The Lives of the Curzon Sisters*, Weidenfeld & Nicolson, 2000

The Dowager Duchess of Devonshire, *The Garden at Chatsworth*, Frances Lincoln, 1999

Didion, Joan, *The Year of Magical Thinking*, Fourth Estate, 2005

Duff Gordon, Lucy, *Discretions and Indiscretions*, Jarrolds, 1932

Egremont, Max, *Siegfried Sassoon: A Biography*, Picador, 2005

Eliot, T. S., *The Waste Land*, Hogarth Press, 1923

—— ed. Valerie Eliot, *The Letters of T. S. Eliot*, Vol. 1, Faber, 1988

Ellsworth Jones, Will, *We Will Not Fight: The Untold Story of World War One's Conscientious Objectors*, Aurum Press, 2007

Emsley, Clive, 'Violent Crime in England in 1919: Post-war Anxieties and Press Narratives', *Continuity and Change*, 23(1), pp. 173–95

Etherington-Smith, Meredith, and Pilcher, Jeremy, *The It Girls*, Hamish Hamilton, 1986

Ewing, Elizabeth, *A History of Twentieth-century Fashion*, rev. Alice Mackrell, Batsford, 2005

Feo, Katherine, 'Invisibility: Memory, Masks and Masculinities in the Great War', Design History Society, 2007

Fisher, Kate, *Birth Control: Sex and Marriage in Britain 1918–1960*, Oxford University Press, 2006

Fitzgerald, F. Scott, *This Side of Paradise*, Charles Scribner's Sons, 1920

Fox, James, *The Langhorne Sisters*, Granta, 1998

Fraser, Rebecca, *A People's History of Britain*, Chatto & Windus, 2003

Fussell, Paul, *The Great War and Modern Memory*, Oxford University Press, 1975

Garnett, David, *The Golden Echo*, Chatto & Windus, 1953

Gavaghan, Michael, *The Story of the Unknown Warrior*, M & L Publications, 1995

Gibbs, Philip, *Realities of War*, Hutchinson, 1919

Gillies, Harold, *Plastic Surgery of the Face*, Oxford University Press and Hodder & Stoughton, 1920

Glendinning, Victoria, *Vita: The Life of Vita Sackville-West*, Weidenfeld & Nicolson, 1983

Graubard, Stephen Richards, 'Military Demobilisation in Great Britain following the First World War', *Journal of Modern History*, Vol. 19, December 1947

Graves, Robert, *Goodbye to All That*, Jonathan Cape, 1929

—— and Hodge, Alan, *The Long Weekend: A Social History of Great Britain 1918–1939*, Norton, 1940

Gregory, Adrian, *The Silence of Memory: Armistice Day 1919–1946*, Berg, 1994

Grigg, John, *Nancy Astor*, Sidgwick & Jackson, 1980

Guinness, Jonathan, with Catherine Guinness, *The House of Guinness*, Orion, 1984

Hanson, Neil, *The Unknown Soldier: The Story of the Missing of the Great War*, Doubleday, 2005

Hawthorne, Jennie, *East End Memories*, Sutton, 2005

de la Haye, Amy, and Tobin, Shelley, *Chanel: The Couturiere at Work*, Victoria & Albert Museum, 1994

Holdsworth, Angela, *Out of the Doll's House: The Story of Women in the Twentieth Century*, BBC Books, 1988

Holroyd, Michael, *Lytton Strachey: A Critical Biography*, Vol. II, Heinemann, 1968

—— *Augustus John*, Chatto & Windus, 1996

Holtby, Winifred, *Letters to a Friend*, Collins, 1937

Hopkins, Eric, *A Social History of the English Working Classes 1815–1945*, Hodder & Stoughton, 1979

Horn, Pamela, *Life Below Stairs in the Twentieth Century*, Sutton, 2001

Horne, Eric, *What the Butler Winked at*, T. Werner Laurie, 1923

—— *More Winks*, T. Werner Laurie, 1932

Houlbrook, Matt, *Queer London: Perils and Pleasures in the Sexual Metropolis 1918–1957*, University of Chicago Press, 2005

Hughes, Molly, *A London Family Between the Wars*, Oxford University Press, 1940

Hustwitt, Mark, 'Caught in a Whirlpool of Sound: The Production of Dance Music in Britain in the 1920s', *Popular Music*, Vol. 3, no. 1, January 1983

Hynes, Samuel, *A War Imagined: The First World War and English Culture*, The Bodley Head, 1990

Imperial War Museum Guide Book

Jackson, Stanley, *The Savoy: The Romance of a Great Hotel*, Frederick Muller, 1964

Jupp, Peter C., *From Dust to Ashes: Cremation and the British Way of Death*, Palgrave Macmillan, 2006

—— and Gittings, Clare (eds.), *Death in England: An Illustrated History*, Manchester University Press, 1999

Keegan, John, *The Face of Battle: A Study of Agincourt, Waterloo and the Somme*, Jonathan Cape, 1976

Kellaway, Deborah, 'Pugs, Peacocks and Pekingese: The Garden at Garsington Manor', *Hortus*, Spring 1993

Keynes, John Maynard, *The Economic Consequences of the Peace*, Macmillan, 1920

Kipling, Rudyard, 'Mary Postgate', *Century Magazine* and *Nash's Pall Mall Magazine*, January 1915

Kitchen, Penny (ed.), *For Home and Country: War, Peace and Rural Life as seen through the pages of the WI Magazine 1919–1959*, Ebury Press, 1990

Kohn, Marek, *Dope Girls: The Birth of the British Drug Underground*, Lawrence & Wishart, 1992

Kubler-Ross, Elisabeth, *On Death and Dying*, Tavistock, 1970

Langley, John, *Always a Layman*, Queen Spark Books, 1976

Lawrence, A. W. (ed.), *T. E. Lawrence by His Friends*, Cape, 1937

Lawrence, D. H., *Lady Chatterley's Lover*, privately printed in Italy, 1928; Penguin, 1960

Lawrence, T. E., *Lawrence of Arabia: The Selected Letters*, ed. Malcolm Brown, Little Books, 2007

Lee, Christopher, *This Sceptred Isle: The Twentieth Century*, BBC Worldwide, 1999

Lee, Georgina, ed. Gavin Roynon, *Home Fires Burning*, Sutton, 2006

Lee, Hermione, *Virginia Woolf*, Chatto & Windus, 1996

Lees-Milne, James, *Harold Nicolson: A Biography*, Chatto & Windus, 1980

Lloyd, David W., *Battlefield Tourism: Pilgrimage and the Commemoration of the Great War in Britain, Australia and Canada 1919–1939*, Berg, 1998

Londonderry, Edith Marchioness of, *Retrospect*, Frederick Muller, 1938

Lovell, Mary S., *The Mitford Girls: The Biography of an Extraordinary Family*, Little Brown, 2001

Lycett, Andrew, *Conan Doyle: The Man who Created Sherlock Holmes*, Weidenfeld & Nicolson, 2007

Macmillan, Margaret, *Peacemakers: Six Months that Changed the World*, John Murray, 2001

Marwick, Arthur, *The Deluge: British Society and the First World War*, Macmillan, 1965

Masters, Anthony, *Nancy Astor: A Life*, Weidenfeld & Nicolson, 1981

Masters, Brian, *Great Hostesses*, Constable, 1982

Melba, Nellie, *Melodies and Memories*, Liberty Weekly, 1925

Micale, Mark S., and Lerner, Paul, *Traumatic Pasts: History, Psychiatry and Trauma in the Modern Age, 1870–1930*, Cambridge University Press, 2001

Illustrated Michelin Guides to the Battlefields: The Somme, Vol. 2, 1918

Miller, Andrew, *The Earl of Petticoat Lane*, Heinemann, 2006

Moran, Paul, *The Allure of Chanel*, Hermann, 1976

Morrell, Ottoline, ed. Jonathan Gathorne-Hardy, *Memoirs 1915–1918*, Faber, 1974

—— *Lady Ottoline's Album: Snapshots and Portraits*, Michael Joseph, 1976

Mosley, Nicholas, *Julian Grenfell: His Life and the Times of his Death, 1888–1915*, Weidenfeld & Nicolson, 1976

Muir, Ward, *The Amazing Mutes: Their Week in Lovely Lucerne*, Stanley Paul, 1910

—— *Observations of an Orderly: Some Glimpses of Life and Work in an English War Hospital*, Simpkin Marshall Hamilton, 1917

Nicholson, Virginia, *Singled Out: How Two Million Women Survived Without Men After the First World War*, Viking, 2007

Nicolson, Harold, *Peacemaking*, Constable, 1933

—— *King George V*, Constable, 1952

—— *Diaries, 1907–1964*, Weidenfeld & Nicolson, 2004

Nicolson, Nigel, *Portrait of a Marriage*, Weidenfeld & Nicolson, 1973

Noakes, Daisy, *The Town Beehive: A Young Girl's Lot, Brighton, 1910–1934*, Queen Spark Books, 1975

Noakes, George, *To be a Farmer's Boy*, Queen Spark Books, 1977

Oliver, Neil, *Not Forgotten*, Hodder & Stoughton, 2005

Onions, Maude, *A Woman at War: Being Experiences of an Army Signaller in France, 1917–1919*, privately printed, 1928

Parsons, Brian, *The London Way of Death*, Sutton, 2001

—— *J. H. Kenyon: The First 125 Years*, FSJ Communications, 2005

Patch, Harry, with Richard Van Emden, *The Last Fighting Tommy: The Life of Harry Patch, the only Surviving Veteran of the Trenches*, Bloomsbury, 2007

Pope Hennessy, James, *Queen Mary*, Allen & Unwin, 1959

The Duke of Portland KG GCVO, *Men, Women and Things*, Faber, 1937

Pound, Reginald, *Gillies: Surgeon Extraordinary*, Michael Joseph, 1964

Pridham, Vice-Admiral Sir Francis, *Close of a Dynasty*, Allan Wingate, 1956

Rémi, Henriette, *Hommes Sans Visage*, Editions Spes, Lausanne 1942

Ridley, Jane, *The Architect and His Wife: A Life of Edwin Lutyens*, Chatto & Windus, 2002

Roberts, Robert, *The Classic Slum: Salford Life in the First Quarter of the Century*, University of Manchester Press, 1971

Rose, June, *Marie Stopes and the Sexual Revolution*, Faber, 1992

Rose, Kenneth, *King George V*, Weidenfeld & Nicolson, 1983

Sackville-West, Vita, *Pepita*, Hogarth Press, 1937

Sambrook, Pamela, *Keeping their Place: Domestic Service in the English Country House*, Sutton, 2005

Sassoon, Siegfried, *Memoirs of an Infantry Officer*, Faber, 1930

Savage, Jon, *Teenage: The Creation of Youth Culture*, Viking, 2007

Sayers, Dorothy L., *The Unpleasantness at the Bellona Club*, Gollancz, 1921

Schoenberg, Bernard, with Irwin Gerber, Alfred Wiener, Austin H. Kutscher, David Peretz and Arthur C. Carr, *Bereavement: Its Psychological Aspects*, Colombia University Press, 1975

Seaman, L. C. B., *Life in Britain Between the Wars*, Batsford, 1970

Seeling, Charlotte, *Fashion: The Century of the Designer, 1900–1999*, Könemann, 2000

Seymour, Miranda, *Ottoline Morrell: Life on a Grand Scale*, Hodder & Stoughton, 1992

Shone, Richard, *Bloomsbury Portraits*, Phaidon Press, 1993

—— *The Art of Bloomsbury*, Tate Gallery Publishing, 1999

Sitwell, Osbert, *Laughter in the Next Room*, Macmillan, 1949

Slobodin, Richard, *Rivers*, Sutton, 1997

Stevenson, John, *The Penguin Social History of Britain: British Society, 1914–1945*, Allen Lane, 1984

Stone, Norman, *World War One: A Short History*, Penguin, 2007

Stopes, Marie, *Married Love*, A. C. Fifield, 1918

A Survivor, *Life Without Servants or The Re-discovery of Domestic Happiness*, Mills & Boon, 1916

Sutherland, John, *Stephen Spender: The Authorized Biography*, Viking, 2004

Sykes, Christopher, *Nancy: The Life of Lady Astor*, Collins, 1972

Tanner, Andrea, 'The Spanish Lady Comes to London: The Influenza Pandemic 1918–1919', *London Journal*, 27 (2), 2002

Taylor, Lou, *Mourning Dress: A Costume and Social History*, Allen & Unwin, 1983

Tebbutt, Melanie, *Women's Talk: A Social History of Gossip in Working-class Neighbourhoods, 1880–1960*, Scolar Press, 1997

Thomas, Alison, *Portraits of Women: Gwen John and Her Forgotten Contemporaries*, Polity Press, 1994

Thomas, Helen, *As it Was*, Heinemann, 1926

—— *World Without End*, Heinemann, 1931

Trefusis, Violet, *Don't Look Round*, Hutchinson, 1952

Turner, E. S., *What the Butler Saw*, Michael Joseph, 1962

Waugh, Evelyn, ed. Michael Davie, *The Diaries of Evelyn Waugh*, Weidenfeld & Nicolson, 1976

West, Rebecca, *The Return of the Soldier*, Nisbet, 1918

Wilkinson, James, *The Unknown Warrior and the Field of Remembrance*, JW Publications, 2006

Williamson, Henry, *The Patriot's Progress*, Geoffrey Bles, 1930

Wilson, Jeremy, *Lawrence of Arabia: The Authorized Biography of T. E. Lawrence*, Heinemann, 1989

The Duke of Windsor, *A King's Story*, Putnam, 1947

Woods, Joanna, *Katerina: The Russian World of Katherine Mansfield*, Penguin, 2001

Woolf, Leonard, *Downhill All the Way: An Autobiography of the Years 1919 to 1939*, Hogarth Press, 1964

—— *Beginning Again: An Autobiography of the Years 1911–1918*, Hogarth Press, 1967

Woolf, Virginia, *Mrs Dalloway*, Hogarth Press, 1925

—— *The Diary*, Vols. I and II, Hogarth Press, 1977 and 1978

—— *The Letters*, Vol. II: *1912–1922*, Chatto & Windus, 1980

Ziegler, Philip, *Diana Cooper*, Hamish Hamilton, 1981
—— *King Edward VIII: The Official Biography*, Collins, 1990
—— *Osbert Sitwell: A Biography*, Chatto & Windus, 1998
Zinovieff, Sofka, *Red Princess: A Revolutionary Life*, Granta, 2007

Index

Daily Mail: sends Christmas puddings to troops, 15; censorship, 20; on dances, 154; on jazz bands, 158; Ideal Home Exhibition (1920), 206; sponsors wireless broadcasting, 214
Daily Mail Cookbook, 207
Daily Telegraph: on Devonshire House ball, 227
Dalton's (club), Leicester Square, 160
dancing: popularity, 151–8
Dancing Times (magazine), 154
Davidson, Emily, 2
Davies, George Llewellyn, 264
Day Lewis, Cecil *see* Lewis, Cecil Day
death: Collins on nature of, 8
debutantes, 104
Del Cot (London store), 176
demobilisation, 69, 70, 73–4, 76–7, 188
Desborough, Ethel Anne Priscilla (Ettie), Lady: loses sons in war, 5, 14; and Armistice, 37; congratulates Violet Elliot (Astor) on remarriage, 46
de Veulle, Mr (dressmaker and actor), 133–4
Devonshire, Evelyn Emily Mary, Duchess of, 7, 46, 221
Devonshire, Victor Christian William Cavendish, 9th Duke of: property and estates, 221–9
Devonshire House, Piccadilly, 195, 221–2, 227–9, 231
Diaghilev, Serge, 34, 36, 215–17
Dickens & Jones (London department store), 177
Didion, Joan, 4
Dinham, Sergeant Jack, 22
disablement: pensions, 47; treatment and compensation, 47–8
disfigurement (ex-soldiers): repair and concealment, 48–56; *see also* faces
disillusionment, 129
dissatisfaction, 123–8
divorce: rise in, 44
Dormeuil, Edmée, 149
Dowson, Ernest, 241
Doyle, Sir Arthur Conan, 33, 97, 250–1
Doyle, Kingsley, 97

Doyle, Louisa, 97
dress: among poor, 132, 207; informality, 158–9
Dreyfus, Alfred, 220
drinking, 49, 184–5
drugs (recreational), 133–6, 160
Drummond, Canon, 158
Drusilla's (tea shop and zoo), East Sussex, 200–1
Dudley Ward, Freda, 164, 181
Duff Gordon, Lucy, 30, 123, 184
Durham, Bishop of *see* Moule, Handley Carr Glyn

Earle, Lionel, 231
Education Act (1918), 201
Edward VII, King, 7
Edward, Prince of Wales: watches erotic performance in Calais, 24; friendship with Gladys Cooper, 45; meets resentful returned troops, 72; on murder of Russian royal family, 82; role and activities, 128–9; on Queen Alexandra's unpunctuality, 141; visit to USA and Canada, 145, 162–4; dancing, 153; and Freda Dudley Ward, 164, 181; women friends, 164; public commitments, 166; on Christmas, 180; proposed tour of Australia, 181; returns from overseas tour (October 1920), 258
Edwards, John, 59
electorate (parliamentary): increased, 74
electricity: in home, 206
Eliot, Thomas Stearns, 127–8, 179, 189, 218, 236–7; *The Waste Land*, 128, 218, 265
Eliot, Vivien, 127, 218, 236
Ellieson Carrier Electric Invalid's Carriage, 47
Elliot (under-keeper at Beeley), 225
Endurance (ship), 150–1
Ennever, William Joseph, 98
Eton College: war casualties, 15
Evening Standard, 190
Everest, Elizabeth (Churchill's nanny), 222